Lawyer, Miner, Sailor, Dreamer

John McCormack, 1933-2022

Edited by Gavan McCormack

"John [McCormack], barrister, solicitor, opal miner, yachtsman, lived life on his own terms and was enthusiastic with all his pursuits in life, not afraid to make substantial changes to his lifestyle and living conditions, to pursue his dreams."

Duncan Bell, Darwin, *Northern Territory News*, 9 December 2022

Copyright © 2024 Gavan McCormack

All Rights Reserved.

No part of this publication may be reproduced, stored or transmitted without the written permission of the Editor, except for Fair Use as per Copyright law.

Photographs are, unless otherwise indicated, the property of the Author and Editor.

The Editor may be contacted at 53 Froggatt St, Turner, ACT 2612, Australia.

ISBN : 978-0-6458361-4-1

Polarity Press
PO Box 316
Childers Qld. 4660
Australia
polaritypress.com.au
polaritypress@mailstar.net

Table of Contents

Introduction—Author Life 1

PART ONE—Beginnings 5

    Chapter 1: Early Days [1933 -1950] 5

    Chapter 2: Student Years, University of Melbourne [1951-1955] .34

PART TWO—The Law 73

    Chapter 2: The Law, 1, Articles and Induction [1956-1960] 73

    Chapter 4: The Law, 2, Collins St [1960-1963] 83

PART THREE—Opals 111

    Chapter 5: Andamooka 1, Opals [1963-1968] 111

    Chapter 6: Andamooka, 2, The Blitz Buggy and Woomera 121

PART FOUR—Darwin and the North 139

    Chapter 7: Transition to Darwin, 1968 139

    Chapter 8: The North, Politics, the Future [1968-] 181

    Chapter 9: Charlie's of Darwin 224

    Chapter 10: Meeting Mother Teresa 238

PART 5—Sailing 251

    Chapter 11: Sailing, 1 [1958-2000] 251

    Chapter 12: Sailing, 2, Bathurst Island Weekend 331

PART SIX—Looking Back 343

    Chapter 13: Upon Retirement 343

Introduction—Author Life

John McCormack was born in Melbourne in 1933, and educated at Catholic parish (Our Holy Redeemer, Surrey Hills) and Christian Brothers (St Colman's, Fitzroy, 1946, Parade College, East Melbourne 1947-1950) secondary schools.

He studied law at the University of Melbourne (1951-1955, his "golden years") and became an articled clerk and then lawyer in Melbourne (1956-1960).

In 1960, he abandoned the Law and from 1963 he spent five years as an opal miner at Andamooka and Coober Pedy in South Australia, including spells as Chairman of the Andamooka Town Progress Association and founder of the Australian Opal Miners Association.

In 1968, meeting by chance with a prominent businessman and former Melbourne University friend (Keith Compton Gale) in Sydney, he was offered the position of Darwin representative of Gollin Kyokuyo joint Australia-Japan fisheries company (1968). In something short of a year, however, he resigned, probably a wise decision because the Gollin companies collapsed, spectacularly, and Gale was sent to prison. John McCormack then returned to the Law as a barrister and solicitor in Darwin (1970-2013). Once in Darwin, he also turned seriously to sailing, including participation in several successive Darwin to Dili and Darwin to Ambon ocean races.

After more than forty years practicing as barrister and solicitor in Darwin, in 2013 he retired to Scottsdale, Tasmania. He chose it, though he knew no one there, because he concluded that it was the best place in Australia for a semi-invalided pensioner without significant means (his condition at that time) to live. Once in Scottsdale, his health problems slowly worsened. He lost speech and mobility, followed by death in

November 2022. Cause of death was recorded as "motor neurone disease for more than 10 years," but he always contested this and believed he suffered some variant of Parkinson's.

He devoted the last years of his life to writing this autobiography, picking it out painstakingly, letter by letter, on his computer, circulating draft chapters among his siblings. He did not live to complete his life story, which is here pieced together from those draft chapters, edited by his younger brother, Gavan McCormack.

So far as we know, John McCormack never found any opal. He was constantly sea-sick on his yachts, and he died penniless, in a nursing home (after repeated disastrous investments) and without a will. Whether such life was "success" or "failure" is for readers of this book to decide.

The following note, written in 2018, may serve posthumously as the author's introduction to his book.

"I am in my 85th year [2018]. My life has differed from most. I hope readers will be entertained by my story. They might even learn something useful. I have enjoyed writing it. I have gained insights in reliving some of the episodes described. Most of those named have passed on. At my age I cannot expect not to pass on in the proximate future. Provided my memoir is completed I will leave this life content. It is something of an end-of-life review. If I had not been invalided over the past few years it would never have been written." (John McCormack, Scottsdale, Tasmania, 2018)

"My voice has been destroyed—by some kind of Parkinson's disease. This has complicated my task. It has prevented me getting in a ghost writer to do an extended interview. Each word has had to be picked out with one finger on my computer keyboard. Perhaps the discipline of slow writing has helped to clarify my thoughts. My story is based on recall and reflection.

Personal records that would have assisted went into storage in Darwin in 2012. Since then, I have been resident in Scottsdale Tasmania, latterly in a nursing home. You might say I was a refugee from Darwin's high rentals, but the root cause is my failure to retain my own accommodation. ...

My balance started to deteriorate from around late 2007. A walking frame became necessary. Deterioration of my throat and digestive tract followed, and then my loss of voice. Then came a fall in late July 2016 and consequent broken hip that post-surgery failed to heal enough to enable me to stand. After eight weeks of "physiotherapy" as hospital inpatient I was transferred to Scottsdale hospital and about a month later to the adjacent James Scott Nursing Home. I was aged 83 (in 2016)."

[I then set about writing my story. Please read on]

PART ONE—Beginnings

Chapter 1: Early Days [1933 -1950]

My entry to life dates from late 1933 in Melbourne. I was first of five siblings, born into a family of Irish immigrants to Australia, part of the potato famine diaspora. My father's father, also John McCormack, born in Ireland in 1860, arrived in Melbourne in the 1880s, accompanied by his mother Honoria (nee Sage) and sister Margaret. I grew up surrounded not only by parents and siblings but also cousins, uncles, aunts and of course grandparents.

Overarching this web and moulding its beliefs and moral code was the Catholic Church. Sunday attendance at the Catholic Mass was a given. Regular use of the church sacraments of Confession and Communion was the norm as well as those supplementing the rites of life passage - Baptism, Confirmation [a sort of Christian Bar Mitzvah], Matrimony, Extreme Unction (an anointing of the dying) and Holy Orders (for those entering the priesthood). In my time, all the growing up extended family attended Catholic schools taught usually by members of celibate religious communities and they had reasonable familiarity with the more actively Church-promulgated New Testament Bible passages and stories.

Christian belief is founded on the bible's New Testament. Yet there was no Bible in the Catholic home I grew up in and I am unable to recall any Catholic home with one. In part this was because of the Irish immigrants' generally limited education, origins of poverty and their positions on the lower rungs of the socio-economic ladder. The clergy, often Irish, were concerned that if the faithful read the bible without guidance they might "wrongly" interpret it and arrive at conclusions contrary to established Catholic doctrine or even worse, promulgate heresy. If they never possessed Bibles and so long as they remained uneducated there was no problem.

Post marriage at the height of the depression (November 1932), my parents (William/Bill 1905-1970) and Teresa/Tessie nee Green (1905-1960) set up in a home my father had bought in May St, Kew. My father's sister Annie (b. 1901) rented with her husband, New Zealander Bert Cunningham [1895-1955], just a few doors down at number 21. Bert, a tram conductor, and Annie, who worked at Myers for most of her life, both died in their sixties at this same address—still rented. My paternal grandparents lived around the corner with my father's other, unmarried, sister Helena [Lena] (b. 1903) at the bottom of Atkins Street.

Aged about 10, (first communion?)

About the time I was born, my mother discovered the mortgage payments failed to cover the interest on my father's mortgage over his May Street property.

My father's parents, John McCormack (1860-1943) and Helena/Ellen (nee Hanneberry, 1869-1955) were an ill-assorted couple. My grandmother was or became a difficult woman. As a young child I would be taken to visit her on the occasional Sunday morning. Grandpa would be half asleep in the bedroom. Into his eighties, he still worked as a nightwatchman. He would appear and sing what seemed to be his favourite song "I've got sixpence." I imagine now it may have been an old music hall favourite. No actual sixpence was ever produced, although I was not devoid of expectation. Soon, he would be banished to the bedroom. Then, Grandma would sing the praises of office employment with 9am to 5pm hours. Occasionally she would vent about the circumstances of her marriage and how she came to marry beneath what she termed her "station in life." She came from a middle class-ish farm background. Her duty was to look after the pigs. One way or the other she became convinced that without drastic action on her part the pigs were to be her lot in life. When a happy go lucky Grandpa turned up at the farm, it was him or the pigs. He never knew what hit him. She was, however, beneath the veneer of permanent disappointment with her husband and his career, a very bright lady. Early in the marriage, around 1902, they took on a hotel (the Whittington Family) in South Melbourne. Grandpa was happy to be close to the amber fluid. She was far from a happy hostess. A clock disappeared. She issued an ultimatum. If the clock was not returned by midnight on a certain date the police would be involved. The clock was returned on the exact deadline — hurled through a window.

Post the hotel venture, John took up a job at the brewery. When he was a carter there he would from time to time take my father out on his round with his horse drawn cart. During World War 11, in his watchman days, he broke a hip when he fell from the very high-set matrimonial bed. Hospitalised initially at Prince Henry Hospital the hip failed to mend. I remember visiting with my father. We took a long neck bottle of beer encased in brown paper. Old John enjoyed his drink. He was transferred to and died in the Ballarat hospital. My father visited him there.

Grandma soldiered on with help from her far from domesticated, unmarried daughter Lena. Uncle Bert chopped the firewood. Auntie Lena worked for Kodak at Abbotsford. Grandma became too much for her. A transfer to Cheltenham Nursing Home followed. My father was a regular Sunday afternoon visitor and occasionally one or two of us children were included. To my eye Grandma in those late years was a happier woman.

At the time of my parents' setting up home at May Street, my maternal grandmother Margaret Green, nee McNamara [1870-1965] lived alone as a widow in largish shop front premises at 312 Canterbury Road, Surrey Hills. She had been widowed quite early in the marriage and left with three young children. Her family then lived some miles the other side of Dandenong, east of Melbourne. Her husband, John Green (1847-1915), had gone into surgery for removal of a diseased kidney. When she visited him after the operation all seemed well, but she returned home to a telegram advising of his death. He had had only the one kidney. His photograph in an oval frame hung in the hallway of our later home at Union Road.

One way or the other, including a stint as a gaol wardress at Beechworth, Grandma Green (or "Mima" as she came to be known) managed. Then, she had come to an arrangement with an invalided woman, Mrs Bonas. In return for full time nursing care, she would get accommodation for herself and family at the Bonas residence at 312 Canterbury Road. On the death of Mrs. Bonas, she would inherit the property. About the time of my birth, Mrs. Bonas had died. My mother's two brothers had already by then left home.

After selling May St, the young McCormack family moved to Canterbury Road. The first family residence of which I have memory, it fronted directly on to the street. The glass shop front was painted grey. There was a suggestion it had been some kind of wine saloon. A veranda covered the footpath. In my early schooldays I used walk from there to the Holy Redeemer convent school at Corner of Mont Albert Road and Barton Street Surrey Hills. The Canterbury Road-block was quite large, with a substantial shed that took up much of the back yard. This property was soon sold to developers. For a short time, we moved into rented premises upstairs at the rear of the Union Road Surrey Hills Pharmacy. All I remember of this locale is the Roman Rings in the small backyard, where Uncle Bert once demonstrated his prowess. Soon afterwards (1940?) it was up the hill to 189 Union Road, the former residence of Mrs. Wedge an elderly widow of a pastoralist.

This was a three biggish bedroom, weather board house with a large kitchen, where the family spent much of its time and an even more liberally dimensioned dining room, used, as such only for bigger family events when the mahogany extending table was fully utilised., A pantry was located between these two rooms. Otherwise, the dining room was a tranquil environment for study, school homework, radio listening or just reading. It housed a glass fronted bookcase mounted on a cabinet now located in the home of my brother Bill at Maldon in central Victoria. Several large illustrated ancient volumes of Shakespeare and the *History of England* acquired from Mrs Wedge accompanied the bookcase to Maldon. My father's taste was more inclined to Westerns and to the works of Edgar Wallace, including *The Four Just Men* and other classics. In winters a coke fire set in the fireplace kept the room cosily warm.

A sleepout or bungalow cum the only toilet was close to in the backyard. A separate lock up garage headed the driveway. There was a chook pen with the wheat feed stored in a bin in the bungalow. I still have vivid memory of a visiting Uncle Charlie Daly carrying out his commission from the womenfolk one Christmas day to kill a hen for the lunch feast. I was deputed to assist. An axe was our tool of execution. When the hen proved uncooperative, a dance macabre ensued around the chopping block behind the garage before Charlie could deliver the *coup de grace*, followed by delivery of the corpse to the impatient kitchen.

Overlooking the roadway was a glassed-in veranda not really used at all. I notice from the internet property listings the glass has been removed. The property last changed hands in May 2013 for $1.48M. Estimated current price is $2.2 to $2.9M. The family purchase price was of the order of 2,200 pounds, as I know from having stumbled across a box of old papers in the garage. Included was a receipted account for the conveyancing bill from family solicitor Tom Brennan.

From 189 Union Rd, my school was a stone's throw away, just around the corner. Although my mother's then single brother Pat lived in the bungalow, we saw little of him. Grandma Green lived with us and had her separate room. Perhaps she contributed to the price. I shared one of the large bedrooms with my two brothers.

A word here about my primary school, Our Holy Redeemer, Mont Albert Road, Surrey Hills. It was from there I and my siblings received from the nuns a solid grounding in the alphabet, the multiplication and division tables, English grammar, the Ten Commandments and the Catholic religion. History was limited to being appraised of the sailing adventures of Portuguese caravelles, sponsored by landlubber Prince Henry the Navigator, around the Cape of Good Hope to India and Asia. Indirectly we picked up the names of Henry V111 and Martin Luther more as epithets than anything else. Henry had too many wives and Luther's one, a nun, was too many for a priest. The Reformation was an unspeakable assault on the Catholic Church. It resembled the approach to science in Form V at Parade College in about 1948, when we the pupils and the Victorian curriculum makers, all knew the atom had been split but the new science was yet to be reduced to teachable form. So the teaching was left unchanged from the era when the atom was the smallest indivisible particle. I could never adjust to the new order in my Form V1 year. It substantially contributed to my change of career orientation from engineer to lawyer.

Individual nuns may have possessed the capacity to deal with the complex swirling issues of biblical translation, the Reformation and the build up to it, Luther & the forces that drove him, Henry's break with Rome and the development of Protestantism, but obviously as a matter of policy the decision had been taken at a high level to teach at the level I had experienced. I well recall the nun who taught my grade 5 class. She had done a teaching stint in New Zealand and loved it as she told us. Along the way, she commenced to read us extracts from what I now know to have been from W, Ramsay Smith's "Myths and Legends of the Australian Aborigines." I was fascinated but, abruptly these readings ceased without explanation. Though I begged for more, I was brushed off. I infer now she had been reined in, probably by our parish priest, Irishman Timothy Fitzpatrick (parish priest 1941-1972), following a parental complaint.

At the time we never had any real appreciation of its enormity the Christian message involving the Trinity, placement of God the Son on earth via the Virgin birth, Christ's crucifixion as a redemptive atonement for man's exercise of his free will to breach the commandments, and his resurrection three days later all as prophesied. It adds up to a stupendous tale if told properly. And it is all constructed from the bible.

Nowadays trendy Christians, tired of having to acknowledge sin and the need for divine forgiveness for entry to a preferred hereafter are tinkering with atheistic Buddhism. I suspect this is because of its non-judgmental nature. The implications of the attainment of nirvana are obscure. To attain this blessed state involves compliance with something akin to the 10 commandments. If you accept Pascal's wager, the Christian road seems to me a safer bet, requiring roughly the same self- disciplinary input. The Catholic sacraments provide indispensable assistance. If you make heaven all problems solved. The Buddhist way promises endless stressful recycling until nebulous nirvana is achieved.

As to Timothy Fitzpatrick he was a placid man, who seemed to think an announcement on St. Patrick's Day that the saint was not an Irishman would stun his flock. Or that a reading from the pulpit of the life of a saint as presented in the printing of the banal Six O'Clock Saints was solid spiritual fare for his flock to chew over for the ensuing week. Never mind that author Graham Greene in his novel "The Power and the Glory" had gone out of his way to rubbish the Six O'Clock series as silly projections by unworldly refugees from the real world. Instead of taking a leaf out of the Six O'Clock saints and standing nobly, calmly, doubt-free sinless and elegantly and gorgeously attired as he faced his end, Greene's deeply flawed whisky priest met his end dirty, dishevelled. and fearful, cringing before a ragged firing squad. The attendant commotion causes Greene's toothache-distracted protagonist to look out to view the squalid scene in the courtyard below the window of his surgery. Timothy would most likely retort that at least one of Greene's novels is on the infamous Papal banned Index, as Greene reported he was once told by a Cardinal at a social gathering.

There is no denying Timothy was a good priest in administering the church sacraments and being at the beck and call of his parishioners. The pulpit was not his forte. His unfortunate preoccupation there was with money - the Parish debt and the Building Fund for extensions and improvements to his church. His flock were browbeaten *ad nauseum* about one or the other most Sundays. A silent collection was much heralded. Notwithstanding that the printed list of Parishioners' individual donations for Easter dues was freely available the whole shebang was read from the pulpit. A true innocent, Timothy kept his hard gained cash in a standard parish account accessible to the Melbourne archbishop's exchequer. Like a prize rose in full bloom it was casually plucked by that exchequer to help deal with a financial emergency. Not a cent remained. Not a cent would be returned. A heartbroken Timothy broke the news to his flock.

What my original nuns' school may be unaware of is that, for a brief period, it taught a future High Court judge. When I was aged about 12 or 13 in grade 8, I shared the class with one Merle Toohey. She sat in a desk directly behind me, and her sister Deirdre was in grade 7 which shared the same room. They were brownettes. About 12 months after they started at the school their younger brother John materialised in a lower class, likely two or three. He was said to be a wonder-child, good at everything. I caught no more than occasional glimpses of John, even then always surrounded by admirers. Then one day in about 1946, the Tooheys disappeared, gone—it was said - to Western Australia. John, who would have attended the school for no more than around 6 months, went on to become a prominent and much loved Western Australian barrister, thence for a brief spell in Broome with Aboriginal Legal Aid. From there he was appointed an Aboriginal Land Rights Commissioner with collateral appointments to the Northern Territory Supreme Court and the Federal Court. Appointment to the High Court followed (1987). He lived in Darwin quite close to my home. I had the occasional chat with him at legal social functions but never realized the linkage with Surrey Hills, which only dawned on me too late to have any opportunity to discuss it with him.

When Grandma Green was not busy with domestic chores her major interests were negotiating with the local illegal SP (starting price) bookmaker in Barton Street, discussing the relative skills of different jockeys or buying tickets in the then Tasmanian based George Adams' Tattersalls lotteries. Despite these activities, she so inveigled her way into the confidence of the nuns at my school that they enrolled my young brother Gavan at the age of 4—an advantage he enjoyed throughout his academic life. I suspect a gifted pack of cornflakes just after the war when they were in short supply may have tipped the scales. Although I am not aware of her having any great success as a gambler, her Brisbane son, my uncle Jack, won the Queensland Golden Casket twice.

Grandma Green also took an interest in religious relics. And on the occasion of a bakers' strike and with much ado she set out to bake her own bread. Although it never rose, I found it excellent. When bread was delivered by local (Canterbury Rd) baker Conlan it was often deliciously warm. Bread as well as milk deliveries were by horse-drawn cart; the milk ladled into an enamelled lidded container. A son of one of the same Conlan bakery family much later turned up in the Northern Territory Legislative Assembly as an elected Alice Springs member. He had arrived in Alice from Queensland as a radio announcer.

As I write this, I realise the important role Grandma Green played in the household. On the rare occasions my mother was absent or ill or in hospital to give birth family life just went on much the same courtesy of her input—a sort of aged au pair live in. Her sister Mary's son, Uncle Din [Dennis O'Brien] who dairy farmed at Mirboo North in Gippsland came to town occasionally. When he did. he berthed his magnificent, olive-green mint condition 1931 Packard 8 in the empty garage at Union Road but stayed with his mother at the home she shared with two other sisters at Sycamore Road Camberwell. Din never drove his car in town, instead engaging an RACV pilot to guide him from the outskirts of town to Union Road.

The move to Union Road was during World War 11. I remember the local congratulatory furore when a son of the next-door neighbours, the Stevens, was awarded the DFC in the course of his fighter pilot duties in the north. Another, younger, son Murray would sometimes pop over the fence to spar with me. Murray had the advantage of me in weight and width but happily he was in it for the exercise rather than the kill. Since I was on occasion dressed in Melbourne Grammar School gear, Murray must have wondered at seeing me in the pullover and tie of his school.

This oddity in my wardrobe was consequent upon entry into the McCormack household of Nellie Hewitt, a long-time friend of Grandma Green who happened to be in service in the 1950s to the well-known Officer family in Toorak. Auntie

Nellie as we called her was a regular visitor. I suspect she and my grandmother had met in the prison service. When her employer's house had a spring-clean she pounced on items she thought might be useful to us. Hence the Grammar pullover and tie let alone various colourful books depicting the majesty of Britain and its leaders.

When Murray and I sparred, we used battered boxing gloves from my father's artifacts from his youth. There was also an ancient gramophone and a violin and banjo, left over from my father's youth.

On the garage bench there were containers, including an ancient automotive sump, full of nuts bolts and the collected detritus of previous motorcycles and cars from my father's more carefree days. I especially remember a Zundapp spark plug.

Widowed old Mrs Kiely over the back fence seemed to perpetually lurk in her back yard for the express purpose of complaining if we were playing cricket and the ball hit her dividing fence behind the batsman—as it invariably did. The backyard was productive. My father grew tomato, lettuce, onions, carrots and potatoes. There were apple and lemon trees and a passion fruit vine on some trelliswork abutting the garage.

During and after the war we had many week-end visits from children of farming relatives who were making their way in the city. Probably Union Road was one of the few city addresses where they had a connection. My mother was rarely out of the house and always made them welcome. She entertained in the kitchen while she went about her meal preparations. Jack O'Sullivan and his brother Pat come to mind as does nurse Betty Daly. Cousin Don Cunningham and Auntie Annie from May St Kew were others but never together.

I think Uncle Bert Cunningham was my favourite person when I was growing up. Unlike my often-uncommunicative father, Bert was a chatty soul, and he was always making things When I was laid low for months with rheumatic fever, Bert, almost every week, mailed some light reading to help educate me and pass the time.

Visiting was far from one way. When I was about 12, my slightly younger brother Bill and I were taken by Grandma Green for a couple of weeks to the Daly dairy farm at Dalyston near Wonthaggi in Victoria's Gippsland. Getting there involved a trip to the city to catch a steam train from I think Spencer Street Station. On route, the surf at Kilcunda was impressive. Cars were thin on the ground then. These days a road trip from Surrey Hills would be unlikely to take more than 2 hours. I recall too a visit to Spencer Street Rail Station when I was about 12 to see off Uncle Bert and Auntie Annie on the Spirit of Progress locomotive to Sydney. To my eyes the Spirit in its blue livery was a glorious thing.

The Daly farm property was about 200 acres. John Daly presided. I learned only recently that in his youth he had boarded for some years at 312 Canterbury Road while commuting to my alma mater, Parade College in East Melbourne for his secondary education. On our visit Bill discovered a battered "Chums" annual from what appeared to be the early thirties. Monthly covers vividly depicted scenes such as of resolute, clean-cut British lads besieged by fiendish Tartars on horseback, hurling hand grenades. The defence deployed tennis racquets to bounce them back. Not quite as fantastical though as a wartime edition cover of my favoured "Champion" depicting an evil German in a special edition Messerschmitt with beefed-up wings flying to smash wings off Spitfires piloted by baffled, honest, decent British lads. Bill totally immersed himself in the Chums world. Even as I write these words I learn he has acquired through ebay Chums annuals for 1914 and 1916, in excellent condition.

Meantime at then aged 70 (born 1870) Grandma Green lamented she must be close to the end of her days. She lived till 1965 and was mentally alert, mobile and active. But then she became introspective and began to query why she had outlived her friends.

Occasionally we visited the Laidlaw farm, adjacent to the Daly's. where I learned to scamper at speed across a cricket oval dimensioned area between the front gate and the house to evade a rambunctious head-butting ram. This was the time I learned to deploy a ferret down a rabbit hole to flush rabbits into nets pegged around adjacent holes. Taught how to do it, I casually disentangled them to break their necks — something I would have to steel myself to do today. Although in my prospecting days I had little concern driving my car at night in the hills around Glen Innes where the whole road surface was a heaving grey sea of rabbits.

John Daly has passed on some years ago now and his brother Pat, about my age, has taken over. I am told nowadays the business runs to several farms each with a separate manager., with Pat presiding as a sort of uber manager of a large beef cattle business. Save for a short visit on my briefly owned Triumph Thunderbird 650 Motorcycle in about 1953 I have not been back. I was accompanied then by my younger brother Gavan riding pillion.

One of Grandma Green's brothers, my great uncle Jack McNamara, lived in the proximate Barton Street with his wife and three children. The McNamaras were rather more traditional Irish than the McCormacks. The eldest of these three cousins, also Jack, tall and powerfully built with a high forehead, died during World War 11 in a diving accident at Whyalla in South Australia. He had miscalculated a dive from a pier into water that was of far less depth than needed.

Throughout the war, Uncle Jack cycled to work at the Charles Ruwolt (later Vickers Ruwolt) plant at Burnley just over the river Yarra on the direct tramline from Kew to the city. Jack's younger brother Tony was about my height but of heavier build and displaying the same high forehead. He loved football. He became a primary school headmaster at a special school for handicapped children. Although I did one hitch hiking trip with Tony to Tasmania in January when I was about 18, we never really related to each other. Tony was a few years older and at that age a few years makes a big difference. Of that trip, I still remember the night cold when we dossed in the ticket box at the Deloraine racecourse. That was more than compensated for by the hospitality extended to us at the Tarraleah guesthouse, where we fetched up after a long trudge when we were dumped in the middle of nowhere by a joker driver. Tony's sister Cath ran a hairdressing salon at the Mont Albert tram terminus until she married Wally O'Regan.

Early Days [1933 -1950] 21

There was no phone at Union Road. We just couldn't afford it. Likewise, there was no fridge or car, at least until later in our Union Road days. Then, a frig did come on the scene but it was a bargain priced model with a cracked motor head that made it noisy. When it cut in the house lights would dim temporally.

Our new location was fortuitous. The Surrey Hills railway station was located just down the hill and the Mont Albert tramline a little further in the opposite direction. Occasionally, my father would lash out and buy a motorcycle, always Indian, and sidecar outfit, usually in late 1920s model. Up until the thirties Indian motorcycles relied on helical [cogged] secondary drive. It was his claim that that the Indian motorcycle manufactory took a retrograde step when, in the early thirties, it introduced chain instead of helical secondary drive. Unlike Indian's similarly laid out v twin American rival, Harley Davidson, there was no gate for the gearbox lever which was located on the right-hand side of the engine. For a brief time, Uncle Bert also owned a sleek, later model Indian motorcycle outfit.

Adjacent to the cinema was Hansen the grocer, while just up the way from him was Fleming's delicatessen, from where Herbert Adams' "bought" cakes could be had. Over the hotter months we had ice delivered for our ice chest from the Armistead woodyard just down the hill. Fridays were fish and chips days from Della's shop fish shop opposite the woodyard. Then there was the local palace of dreams, the Surrey Theatre. Just up the road from Armistead's was a small library run by two middle aged ladies. For a brief period, this was my favourite place to browse on Friday or

Saturday early evenings to make a selection. Then the Box Hill Council opened a superior lending library. A few more doors down to the rail crossing was a sub newsagency run by a Miss Davies. It was from there I bought my "Champion" English boy's adventure publication to read of the derring-do of the likes of Rockfist Rogan RAF; the 180 pounds of bone and muscle of the Mantamer from Muskrat; and the adventures of Colwyn Dane Detective. The money came from my after-school paper round.

One weekend, possibly at my mother's behest, our father took my brother Bill and I in his then ancient Indian motorcycle outfit to visit Mr. Komesaroff, a former Richmond furniture store employer [presumably Mr Schlomo-Zalman Komesaroff, who had arrived in Australia from Ukraine in 1913]. As I was to learn quite some years later, he was the father of barrister Bill Kaye (1919-2012) who went on to become a Victorian Supreme Court Judge. Another lawyer son who retained the family name invented strata titles to airspace. His legal action against a former staffer who breached his copyright is reported in the law reports. Old Mr. Komesaroff and his wife made us most welcome.

About this time at Union Road my mother prevailed on my father to study for a promotion to tramway inspector. I have always been of the belief he was the smartest in the family. He applied himself and with some assistance from other inspectors in the layout of accident reports was promoted. It wasn't that many years later he rose again, this time to Depot Master.

This latter promotion roughly coincided with my mother's death in 1960 from abdominal cancer. It was an event from which my father never recovered. My mother died at home in the matrimonial bedroom at the front of the house after a lingering wasting illness. My father had moved to a rough sleep-out at the rear, and he never went back.

At the time of my father's initial study the older male children were beginning to have some idea where they might be heading scholastically and even career wise— always subject to winning scholarships to pay for secondary schooling. As the eldest I was establishing a rough modus operandi.

It was my mother who pointed the family in the direction of higher education. Save for a few secondary school graduates, two teachers college graduates and a university degree in civil engineering earned by my father's cousin, Pat Hanneberry, there was little useful information in the family to base future plans around. The immediate objective was to earn scholarships through to university entrance standard. The preferred path was to win what was called a Junior Government Scholarship [JGS]. This was for four years of secondary education. The best pathway to this was said to be via a year a St. Colman's school in Fitzroy. All students there were holders of a one-year scholarship, whose only function was to prepare students to successfully sit for one of these JGS. The success rate was said to be over 90 per cent. The path to the one-year scholarship was via competitive exam. So you could say that this raised the collective odds in favour of winning a JGS. The selection procedure ensured a St

Colman's class was something like the cream of the crop of parish nun's schools around Melbourne.

It was not a course all students chose. At my primary school many students disappeared after completing grade 6 at about 11 years of age. They were not dropping out of the education system. Rather they were moving to secondary colleges that commenced at around the primary school grade 7 level. They were the children of the more well to do to whom winning a scholarship was not a determinant of whether they would have a secondary education.

So in 1946, I took my place at St. Colman's upstairs classroom in north Fitzroy with about 49 other similarly selected male students of the same age. The school included another library area of about the same size as the classroom. At ground level at the base of a steel staircase there was a small asphalt paved yard where lunchtimes we would have competitive tunnel-ball. A similar parallel system at another school was in place for girls. Unlike at my former convent school there were no slow learners. There was just the one teacher, Christian Brother FP Bowler (1885-1970), named behind his back as Percy or Perc. Born in 1885, Perc set up at St. Colman's in 1929 and retired in 1966 at the age of 81. I saw little of him after my year in 1946.

As we were all to find out Perc presided over an intellectual commando course. He lived with the Christian Brothers community at my later school, Parade College, just around the corner in Victoria Parade. Come March every year the entire class would march together representing the school on the St Patrick's Day procession.

Early Days [1933 -1950]   25

The key to our course was the mark book. This was issued to each of us on day one. Virtually everything we undertook was marked and the mark recorded by us in this book. At the end of each week, we were expected to have recorded a plethora of subjects at over 90 per cent. Failure was to invite queueing up for a taste of the strap. Lest any student attempt to falsify his marks, from time to unpredictable time and out of the blue, Perc would announce what he called a raid. Pens would be put down and a particular mark book number recorded individually checked by Perc against the written answers it was based upon as he prowled the classroom aisles. The atmosphere would be electric. Inevitably some unfortunate wretch would be undone. A desperate secretive attempt to rectify an inconsistency might be caught. A scuffle would ensue. The family name of the offender would be called out. The miscreant would end up half out of his desk, even on the floor. As I write this, I realise it was mostly a psychological ploy. No student was ever injured. But there was plenty of barking. And the pressure helped to toughen us up mentally.[1]

Reproduction of geometrical theorems which had baffled us under the nuns became effortless and commonplace. I doubt if any group of candidates for any examination could have been better prepared than we were for the JGS examination at the year's end. There may have been the odd

---

[1] For an account of St Colman's in the year 1949, three years after John McCormack's class, including a classroom photograph, see Geoff Coyne, "Remembering Brother Bowler," 8 March 2019, https://www.oldparadians.com/

one of us who failed to win the coveted scholarship but that would have been it. Latin, which was off our JGS curriculum, aside, the next year of intermediate level [Form IV] High school was a doddle retracing as it did much of the ground we had covered under Percy's pressure cooker tutelage. We even managed to squeeze in a school excursion by train to the Dandenong Ranges. When it came time for Percy to retire a ceremony was conducted to a Cathedral Hall filled with former students overflowing with goodwill. Brian Hill gave the key speech and it hit the nail exactly right. Much merriment ensued during his recollections of a rampant Percy and the pressures of those student days.

Parade College

Ed. Note: From St Colman's, the author proceeded to nearby Parade College in East Melbourne, 1947-1950. It is puzzling that this memoir contains only brief reference to those formative teenage years because the influence of one teacher in particular, Frank McCarthy (1920-2010) seems to have been profound. It continued into a friendship that lasted long after John's school years. McCarthy, a highly literate Cambridge Ph. D., stood out among Christian Brothers of that time for his passionate concern for ideas. He was an intellectual. Many of his pupils, almost all of working-class origin, went on to become prominent professionals and intellectuals. McCarthy, interviewed by The Age in 1997, recalled one class he had taught in the early 1950s that turned out "four professors, three judges, two architects, a colonel, a high commissioner, two psychiatrists and three AFL footballers."[2] It is very likely it was John McCormack's class he had in mind.

---

[2] Margaret Cook, "The old art of teaching," *The Age*, 4 March 1997.

John's discussion of his high school years is brief. The Commonwealth Scholarship scheme to which he refers was inaugurated in 1951 (by the Menzies government), so that John McCormack's cohort was the first to benefit from it.

School Cadet uniform, 1948

Many of my quite small group of classmates from Parade College, a fairly typical group, had been awarded Commonwealth scholarships. At the time any secondary student with a reasonable overall pass in the Matriculation public examinations had a fair prospect of being awarded one. John Howard, later Prime Minister, is one who failed to secure one initially but did so at the completion of his first year of university study.

My small Matriculation class (1950) sent a considerable cohort to tertiary studies and subsequent careers — all bar one courtesy of Commonwealth scholarships. Five became lawyers [myself, Jack Powderly, Noel Purcell, Peter Phelan, Leo Broben]. Of these, Peter Phelan's first career was as a Catholic priest and his last as a NSW District Court Judge. Noel Purcell became a magistrate. Jack Powderly (who tragically died young) became Mayor of Richmond. Others in our school graduating class included one general practitioner (GP) and later psychiatrist [John Garland], two university lecturers/professors [Mick Heffernan and Keith Garzoli], one Arts graduate professional footballer/journalist/history teacher/politician [Brian Buckley], and another who took a position with the Australian Tax Office [Denis Wheelahan].

The Melbourne 1950s real estate industry was sluggish. Blocks of vacant land had agent's display boards on them for ever. One such block on the corner of Union and Mont Albert Roads was occupied for a few weeks by a heavily built, aged and massively bearded tramp believed to be from Russia. He kept to himself, and I caught only the briefest glimpse of hm. Once he was ensconced, the vegetation was so prolix he could not be seen from the footpath. His evening campfires kept the locals agog.

It is amusing to reflect that, courtesy of our political masters and the US abolition of the gold standard in 1971, a purchase and long-term hold of one such block by the early 1940s and nothing else could have provided a comfortable retirement in 2017. Even better, a house like 189 Union Road, which of course could be lived in. The price might mean opting out of real life but the pursuit of money as an end in itself tends to lead to that result anyway. I wonder where this present [2018] age of untrammelled US and European government spending and limitless debt might lead in the next 50 or so years.

There may not have been much money about when I was growing up but there was enough for trammies like my father and Uncle Bert to buy and hang on to a block of land in the Dandenong Ranges 20 miles or so east of Melbourne.

Early Days [1933 -1950]

Living off no more than a tram drivers wage and despite his household of a wife and five children relying on a single income, my father was also able to pay off a block in Bulleen Road on the northern fringes of Camberwell.

There was a tiny investment in forestry, but I don't think there was ever any return. Speculation about the possibilities flared up from time to time. Family solicitor Tom Brennan was consulted.

Australia may have been noticed in the world but its citizens are paying the price for its dumb politicians. Until recently, any citizen of any country has been able to buy into our housing. Try doing the same in many of our neighbour countries. Australians have learned they have to compete in the international marketplace to buy into local housing stock. Local immigrants from Asia are often backed by family money from their often-wealthy countries of origin when they seek out local housing. Add low interest rates, unlimited debt fuelled credit, superannuation money and negative gearing into the mix and you have volatile instability. And don't forget the nature of the generous allowances for your federal member posits a challenge for him or her to convert these into purchases of real estate. It has become fashionable for a trendy young married couple to feel ill done by if they haven't a negatively geared investment house. After all isn't the past real estate boom a mirror to the future?

That money went further is not to say life was easy. My father often worked night shifts for the extra money. Night shifts involved driving what were called "All Nighter" trams. They were different to day trams being set up so the driver collected the fare. I think they ran from around midnight to something like 6am. At these times when he was day sleeping we were enjoined to keep the noise levels down. Fortunately, he was trying to sleep at the front of the house and the kitchen was at the rear. In my early 20s I tried night work from 4pm to midnight but my body clock never adjusted.

There was also a gladioli growing venture on a large vacant block at East Camberwell. It preceded Barry Humphries' use of this prop in his shows. The idea was to sell to American servicemen. But, although production was successful marketing doesn't appear to have been well thought out. The end of hostilities may have contributed.

My mother tried to make sure we always went away for part of the annual school holidays. Usually this was to a Port Philip bayside beach like Parkdale, Chelsea, Mordialloc or Aspendale. Even ocean beach Ocean Grove got into the mix once. Often, we stayed at semi-finished unlined house properties belonging to other trammies. What mattered was the near beach locations. On Port Philip Bay beaches I came to envy the beach box owners who brought out their beautifully painted and varnished sailboats, launched, and sailed over the horizon to return hours later. Canoe hire was occasionally available. When it was, I spent everything I had on hires. The beach proximate to our digs at Ocean Grove was unpatrolled and the surf so ferocious that we never went in the water. It was well before Harold Holt's time but no one aspired to a fate like his (the then Prime Minister disappeared without trace when swimming off Portsea in 1967). Unaware then of the true danger posed by the sun's rays we sought the deepest possible tan in the misguided belief we were thus inoculating ourselves against future sunburn.

We saw next to nothing of our father during these holidays. Absent personal transport, usually the case, such journeys would have called for a major odyssey. He kept the home fires burning. From time to time, he, and a few mates, usually trammies, would disappear to Stony Point on Westernport Bay for week-long fishing breaks. There, catch variety prevailed, unlike in the more convenient Port Philip Bay where it was invariably flathead. Even then, a shark lurking beneath the boat often left only the head.

We lived at Union Road for about 8 years. Then, late one night (1948?) I could hear raised voices from the kitchen. In hindsight, I suspect my father and Grandma Green were approaching a parting of the ways. It was around 1948 that the decision was made to sell Union Rd. The price was to us at the time an incredible 1,300 pounds. These days [2018] it would be well over $1M.[3]

Union Road sold, we moved to 24 Wolseley St. [now renamed Wolseley Close] in the adjacent suburb of Mont Albert. Grandma Green relocated to join her sisters in a non-stop prayer-fest dominated by sister Auntie Annie in their Sycamore Street East Camberwell abode. Location-wise, Wolseley St was about the same distance from the tram and rail station except the station was Mont Albert instead of Surrey Hills. It was a quarter-acre site and the house

---

[3] Almost certainly by now, 2024, well over $2 million.

required an urgent re-block. Different (Mont Albert) rail gates as before were just down the modest decline from the new address.

The house re-block was a monstrous intrusion but once completed life went on much as before. It was similarly dimensioned to Union Road but there was one extra room that formerly would have been taken by Grandma Green. Stables at the top of the driveway were demolished and the timber used to construct a new garage in roughly the same place. There was enough material left over to construct a chook coop. All this demolition & reconstruction was made possible by Uncle Bert in his spare time. Bert was a robust and skilled constructor. It was from this address I undertook my university studies such as they were. A retired English military Captain who lived in the area successfully sought out accommodation for his ancient but solid camp-mobile in the new garage. I noticed new people at the rail station including one who I much later leaned was historian Manning Clark. I undertook my legal articles from this address.

But in about the mid- fifties my father became concerned about his perception of the state of the slate roof. From the manhole in the ceiling, he was able to see patches of sunlight. This notwithstanding, we were never bothered by leaks. I don't believe a tiler was ever consulted. The unspoken assumption was that the cost of a reasonable repair would be prohibitive. Knowing what I do now and as against the cost that my father was later put to because he was forced to move, I suspect a practical tiled roof repair could have been managed more economically. But we children were never brought into any decision making of this nature.

Another actor entered the scene. An estate agent, another retired English army officer, this one from intelligence. My father had signed a written memorandum of terms of sale which when, as an articled clerk, I consulted others who were expert in the area, was adjudged bomb proof. From memory it was a "Section 34" statement. With the experience I have gained over the years, maybe a different result would have ensued but only after a court battle with expensive litigation. There was no alternative but to seek out a new home. Once this was accepted it turned out my father had been no more informed about the state of the real estate market when he signed up unconditionally than he had years before about gladioli. He had put unjustified faith in the agent. His dream of a suitable replacement brick and tile residence was out of the question because of cost.

So it came to pass that the McCormack family moved to 1 Benson Street, back in Surrey Hills—a location I looked on as a serious downgrade from Wolseley Street. No brick and tile here, rather weather board and tin. This notwithstanding, this house, apparently in much the same state as it was when sold after my father's death (in 1970), is valued today (2019) at $1.7M. The new owner of Wolseley St soon demolished the house and constructed two quite mediocre flats. If it turned out to have involved another retired British army connection that would not surprise me.

From Benson St, I took off into a career in the law, while my siblings scattered—to Saigon, Vancouver, Tokyo. Following my father's death in 1970 the house was sold.

Chapter 2: Student Years, University of Melbourne [1951-1955]

In 1951 I commenced my Law degree course at Melbourne University, having turned 18 in late November the previous year. Two older cousins had graduated as teachers from Melbourne Teachers College, but I was the first regular university student from the family. Of my 4 siblings, two were later to acquire degrees from Melbourne University, my younger brother an LL. B and my older sister a BA.

At that time there was only the one University in Melbourne. Commonwealth scholarships were a relatively recent innovation of the Menzies Government in 1951, and any student awarded one (probably four out of five at the time) and enrolled in a course of degree study had all fees and ancillaries paid for the duration of that course, with all faculties open to choice. There were no quotas or barriers to entry, and no requirement for special high marks in particular subjects. As I recall none of my year -12 school classmates had even a university graduate, let alone a professional, in their family tree.

From the 1960s new universities opened, the population grew, commonwealth scholarships were abolished and HEC loans made available instead to cover university fees. Thereafter, to attain a degree, and depending on the duration of a course, the 80 per cent of students who as Commonwealth Scholarship holders had paid no fees found themselves graduating with significant debt burden, conceivably around $100,000 plus interest.

Student Years, University of Melbourne [1951-1955]

To any reader who has not attended university, the difference from High School is not great. It is just that a university student is on his own. There was no law faculty roll call at lectures or tutorials. Attendance at lectures was entirely up to the student. Crunch times came with the Arts History course requiring a 3,000-word essay by a set date; and the end of year written examinations. The student had control of how he wished to apply himself.

When I look back and subject to non-university interruptions, the next four years (1951-1955) was for me a golden time—in the sense of people I met and public events I attended staged by fellow students. On the debit side was the whole purpose of the exercise - lectures and tutorials to attend, essays to write, exams to pass.

I am sorry to admit many were the lectures and tutorials missed, not through debauchery but distraction. This included a deluded belief that poorly presented lectures could be missed with impunity. Indeed, in the case of one Law Faculty lecturer on the subject of Contract Law, the lecturer's persistent ultra-late attendances made it a moot point whether to attend at all.

I became accustomed to desperate third (final) terms, mainly working from Melbourne's Public Library which held stored copies of earlier year test papers. I would get them out for the preceding three years and try to make sense of them. Then it was back to the course and lecture notes [if any of the latter] to try and make more sense.

The problem was to identify the correct legal issue raised by the examiner's always intriguing matrix of facts. My

Private International Law lecture notes from Prof Zelman Cowen [1919-2011, Governor-General 1977-1982] usually stood up best as records of well-delivered easily understood material—good enough for a second-class honour. History lecturer Kitty Fitzpatrick was another exemplar of presentation. My attendances for her lectures came about because in the first years of law a number of Arts subjects were required, the choice optional. I chose Political Science A. and Tudor history in the first year, Political Science B in second year B.

For Political Science B, I was confronted as a tutor with Sol Encel, a cousin of my weightlifting mate Alex Encel. Under Sol's energetic prodding, solemn study was undertaken of the Russian constitutional process at a time when Stalin, not unlike Henry Vlll in an earlier age, was in undisputed control. Sol was something of a personal embarrassment in that he expected his students to have undertaken some study before attending so they could participate as intended.

I have found the knowledge of history from my university days has been almost all courtesy of the internet, I have recently immersed myself in the chequered history of biblical translation into English, the reformation and other antics of King Henry V111 and the power and influence wielded by and the untimely ends of Thomas Cromwell and Cardinal Wolsey.

In an indirect way, I had even paid, outside my Commonwealth Scholarship funding, for essentially unused Newman College law tutorials to the value of 150 pounds. This was the value of an Irish history prize which I had

Student Years, University of Melbourne [1951-1955]   37

mistakenly assumed was cash. I found the first tutorial so uninspiring I never returned.

The source of my Irish History knowledge was 2 volumes I had been given by my teacher Brother Frank McCarthy, who assured me they covered the subject. Over a two-week period at home, I committed the two books to short term memory. I was able to recite any chapter. Unlike with my later law exams, the questions were straightforward. I have never done, or attempted to do, this with any subject before or since.

Passing end-of-year exams was to avoid becoming an addition to the more or less permanent, private income-supported, university presences not necessarily involved any longer with the aspiration for another or indeed any degree at all.

The Law Faculty may have contributed to this. If a student failed to earn a law degree within 10 years, all subject credits up to then were wiped. If the heart and stomach wished continuance it must needs be with a clean sheet. One of my smartest school mates/Commonwealth Scholarship holder so permitted personal distraction that he had attained 10 passes only within the 10 years, leaving him something like 10 short.

A searching set of law exam questions over my years was designed to weed out the memorialists who had quickly boned up on a subject. Even a rough working knowledge, from a reasonable going through of the curriculum, might not be enough to identify the real issue raised by the factual matrices presented in exam papers. Mr. Photographic

Memory, Quiz maestro and later Federal cabinet minister, Barry Jones, just scraped through his law degree in under 10 years. He may, of course, have been studying something less than full time.

Post-graduation, there was one lecture subject that was required for those law graduates who intended to practice law. This was Professional Conduct. My lecturer, Arthur Heymanson, had written a book on the subject. Attendees were mostly articled clerks, and the once weekly lecture was at 5.15pm.

Much of these lectures were given over to the historical individual misdoings of Sydney solicitors Paddy Crick and R.D. Meagher. Then they joined forces in partnership. As fellow attendee Peter Liddell was heard to remark, the outside prospects of an articled clerk with the partnership could not have been enhanced by the association. I enjoyed these lectures and the post-lecture, brisk and chatty strolls down to Flinders Street station in the company of [later Senator] John Button.

As to end of year exams, the desperate law examinee might have to elect to nominate his or her written exam answers for honours. Honours seekers had only to answer 4 instead of the otherwise 5 questions. From memory, there were more than 5 questions on the exam paper. I would be stretching the truth if I claimed never to have sought this way out. The fact of the matter is I managed to collect several honours, although none first class and none sought until after I had taken my seat in the exam room.

Student Years, University of Melbourne [1951-1955] 39

Of late I have had an odd dream. I had belatedly realised at a Law Faculty end of year written exam that I had answered unnecessarily all of the questions. As the time for writing had all but expired, I was desperately attempting to choose which answers to rely upon and whether that number should be 4 or 5. The story faded away without resolution.

The not so golden side of my university years was my need to pick up, at the best pay rates possible, part time work. This was so that I was able to contribute some modest sum for board at home as well as have spending money. The university even had a specialist part time employment service, then a Miss Lemon, to cater for the likes of students such as me. Miss Lemon's office would get out as often as inquiries warranted a listing of available work.

Initially at university there was a tendency to congregate with former Matriculation classmate Commonwealth Scholarship holders from my high school, Parade College. For the non-technical people, like from the Arts, Law and Commerce faculties the universal meeting place was the Union Building coffee-shop or Caf. It was a generously proportioned space for affordable meals and indifferent but adequate coffee. In my day, [earlyish 50s] a workmanlike steak with salad was priced at three shillings and 6 pence— about the same as a gallon of petrol.

In the dryer, warmer, not too hot, months, many chose to relax for the early afternoon spread out on the lush lawns fronting the Union Building. I was never a lawn man.

One bright sunny day, I was traversing this lawn heading in the direction of the Union Building when Barry Humphries emerged with a large bag in hand whose whitish, powdery contents he then proceeded to empty over a reclining male reclining on the lawn. His bag emptied, Barry scurried back through the Union Building entrance. What surprised me most was the almost total lack of response from the victim. Save to dust himself off, he seemed content to return to whatever discussion had been in hand among his group. Maybe it was a commonplace event for Barry, linked to something like the time of day and the phase of the moon—or even DADA.

I mention here early on in my legal studies Barry surprised me when, with a small entourage, he made appearances at a few Law Faculty lectures.

As I got to know more people over the years, it became a rare event to drop into the Caf without meeting up with good company. If I was unthinkingly and blissfully tucking into a steak on a Friday, a mortally sinful matter at the time for a Catholic to deliberately and knowingly undertake, I could be certain to have a non-Catholic friend, such as Bruce McQuaide, take me to task. These auxiliary consciences never waited for any meat to be fully devoured.

More promising were meeting with the likes of poet (and sometime Carlton postman) Bruce Dawe, old classmate Brian Buckley or Malaysian student Ananda Krishnan. Germaine Greer, always in a group, was another regular but, although known to me to greet in passing, we never broke bread together.

Fellow law students were very thin on the ground here, seemingly having a preference for off-campus licensed premises. When not so indulging, they were to be found, if at all, in the Law Library digesting the wisdom of the ages as interpreted by learned judges. A source of fruitful intellectual endeavour might well have been analysing how Sir John Latham's minority [of one] judgment in the Communist Party Dissolution case was justified in following the militarist thoughts and philosophies of English Lord Protector Oliver Cromwell.

I was about as far from being a law library addict as it was possible to be. My knowledgeable citations extended to the sordid facts reported in the 1930s Victorian decision in Cox v Cox and the 1641 [English] State Trials report of the judicial decisions involving the condemned Mervyn Lord Audley and his unfortunate manservant Skipwith.

It stretches credulity that Audley was found guilty for good cause by the Privy Council sitting as a court on basically the evidence of his wife on a charge made by his eldest son. The son made no denial that his sole purpose was to prevent his father dissipating the family fortune. Audley was decapitated 10 days after the verdict.

The Caf was but one section of the Union Building. The actual building complex was just to the right of the apex of the principal university entrance driveway with expansive lawn covering much of the terrain to the right of the driveway and in front of the structure. To the immediate right of the same entrance were to be found the Commerce Faculty buildings.

The ground floor was shared with the cinema/theatre home to the University live theatre and film enthusiast groups. Often there were, of course free, lunchtime screenings of ancient classics such as Battleship Potemkin [1925] and Citizen Kane [1949]. Candidates for the Student Representative Council [SRC] elections were given the opportunity to harangue the mob with their policies from the theatre stage. I well recall attending a packed house there one evening for an entertaining international debate pitting locals against a talented US team on the subject: "That Captain Cook Went Too Far."

When the Melbourne Film Festival was in its embryonic stage, I attended wonderful film screenings there to packed houses. I can even recall the name of an Italian masterpiece "Knights of Cabiria" [1957]. I am unable to so recall the name of a lavish Czech fairy tale type colour production. From a plethora of classy subtitled non-English language films, I was forced to conclude that, with all too rare exceptions, the US movie production scene had abandoned story-telling, character development and dialogue with any subtlety for childish Colosseum type spectacle.

There were commodious toilets, the walls of the male given over, it seemed to me, to a struggle between licentious raunchy poets and censors. Apparently prompted by one bored toilet scribe's cry:

"Where are the bards of yesteryear?"

there quickly appeared a celebratory ode:

"Some condemn censoriously,
Our efforts penned laboriously,

So drop your tweeds,
Fulfil your needs,
Then write and triumph gloriously."

A storm of crude invective could be expected to follow.

In came the censor, to apply a universal coating in a drizzle black and white effect that made the life of a would-be transgressing scribe at least problematic—unless he came equipped with more specialised writing equipment in, for example, the right shade of green. No doubt the war continues.

Upstairs was a more decorous scene. The Warden and his lady lived there. A spacious Men's Lounge with comfortable arm-chairs was to be found. For the lack of any other readily available option. it was the default venue for many debates.

The Debating World (Ed Note)

The Melbourne team for the Adelaide intervarsity debating contest in 1955 comprised John McCormack, John Howes, then a theology student, and T. Ananda Krishnan (then a 17-year old Malaysian Tamil just arrived in Australia under the Colombo Plan to study political science). John and Krish were to become lifelong friends.

In 1958, with his honours degree from Melbourne in hand, Krish proceeded to Harvard University for an MBA. Subsequently, he became a highly successful businessman, recognized a one point as 82nd richest person in the world (and second richest in Southeast Asia). [4]

---

[4] https://www.famous-entrepreneurs.com/ananda-krishnan

Mates Meeting: John and Krish meeting at unidentified airport some time in 1980s or 90s

Among the papers left by John McCormack upon his death in November 2022 was the following, April 2017, emailed poem of greeting from Krish, recalling "the warmth of a fifties Melbourne Irish working-class home" sixty-two years earlier.

Home to Tea

Mr McCormack
    Came home to tea,
    From the tram depot
    And produced second-generation
    Irish kids with Mrs McCormack,
    Who made scones as well.

Mr McCormack sat at the
    Head of the table,
    Said nothing,
    Watching John n Bill n Gavin
    Argue with each other,
    And maybe a sister,
    Groomed to debate
    By Brother McCarthy,
    At Christian Brothers Parade,
    Named after Victoria Parade,

Student Years, University of Melbourne [1951-1955]

Queen of the hated English,
Who sparked that rebellious
Streak in Aussie Irish Catholics,
Starting with Ned Kelly
Archbishop Mannix
And BA Santamaria
Who split the mighty ALP,
Giving the country to Menzies
And sadly ending with a whimper,
In Phil Lynch n Tony Abbott

When Mr McCormack died
His son John wrote me,
Saying the family had not known
This man who sat silently
At home reading the Sun
Was enormously popular
At work and so many turned up
To the wake
That Melbourne trams nearly
Came to a halt that day.

And now I keep demanding
My chefs all over the world
To produce scones
Hot from the oven like
Mrs McCormack's,

And when it happens,
If it ever does,
I shall put butter on that scone
And watch it melt,
Remembering the warmth
Of a fifties Melbourne Irish
Working class home
With children enroute
To a third generation

Lives as lawyers and professors
Thank you,
Brother McCarthy

Ananda Krishnan
With fond memories
Sunday Apr 9 2017
Sixty-two years later

DAV and Debates

Subsequently, and separately from their university affiliation, together with their friend Peter Liddell [1934-2003], John and Krish debated far-and wide. John writes,

Together with Peter Liddell [1934-2003] and Ananda Krishnan [1938-], I entered a team [under the name "New Australian Democratic League," a League of which we were the only members] in the Debaters Association of Victoria [DAV] regular monthly debating circuit. In Victoria in the mid-fifties, the Pentridge Gaol team had been considered almost invincible. On the occasion of our contest with them, our opponents included two convicted murderers (one being the notorious Scotch College graduate and radio announcer, John Bryan Kerr); but we defeated them. In our last debate before my departure from Melbourne in 1963, a McCormack/Krishnan/Liddell New Australian Democratic League team confronted Barry Jones, John Button and Clyde Holding (whose collective name now escapes me). Liddell was later to become a QC and take up raising cattle on Flinders Island, Krishnan became a global tycoon, and all three of our opponents became nationally prominent political figures.

The DAV organisation was very simple, its fixtures and rules all collated in a tiny blue booklet and its arrangements all in the hands of the secretary, Trevor, who also made sure to secure independent adjudicators. It wasn't long before other university-based teams followed our lead. Last time I looked, before I left Melbourne in the early sixties there were 10 university debating teams entered in the DAV competition. The DAV continues to this day and appears to be flourishing.[5]

I well recall attending addresses in the Men's Lounge from serving High Court Chief Justice Sir Owen Dixon [1886-1972] and from well-retired Chief Justice Sir John Latham [1877-1964]. The former, a student philosophy addict, had yet to reach the point of his post-retirement confession to distinguished lawyer mate Eugene Gorman [1891-1973] about his judicial career having been to him "35 wasted years." His preoccupation on the night of my attendance was the plethora of what he described as "fashionable [code for incompetent] counsel" presenting argument before him.

It was in another room opposite, the name of which escapees me, that I played many a game of chess with Alan Hughes or another student of whom I can recall only the surname of Isaacs. The latter could play and win three games, one of which I played, with his back to the boards. For those seeking a quieter milieu there was a comfortable reading library.

---

[5] Debaters Association of Victoria: https://DAV.com.au

This was the location of the somewhat diminutive office of the student newspaper Farrago—no more than a small office really. Above that doorway was emblazoned the words "Abandon Hope All Ye Who Enter Here" from Dante's Inferno. Gavin Dawes and Claude Forell were in command those days.

To me, the Union Building was the heart of the university. There was always something going on. Nights were usually dominated by theatre screenings or plays performed by the theatre group. Last time I visited the Darwin University campus there was no remotely similar meeting place. The result it seemed to me was a campus without soul.

The Union Building was a stone's throw from the Arts building with its lecture theatres used for delivery of lectures to arts/law students. Dominant there was the Public Lecture Theatre with its 400-odd capacity, site for many a lunchtime address from a notable public figure. Politician Arthur Calwell, columnist DGM Jackson and various religious luminaries graced this platform. Barry Humphries even staged a DADA lecture there. It comprised most of the stage taken up by desperates attempting futile tasks, while the presenter droned on.

Earlier, Barry had staged a DADA exhibition upstairs in the Union Building. The exhibits were not unique in themselves but, assembled as they were, combined with their provocative titles, they were intended to startle and amuse. Lest the viewer be too serious, an omnibus range of laughter was loudly and continuously played, ranging from titter to belly laugh.

Two exhibits remain in my memory. The first, a plate of raw liver bore the title Lights Out or the Bowels of Saint Marys. The second, a public-school tie draped around a longneck beer bottle, was entitled Old Fools Tie.

Most, if not all, visiting speakers in the lecture theatres were open to questions after their main speech. I was always quick to make the best of such opportunities. Arthur Calwell, especially, was to establish an easy and to me surprising, rapport with a rambunctious student audience.

John Gorton, a minor player at the time, spoke in one of the smaller lecture theatres as Minister for the Navy. He displayed then such an awkwardness and diffidence that it was difficult to believe his much later public persona as Prime Minister was the same person.

It was a short walk north from the Caf to a section of smallish car park where I chose to leave my transport de jour. I shared this space with vehicles of distinction such as a two-seater Bentley 8 from the early thirties and my Law School Professor David Derham's A-Model Ford sedan of about the same vintage. Another occasional presence was a late thirties Hupmobile owned by a senior law student. There was even a very trim 350cc horizontally opposed twin-cylinder water-cooled Douglas motorcycle with shaft drive. The carpark at Newman Residential College ran to a mint Stutz Bearcat an equally pristine early thirties Studebaker (owned by Basil Rice).

Hupmobile is noteworthy for three things. Henry Ford paid the Hupp 20 of 1910 what seemed a compliment. "I recall looking at Bobby Hupp's roadster at the first show where it was exhibited and wondering whether we could ever build as good a small car for as little money." Henry implied that the Hupp was being sold at a sub-economic price. The Hupmobile was the first all-steel bodied car, but it failed to patent the process. Cars built to the design that had been publicly released were un-patentable.

Obviously, a superior all steel body construction was later the subject of patents such that when Andre Citroen came to build his revolutionary L15 in the mid-thirties a license fee was paid to a US patent holder. The VW Beetle engine was also the subject of a US patent whereby the patent holder was paid a licence fee by the manufacturer.

It was in the same university car park late one afternoon I bumped into my former school classmate, Brian Buckley [1935-2013]. He owned a top of the range Matchless 500 twin motorcycle. With its fully sprung frame, its value was far beyond the price of any bike I could have afforded. On this occasion Brian was obviously affected by alcohol and darkly aggressive to the world. He made a few desultory attempts to kick start his bike. Then, his attention otherwise diverted, I made the decision to disconnect his sparkplugs, thinking to save him from the hazards of the road. Meantime, he was attacking an adjacent paling fence with bare fists.

On another later occasion, I had been twice un-biked, by slippery tram tracks, from my Aerial 600. Fortunately, I had been uninjured thanks to my conscript-issue Melbourne University Regiment military greatcoat.

Sporadic cash emergencies saw me in and out of a number of two, three, and four wheeled vehicles over the

Student Years, University of Melbourne [1951-1955]   51

years. My best university car park showings over my years were a brilliant red extreme low mileage 1947 1200cc Harley Davidson sidecar outfit and a low mileage 1936 Hudson Terraplane, two-door, soft-top, indifferently coloured with severely worn brown paint. The previous owner may not have done the miles, but he had taken a heavy toll on the paintwork.

John with Harley-Davidson motor-bike and sidecar, ca 1953

The former had been one of only 3, specially imported for escort duties for the aborted 1947 Royal Tour. Mine had run in about 3,300 miles on the odometer and came into my ownership quite fortuitously. I had submitted a very modest price (70 pounds) in response to an invitation by the Police for public tenders. The Harley was in my charge for no more than about 12 months. I sold it for profit of about 150 per cent to Elizabeth St motorcycle dealers, Mayfair Motors, where I think it became a collectable. It was no speed machine and used about 1 gallon of fuel for 35 miles.

I would have liked to remove the sidecar and fit solo gearing and a side prop stand but cost always got the better of me. Moreover, if the square-edged car type tyres had not been changed to enable secure heeling in the course of cornering, it would have been quite dangerous. All these modifications would have been prohibitively expensive to me individually, let alone collectively, at the time.

This was well before Harley ownership became something of a cult. Even former Chief Justice of the NT, Trevor Riley and a fellow Rotarian and chief Northern Territory Salvation Army officer, Dudley, rode large modern solo Harleys, with overhead valved engines and telescopic forks, I think they may also have been equipped with belt, as opposed to chain, final drives. Their rides were for relaxation as distinct from daily drives. The acme of my motorbike desire back in those days was an unaffordable BMW flat twin R69 with shaft drive.

On reflection, my Harley had three graces. It was basically a replica of the 11 year earlier 1936 model by the same marque if you liked that sort of thing. The consequence was a large lazy side-valve V twin configuration engine representative of the late twenties. It was fitted with reverse gear and had a wondrously comfortable plunger-sprung bucket seat. On the cost side, it needed a proper windscreen to avoid a bare headless look. My only photos show mine sans the screen. Another Harley rider I met on the road, Fred, made up a suitably impressive and practical screen for me. To my eye, any screen-less, larger motorcycle looks just wrong.

In a right-hand drive country like Australia, there are few things more disconcerting for an unprepared first-time motorcycle outfit rider than a left-hand turn. The problem is that there is next to no weight on the left-hand side to prevent the outfit from turning turtle.

When Brian Buckley was taking his only ride on my Harley, fortuitously in the Royal Park area adjacent to the university, coming to his first left hand bend he finished up stationary, off the road, on the right-hand side, hard up against a wire mesh fence. I had warned him. Fortunately, no real damage was done except perhaps to his ego.

Brian was engaged for much of his time away from lectures assisting Gerard Heffey in the production of the *Catholic Worker* periodic newspaper. That paper was devoted to social justice as defined in various Papal encyclicals. If I read the situation correctly, its line was different to that of its original founder B.A. Santamaria whose more assertive anti-communist ideology at the time was expressed through the pages of *News Weekly* and the secret influence of "The Movement" through positions of influence in the Trade Union organisation.

The Movement had secured the backing of the Australian Catholic bishops, albeit it seems they sleepwalked into it without understanding the political implications. It led to the Labour Party split on sectarian lines in 1959, which kept it out of power federally for 23 years.

In 1950/51 the communist party dissolution legislation dominated Australian political debate. Passed as it was in 1950, it was declared invalid, giving the executive powers that were unexaminable by the judiciary, in March 1951 on an application by ten Trade Unions to the High Court. There followed a double dissolution of the federal parliament, and in April 1951 return of the Menzies lead coalition. In June Labour leader B.J. Chifley died and was succeeded by H.V. Evatt.

Not satisfied, PM Menzies went to the people with a referendum seeking to validate the unexaminable power of the Federal cabinet under the Dissolution Act. In September 1951 that referendum failed.

When political feeling was running at its highest over this issue, I attended a lively public political meeting addressed by PM Menzies at a hall in Canterbury. It was my one and only sighting of Country Party leader Arthur Fadden, in all his foghorn-like electronically unassisted rhetorical glory.

Opposition to the Act was founded in part on its incompatibility with the rule of law. Not only could a person be declared a communist by the executive but also that unexaminable decision was not on what he had done but what he was believed to believe. If the named person was to dispute the decision, the onus of proof lay on his shoulders. As had happened in the US, accusation would then surely replace debate. Not unlike US Senator Joe McCarthy, PM Menzies had his own "list of 53 avowed and alleged Communist trade union leaders" referenced in the course of privileged parliamentary debate before passage of the original bill.

About the time the university and I parted company and courtesy of a gift from the estate of Sir Frank Beaurepaire, a marvellous modern sports complex had become operational. It was located abutting my car park and at the edge of the University Oval. It included a heated, glass enclosed, 25-

Student Years, University of Melbourne [1951-1955]   55

metre pool, to which I was privileged to have access. I seemed to have the wrong physical make-up for apparent fuss-less, all but splash-less, effortless gliding through the water. Nonetheless, over the years since, especially in Darwin, as other forms of aerobic exercise requiring balance and unsupported standing became beyond me, I have used swimming at the Parap Olympic sized Pool as my basic exercise routine.

On the far side of the university oval that abutted the north side of the Beaurepaire Centre were to be found a number of shed-type structures that were able to be used as sports dressing areas. Inside one was a full-size boxing ring and professional weightlifting equipment. Old Parade College mate Philip Hartnett and I wasted many an hour that should have been spent attending law lectures lifting weights and sparring in the ring. Gloves and head protectors were all found on site.

Regular weight patron visitors included Australian weightlifting champion Len Tregonning and appliance and electronics entrepreneur-to-be, Alex Encel. I was to meet Alex's father at his modest jewellery outlet in St. Kilda. I bought an opal from him and split it to make two opal stones.

Brian Buckley was something of a champion boxer as well as a VFL footballer. One fateful day, I invited him to join Philip and me for a spar. In individual rounds with Brian and at the cost of some physical discomfort, we were introduced to a new full-on boxing dimension. We never asked Brian to return. In the ring that day, the thought did cross my mind that even an alternative attendance at the most boring law lecture was to be preferred to a "quiet" spar with Brian.

From an early age, Brian had been introduced to regular sparring sessions with his father. Over the years, he became consumed by such a desire to win one day that, when he did, in his later teens, his father became at risk of serious injury.

A squash court lay about 70 metres or so west of the car park. Use involved getting the key from a source in the Union Building. I was never a squash addict, nor did I ever own a racquet, but somehow I managed to have a few entertaining games.

Beyond the oval and to its north were to be found residential colleges such as Trinity, Newman and Ormond. Slightly further north, on the other side of the main thoroughfare bounding the western campus border, International House was located.

At the invitation of boarder Ananda Krishnan, I attended the occasional meal at Trinity. Ken Mason presided as Rector at the high table, reciting Grace in Latin before the meal. The same Ken was appointed Bishop of Darwin about the time of my arrival in that city in the late 1960s. Through our mutual membership of Rotary we were to meet up and share many a lunch at Charlie's restaurant.[6]

Less decorous was my first meeting with John Pasquarelli.[7] During an evening meal at International House

---

[6] See below, chapter 9.
[7] John Pasquarelli (1937-) was a prominent Melbourne University contemporary of John McCormack, a "larger than life" figure, also at some point an opal miner,

to which I had been invited, John had been bobbing about under dining room tables to the displeasure of the Warden. John was to achieve a measure of undergraduate fame when his mother arrived in her Daimler coupe to settle his outstanding gambling debts. A queue quickly formed outside his room. The creditors were ushered individually into the room where John sat at a table beside his mother.

John as a card gambler was one to push his luck with some success. All-night poker schools playing three and four-card stud with betting on each individual card after those dealt face down was his forte. Such games required nerves of steel to even get a hand and the betting pool with a half-jackpot limit could be quite large.

In due course John teamed up with Alan Hughes. Alan, although very clever, became besotted for a time with what he saw as the opportunity for enrichment through operating a horse racing system. What was sold as Form Plan became the apple of his eye. So far as I understood it, a bet was to be placed on the second favourite in two-year-old races. Alan on one occasion organised a syndicate to apply the system on a meeting in Canberra. Apparently, Melbourne was devoid of suitable betting facilities. The decision was made to finance John to fly to Canberra to select and place the bet. According to the post-race media available, the syndicate's horse won, so an exultant group congregated at Melbourne Airport to greet John's return. They were to meet a deflated

---

subsequently a crocodile hunter in Papua New Guinea, member of the PNG House of Representatives (1964-1968), then adviser to Australian politician Pauline Hanson.

warrior. The media failed to report the actual state of play in the betting odds. The result was that the system selection, as made trackside differed to the system selection made relying on the subsequent media report.

I leave campus activity here to review my part-time university employment, an important extracurricular window on the world for an early 1950s student. I became a regular visitor to Miss Lemon's employment office to scan her lists.

There were slack times when next to no work was available and the occasional job offered was hardly worth bothering with. One such was wattle bark stripping. I now puzzle over this. I spent at least one night at the digs offered for workers after I had driven about 160 kms roughly northeast from Melbourne to take a look. I was kept awake by the noise a shivering Asian student made as the bones of his body rattled with the cold against the bare floorboards upon which he lay to sleep. Truth to tell, I was little better off myself for it was desperately cold, but at least I was inside an [indifferent] sleeping bag.

I was on the return road the next day after my survey of the available target wattle trees had revealed them to be few and far between. Yet the advertisement persisted for many months.

Another university job was with a spinning mill located off Warragul Road about seven miles south of the McCormack family residence. The work was on weeknights from 4 pm to about midnight. In a sense it could have been maintained throughout my university course, but I found I was not cut out for shift work, let alone in the summer months when wall mounted humidifiers blasted moisture into what was already sticky air inside the mill. The objective was to help prevent the fracture of the threads being spun. Unlike Philip Hartnett, another law student mate who joined me at the mill and seemed to be able to function with next to no sleep, I found I was operating at about 70%.

Fortunately for me, there was another side to the mill job. Lou Dyson was a co-worker who rented a room close to our homes. He drove a lovely near new silver Jaguar as if no speed limits existed and was happy to pick us up on route. Along the way, in about December, he convinced me to buy from him for 200 pounds a rotary hoe-cum-ute combo on the understanding that it could be profitably operated. The going rate was 30 shillings an hour with a minimum charge of two pounds ten shillings. All that was needed was insertion of suitable ads for work in the local free presses.

The hoe was a Howard Junior powered by an air-cooled single cylinder side-valve motor of about 600 cubic centimetres. It had seen better days but over the ensuing months of challenging work it proved to be sound.

The ute, a 1928 Whippet, was something of an antique at a time well before such commanded high prices. And it had an excellent body, somewhat let down by an indifferent engine. The weakest link was the tail-shaft connection which was secured by a bent nail and would occasionally become disconnected when one end fell to the road. Still, the ute never let me down. If the tail-shaft did, it was simple to get underneath and reconnect.

As I was to learn, the biggest fault with the kit was the absence of an available option of reverse gear on the hoe. I made up a large "Rotary Hoeing" sign attached to the ute tray with my home phone number—WX1869. For most of that summer university vacation I became a domestic rotary hoer. It was not unusual to be flagged-down on the road and booked for jobs. My mother took phone messages by day when I was out, and since this was most of the time, she became my de facto unpaid secretary. The work was hot, hard and dusty. Often at day's end it was all I could do to stand up. The biggest and most physically draining part of the job was when the hoe jammed up against a boundary such as a fence and had to be dragged back without the aid of a reverse gear.

Before commencing this exercise, I had no experience with hoes or gardening. It was before the internet information era. The best I could do was inquire. Little old ladies, with what to my eye looked perfectly reasonable lawns, seemed obsessed with having them hoed up. In one backyard I planted a new lawn deploying a water filled 12-gallon drum as my roller.

It was a delight to return to university around Easter. And then the kit had to be sold.

One year later, there being no reasonably well-paying work available through the University Employment Office, I tried to replicate the hoeing venture. This time I had to find utility and hoe separately on the open market. The new hoe was a khaki replica of the Howard I had used earlier. The ute was a Ford Model A of about 1929 vintage which I repainted in green with black mudguards and to which I fitted new piston rings.

This time my luck ran out. Mid way through several acres of orchard, the hoe motor gave up. It had to be rebuilt. When I was able to return to finish that job, I found it had been completed by a competitor operating a tractor mounted hoe. Then, when it came to sell off the kit, a middle-aged English émigré engaged me in lengthy conversations over considerable time before, armed with his exhaustive knowledge of the market gleaned from me, he purchased a brand-new kit built around a considerably lighter model Howard.

Another less demanding shift job was that of weekend watchman at the Commonwealth munitions factory at Maribyrnong. My duties were shared with a printer [whose name escapes me now] establishing a new business. It was mid-winter.

Every hour or so one of us had to punch a number of time clocks located around the extensive factory grounds. If we failed, we were told the Fire Brigade would turn up at our watch-base. This was the early fifties. Melbourne was then a much more placid place than now and we never saw any sign of life on our bleak rounds.

Other employment came up closer to home in Box Hill. Whilst establishing my hoeing venture one year I took up a labouring job at the then under construction Box Hill Hospital. This was hard and apparently aimless work. Fortunately, the hoeing venture picked up after a week or two.

Then there was the labouring job at the Box Hill Brickworks. That work was demanding but compensated for by the people I met and had discussions with during breaks. Production at the time was focused on terra cotta tiles. I recall the earnest Christian Scientist co-worker who provoked me into a trial sampling of the Christian Science Monitor newspaper.

A more intriguing job came up with plumber Vic Burden one shorter vacation. Vic's base was somewhere around Nunawading. A few challenging months were spent as a secondary school history teacher at Nunawading High School. That brief experience taught me that to teach properly at the junior level, as I was attempting to a restless undisciplined class, the subject must be well known at a higher level.

Then there was the job as roustabout at the headquarters of the Melbourne University Regiment [MUR]. Gardening and chopping firewood were the main tasks I remember. Something like 15 hours a week was involved, and I could choose my hours. In many ways this job was ideal, located as it was on campus. Alas, I had no green finger and I never felt any confidence about what I was doing in the garden. Indoors there was a large what I would style mess-hall. Invariably the long table was covered with the detritus of banquets past—mainly part filled glasses of wine and stale beer. My duties did not extend to cleaning the Mess.

Oddly enough I had to fight for this job when I had to relinquish it to undertake my compulsory 3-months National Service at Puckapunyal whence I was transferred to the MUR for the term of the subsequent compulsory two or three annual 20-day January camps. But in my absence an interloper had ingratiated himself into my position. I was not welcomed back. I had to remind an ill-tempered commanding officer that it was the law that no compulsory National Service should diminish any worker's position.

My annual 20-day January compulsory camps were the source of a problem when I tried to return to Peters Ice Cream. One end of year vacation, I had worked as a freezing chamber hand at Peters at Burnley. The hours were long and the work spasmodic but hard. The pay was good.

When I sought to return the following year I was asked in early December, as a condition of a return, whether any such camp was in the offing for me in January. My denial followed by my later contrary admission when the camp came up resulted in me being told not to come back.

At the actual camps, so far as I could assess, most of the MUR people, unlike me, simply suffered mild interruption to their idle, parent supported, university holidays for which they enjoyed welcome holiday military pay. For me, however, the military pay was about seven pounds per week as against around 45 pounds after tax from Peters.

The American novelist Tom Wolfe in his Dickensian opus "A Man in Full" described his fallen anti- hero working in a US freezer environment as tantamount to Siberian slave labour. Wolfe's freezer workers were afflicted with all manner of lung associated disorders. My experience was different. Chamber hands had to spring to it when needed. The temperature was 20-30 degrees below and often the blast fans were at full bore. We had to stack on the freezer shelves newly minted ice cream in all of its varieties or load up using the same conveyor belt in reverse to meet orders being trucked out. We were well suited up with flying suit inners and balaclava head gear. When each task was completed we were permitted to rest outside the freezer door to "warm up."

I still chuckle to recall Rene, the ebullient doyen of the Tutti Fruiti machine, proclaim [with a laugh] as she hand sliced the bars extruded from the machine for fancy individual wrapping to the Peters jingle about ice cream untouched by human hands, "We ain't human."

Among the permanent chamber workers two stand out in my memory. The Irishman, Joe O'Donnell, by my estimate in his early thirties, spoke a wondrous new language. Sure, it was English, but, using a non-repetitive and original assortment of innovative phrases spoken in a manner that I have never heard before or since. He had a seemingly inexhaustible catalogue of what were, to me, completely novel, lyrical phrases and descriptions. Poetry it may not have been, but, on the other hand, it was deeply poetical. I would not have been surprised if Joe had bobbed up on the Australian literary scene in later years. But if that happened and I hope it did, I heard naught of it.

Adolf Sporkert was cut from different cloth. Then in his fifties, he was given to sitting in isolation in our worker's tea room, mumbling and chuckling to himself in what I assume to have been German. It appeared that he had been a submariner in the final stages of World War 11. At a time when the life expectancy of a U Boater was truly short, Adolph had participated in one of the great submarine epics of World War 11, as one of the crew of U-977. At close to—or perhaps just after - war's end, U-977's captain had ordered his crew to down periscope and take course for South America. There was sufficient fuel and food. Given the nature of the decision, it seems likely that it was privy to those on board U-977 only.

From the little Adolph told me, the voyage although successful had been fraught. It seems probable his odd, solitary behaviour and his penchant for talking to himself were manifestations of what we would now call post-traumatic stress disorder. This was in about 1953, when World War 11 was still more than a distant memory.

Recently detailed U Boat records like crew lists and boats have been published. Sure enough on my checking one such in a book-store, up came the name Adolph Sporkert. As to the voyage, what little I had gleaned from Adolph pointed to his submarine having been U-977, under the command of Heinz Schaeffer. It was one of two German submarines which landed in Argentina, in apparent disobedience to a surrender order in May 1944. Schaeffer wrote a book about the voyage, which was prompted by a number of factors.

Though the surrender order had been received, albeit faintly, it seemed so alien to the usual emanations from the submarine High Command that it aroused Schaeffer's suspicion. It might have been a trap set by the allies. Then, Goebbels had made a speech, also received by radio on U-977, outlining the treatment Germans could expect if their country was defeated. Germany would be a goat paddock, its males enslaved and sterilized. Germans still had memories of the delay in returning its POWs after World

War 1. Schaeffer and some of the crew had relatives in Argentina where there was a large German community. Married crew were given the choice to be put ashore in Europe. Sixteen of the total of 48 crew took that choice and were put ashore in Norway at night. From there, the Captain had decided to remain submerged from then until they reached the equator. At the time, a voyage of such length had never before been attempted by any submarine. The route was a north rounding of Scotland thence down the west coast of the British Isles. The plan was to cruise at a depth of 25 fathoms [about 50 metres] by day and ten fathoms by night and limit the cruising speed to 3 knots to conserve fuel. Part of the voyage involved 66 days underwater—the second longest such voyage ever undertaken by a submarine at the time and only by a two day margin.

Another U boat, U-530, travelled for 68 days also Argentina-bound at almost the same time.

Living conditions became hellish. Rubbish could not be discarded. Filth, flies, vermin, rotting smells and diesel fumes filled the air, and breathing was difficult, even the bulkheads turning green. Clothing stuck to the bodies of the crew. Saltwater washing led to skin complaints even boils. The U-977 crew became mutinous.

The upshot is that the voyage of U-977, like U-530's to Argentina about the same time, became the stuff of enormous speculation. Had the subs transported Nazi gold, or even perhaps key High Command figures including Hitler and Eva Braun? Had Nazis been put ashore, in Antarctica of

Student Years, University of Melbourne [1951-1955] 67

all places, before the formal surrender to the Argentine naval vessel "Belgrano"?

One enterprising woman journalist in Argentina published a purported "interview" with Hitler and Eva Braun from Patagonia. Were U-530 and U-977 part of a much larger ghost fleet added to by so called "black" submarines engaged in wholesale transportation of the Nazi elite and their ill- gotten gains? What had happened to Adolf at that time?

Eventually, U boats 977 and 530 were delivered by Argentina to the US, where they were used and destroyed during gunnery and torpedo practice drills. The Belgrano itself, ill-fated, was torpedoed and sunk with major loss of life by a British submarine during the Argentinian Falklands war.

I should add in passing that the modern much larger American atomic submarine make common patrols for six months without surfacing. Amenities can include a swimming pool. Range is limited only by food.

The hulls of these subs, as are the modern Russian subs, are based on the advanced German designs which never saw construction until the war was all but over. Like Willy Messerschmitt's ME-262 jet, they were ready to build in 1940, but were shelved on the ground of cost and a "what we have now is good enough for the job" mentality.

I also worked for at least several months as a Friday afternoon motorcycle ad collector for the Melbourne "Age." This involved a north-east quadrant of the city and was usually completed around 5.15 at the Age office. I had to use my own motorcycle and this was no hardship. I was expected in the various newsagencies so it was quickly in and out. All weathers had to be faced. On one particularly cold wet and miserable Melbourne Friday afternoon my bike electrics became waterlogged. A call was made to the Age. Within an astonishingly short time an Age man cosily ensconced in a warm dry car met up with me, took over my collected ads and was gone.

I recall here also English migrant Alan Etherington's commercial endeavours. Alan was himself a student of more mature age than most. I first crossed paths with him when I became one of his timber cutters at a property at Gladysdale in the Dandenong Ranges east of Melbourne near Healesville. Trees had been felled and Alan wanted them cut up into firewood-compatible pieces which he could deliver to suburban customers. Possibly he owned the property. There was a shack where I spent Saturday evenings. There must have been cooking facilities because I never ate out then. Wielding an axe against the timbers was great exercise.

This job was brought home to me when in Darwin many years later I had a phone call from a McCormack, not a kinsman, who was on the Law Faculty staff at Melbourne University. He had a faculty photograph of among others former Dean Prof Zelman Cowan at a Law event at Healesville. He had been given to understand I probably was one of the "others" in that photo.

This was before the age of the internet and digital photography when a copy of the image could have been emailed. Then, I was able to recall visiting Healesville for a

Student Years, University of Melbourne [1951-1955] 69

Law Faculty function from my workplace not far away at Gladysdale. My caller seemed singularly unimpressed by the linkage of my visit with wood chopping.

I have hazy recollection of from time to time sharing the Gladysdale shack with a law graduate and wood chopping with him. Alan would turn up occasionally. Once he left Bushman brand saws which he considered would be more efficient than axes for what we were doing. He was probably correct. But changing to the saws was not attractive. A modern chainsaw would have increased our efficiency exponentially.

It was about this time Alan set about anti-termite home spraying with dieldrin. His workers, myself included, used knapsack pressure spray units to go around the house perimeters at ground level. We were told to exercise extreme care to ensure we avoided skin contact with the dieldrin.

When the family lived in Wolseley Street our next door neighbour was involved as a working investor with a company trading under the name Nonporite, which specialised in the manufacture of coatings for reverberatory furnaces. I found employment as a labourer in the Nonporite factory during a shorter vacation. There was no connection with the neighbour to secure the job, nor did I ever sight him during my short stay.

Looking back now, I realise the principal direction of my earned funds was to purchase various cars and motorcycles over the years all of which, for differing reasons became beyond my capacity to keep. The cause was my making something of a futile week-end hobby of looking out from the pages of the Saturday Melbourne *Age* newspaper vehicles that interested me. All were to a degree distractions both from the study of law and the real business of living but part of the tapestry of my life during those "student" years.

This weekend pursuit kept me well informed though about the Melbourne used car and motorcycle markets, as well as giving me hands on experience of the advances in automotive engineering and technology post 1926. How many people can claim, as I can, to have personally undertaken two successful car new piston ring fitting jobs let alone the [probably unnecessary] decarbonising and valve grinding of an Aerial Square 4 motorcycle?

My dark blue 1937 Nash Ambassador twin ignition 4 door sedan was one example of futility. Lovely car as it was in all other respects, the motor was subject to engine knock. Carefully driven, that knock was not so intrusive, but it was apparent to my attentive ears. Eventually, this would have led to a major immobilising, destructive engine event.

The obvious cure was a complete engine rebuild - rebore, fitting new pistons, a crankshaft regrind, new big end and gudgeon bearings and ancillaries—all to my mind out of the question by reason of cost. Compared to the A$15,000 cost as of ten years ago, including labour, of rebuilding a Mercedes 280 double overhead cam engine, relatively inconsequential, but too much for me. It had to be, and was, sold.

The Nash even was able to cruise effortlessly, albeit dangerously given the state of the engine, at 70 mph (recorded on my return trip to Melbourne from my wattle bark stripping job survey). Mid this trial, another unmarked vehicle materialized, hard on my tail. At the instant of its first sighting, I released my foot from the throttle hoping, if it was an unmarked police patrol, it would have needed to so accelerate to catch up had not had the time to properly record my speed. I dared not use the brakes lest my stoplights alert my pursuer. After a few tense minutes at 50 mph my follower disappeared.

Other road machinery of note include my Fisher bodied with a windup windscreen 1926 [or thereabouts] Chevrolet Sedan, of low mileage but sold because of uncontrollable front wheel shimmy; my 7 passenger Studebaker of around 1930, sold because of its high fuel consumption; my Triumph 650 Thunderbird motorcycle sold because it was unaffordable; and my 2 Ariel Square 4 motorcycles, the latter a blue, SU carburetted, 4 port header, sold because I was finding the roads too dangerous for two wheels.

Others, that I "nearly" bought, and would have had I not been short of twenty pounds or so, included Greg Armstrong's near new Vincent 1000cc Rapide motorcycle and an extraordinary darkish blue 6 wheel Packard of 1931 or so vintage that still smelt and drove like new with the original paintwork in showroom condition. The last was far too good for my later outback driving and I could not afford to store it. Still, the test drive was a privilege.

PART TWO—The Law

Chapter 2: The Law, 1, Articles and Induction [1956-1960]

To work as a lawyer, one must first serve "Articles," a kind of apprenticeship. This meant finding a solicitor with a full practising certificate who was prepared to show a rookie the ropes for 12 months—basically to have him as understudy. Once matched up the pair would enter into a set form of written articles of agreement to this effect. Generally, this meant a partner in a larger law firm. It was only on completion of articles that a young lawyer could make application for a full practising certificate and be able to consider independent career options.

These options included practice as a private solicitor or government lawyer or opting to become a barrister. At that time the Melbourne University Law Faculty had printed booklets analysing the hazards of the respective careers of solicitors and barristers. Under the direction of Professor David Derham [1920-1985] appointments were made for interested graduates with principal lawyers offering articles. Graduates with particular, specialist ambitions could even be matched to potential masters practising in the relevant area. Fortunately, at the time there was little difficulty in finding matches. My understanding is that this is far from being the case today (writing in 2018). To a certain extent the profession has found a way around this by providing a course of practical training of prospective degreed lawyers which is accepted in lieu of articles for the purpose of admission to practice. No doubt real world training must be the preferred choice.

Before my time a prospective lawyer was expected to pay for the privilege of articles. While this custom had ceased and articled clerks were paid the actual wage was to say the least modest. During my interview with Weigall and Crowther senior partner John Adam which led to our entry into articles eight pounds per week was discussed. During that discussion John used the office intercom to contact another partner to alert him what was afoot before mentioning the eight pounds per week and then hanging up to pre-empt further discussion. I think I learned the reason when my first pay was delivered in the presence of Michael [WMR] Kelly, my predecessor in articles who had just completed his term. I was indiscreet to let Michael see my first wage payment. Since his wage envelope contained one pound ten shillings less tax, he was far from pleased. He went on to the bar, however, and concluded his career as a County Court judge.

Weigall and Crowther was one of Melbourne's then bigger law firms. Weigalls and I found each other through the good offices of professor Derham. The firm has since been merged into another entity Norton Rose Fulbright. The office was located at 459 Little Collins St, This was directly opposite the entrance to Selborne Chambers, then an ancient two-story arcade style building that ran through to Bourke St - a distance of 100 to 200 metres. Individual barrister's rooms with their names on the doors were on either side. The upstairs level replicated the downstairs layout except the upstairs galleries were enclosed by balustrades to hip height so the space above the walkway was clear to the ceiling. So far as I could make out the entire structure was of timber. About mid-point on the ground floor there were a few steps up to allow for the elevation to Bourke St. At the top of these on the left proceeding to Bourke St. was a larger room probably the best in the building emblazoned with the name RG Menzies QC [never there in my time] underneath which was the name Ninian Stephen [1923-2017, Governor-General of Australia, 1982-89]. Every trip to the Supreme Court and there were many for me usually to the registries involved a double traverse of the Selborne Chambers walkway On route, time of day was exchanged with out of court barristers hovering just outside their chambers chatting with each other ears attuned to their phones.

Other considerably smaller barristers' chambers were located over two floors in a more conventional building known as Equity Chambers located on the north side of Bourke St. It was the home of 20 or 30 barristers. It was not regarded as an auspicious address for an aspiring young barrister but the late ED [Woods] Lloyd took his first steps there as counsel and prospered - a fact that I believe says as much about his great ability as of his location. Woods also had the unusual advantage for a young barrister of having had some years life experience remote from study and the law. Moreover, his father came from Ireland and as Woods remarked the solicitor's names in his fee book could have been from a casualty list from the Battle of the Boyne.

During my time at Weigalls, my master in articles and firm partner, John Paterson Adam, shared the ground floor with George Crowther, William Weigall, and the accounting department. George owned the office building and I never saw evidence of his activity on behalf of the firm. William, an irregular office attendant, was quite aged and seemed to be in genteel retirement. Halfway up the staircase from the ground floor offices there was a mezzanine floor where corporate lawyer Edwin Colquit Kennon plied his trade with assistance from secretary, Mrs. Miles. David Adam, son of John, occupied an area at the rear of a covered-in bridge over a laneway at the rear of the building. Conveyancer Miss Kennedy worked from the main office area proximate to the bridge.

Together with his Irish-born secretary Mrs Mangan, John Adam managed a prodigious and unrelenting output using every minute of every working day with the accent on building dispute cases. When these came to trial, it was the privilege of the articled clerk in lieu of John to sit beside his counsel in the role of instructing solicitor take notes, orally report to John Adam at the end of each day and learn.

I learned of John's selections of counsel to brief. As best I can recall now, preferred names were Bob Brooking, Steve Strauss, Ted Woodward, John Greenwell, John O'Sullivan and for divorce Charlie Lucas. So far as I could make out all were hard workers. Even when it was apparent a case was doomed, if John even suspected his counsel de jour was not fighting to the last he would be unlikely to be re-briefed.

In that time a divorce was granted only on proof of an offence such as adultery, habitual drunkenness and the like. Sitting in the court for undefended divorce hearings, as I often did, it was difficult to know if the presider, Barry J, was awake until there was even the slightest slipup in the presentation when the judge immediately became highly pro-active. Charlie was always ultra- careful with his cases in which I was instructor.

I shared an office on the first floor initially with Michael and Gay Tolhurst. Gay's middle name was Vandaleur and he preferred to be addressed as Van. He was completing two years, the first for Articles, with Weigalls, when I arrived. He left to go to the Bar very soon after. He died very young from natural causes. During my 12 months, Michael stayed on for a second year and we shared our room with various other men of law including English managing law clerk Mr. Salter and Dr. Fraenkel. My out-of-court time was devoted to handling agency work for sundry country law firms, minor debt collections, filing court documents, attending the Supreme Court as instructor and attending list call-overs in the Supreme and County Courts. To eke out my modest income, on one or two nights a week I would serve the firm's summonses using my vehicle de jour, then a 1930 Pontiac sedan. I knew my way reasonably well around Melbourne, but I came close to taxi driver knowledge from serving process.

My master John was always cautious when his court antagonist was represented by Arthur Secombe. Arthur was about John's age and managed a heavy workload in his prime. When I watched him instructing, his voice was impeded, probably through Parkinsons Disease and his voluble, high pitched, noisy, but to me indecipherable observations made to counsel to promote his client's case seemed to me to be eccentric. I passed these observations on to John. He told me Arthur was in his experience in court likely to be up to something. Arthur's client won that case.

Ex Governor-General and High Court Judge Ninian Stephen was buried in 2017 aged 93. As an articled clerk I once sat opposite Stephen at the bar table instructing another UK émigré Bob Brooking in a Supreme Court boat building dispute. The trial went over eight days and was before a Judge sitting alone. The judge, Alistair Adam, was the younger brother of my master in articles. My firm's defendant client was the boat owner. The plaintiff was the builder. The dispute was over the construction of a 42' catamaran sailboat quite a revolutionary craft for the times. It put me on the road to sailing after I wangled a sail on the craft the subject of the litigation. Master of Pleadings, as Stephen was described to me by Frank Costigan QC [1931-2009], he may have been, but he was equally an eloquent advocate with a mellifluous voice. A reserved judgment awarded victory to my client.

Another case I recall involved John's client Mr. Allen, a builder, locking horns with one O'Keefe. O'Keefe was out to prove a minor point to do with a building advisory service he ran. After about five days into an eight-day trial he admitted as much in evidence. This provoked a response from the trial judge Norman O'Bryan that he had chosen an expensive way of going about his point. Norman had a deep, rumbling voice backed up by strong personal presence. Mr. Allen was successful at trial. Whether O'Keefe paid any of the costs awarded against him I do not recall.

The Supreme Court registry office was a busy place even in in those days. Prothonotary Percy Malbon sat in a telephone box-like structure and those wishing to file or issue documents queued for their turn. Percy would cancel the duty stamp and make an entry of record in his registry. You were handed your writ and that was that. My later Northern Territory experience of the same procedure has been sadly lacking.

Supreme Court Building disputes and the more esoteric civil cases were usually, at the election of the plaintiff, tried by a judge sitting alone. The bulk of the civil list comprised motor accident personal injury cases of little legal complexity and these were invariably set down for trial by a jury of 4. Many of these cases were settled on the day of trial. I learned of the unpredictability of civil juries when after a brilliant performance by barrister Tony Murray on behalf of the third-party insurer the jury entered a record damages award to barrister John Mornane's plaintiff client.

John Adam's cases were not so easily amenable to settlement, and it was commonplace for them to go on for at least several days. I think the longest I sat in on went for 8 days. The usual motor accident personal injuries damages case that went to a hearing was resolved within one day.

Upon completion of the 12 months of articles formal court admission procedure followed. The usual first admissions date for the year is at the first March Supreme Court sittings. The papers are prepared and filed. Each applicant is represented and a formal oral application made. In my case an Old Paradian, Jim Gorman, moved the application. The ceremony completed, it was a race to the Federal Court Building in Little Bourke Street to sign the high Court roll.

Those earlier in the queue have Federal court seniority over the later signatories.

I could see no future for myself at Weigalls. My articles completed; I was off to 2 other single principal firms where I obtained more diverse but considerably less exotic experience. There Supreme Court trials were a rarity. If one did come up, the principal sat at the bar table as instructor. Now I realise my experience at Weigalls was an extraordinary opportunity especially for a budding barrister. I was privileged to be given a rare insight into the law and some of its personalities.

Two events come to mind. One involved an older Supreme Court Judge, the other the later days of a doyen of the Victorian bar. It was a Friday afternoon unopposed urgent application for a special chamber order. My counsel was Arthur Adams. Charles Gavan Duffy [GD, 1882-1961], the Judge, was already an old man. As Arthur droned on GD slipped off his chair under the bench. Up came Mr Chad, wig askew. This happened several times, with Arthur droning on. Then GD nodded off. Arthur dropped books on the bar table to try and arouse him. Finally, the Order was made, and GD tottered off to his chambers. Back at the office I got a call from GDs associate. If I wanted the order signed, I should be quick. I set forth immediately and secured the signature. GD died days later.

The younger GD was said to have been of urbane temperament and great personal charm as well as having a sound legal knowledge and being gifted as an advocate During WW1 he had served at Gallipoli as a second Lieutenant and later on the western front where he was gassed. After seven months treatment for this, he returned to the front and was wounded again. By the time he returned home, in 1919, he was a major. He married soon after and the only children, twins, died at birth. From what we know now this may have been related to his exposure to chlorine gas. He was appointed in 1933.His later years were plagued by ill health. Not long before the episode narrated above GD was hit by a tram.

I was called upon to make a brief visit to Eugene Gorman QC to his Equity Chambers rooms on some minor but now obscure professional matter. Unbeknown to me at the time of my attendance I was meeting a man who post World War 11 had essentially abandoned the practice of law. This was by a man who had dominated the criminal bar in the 30s. Instead, he had chosen a gregarious lifestyle and freewheeling career choices as race-track aficionado Truth newspaper director and journalist and Australian Dried Fruits Association chairman and company director cum one man sphere of significant influence. His National Biography entry, written by Barry Jones, describes him as one who as a barrister had a large commercial and criminal practice winning recognition as one of the best criminal barristers of his time. The room I entered was enormous about three times the size of a moderately large office. At the end was a kind of raised dais where he sat at a huge desk. Racehorse photographs filled the walls. I was hugely impressed by the man's charisma.

John Nimmo, at the time QC but later a Federal Court Judge and, like Gorman, an Equity Barristers Chambers denizen, told me of a celebrated divorce case in which as a young barrister he was junior to Gorman. Throughout, the

Melbourne media was agog with the salacious revelations from the witness box. After the first hour or so of proceedings Gorman slipped away never to be seen by Nimmo until the closing stage many days later. Then, he delivered what Nimmo described as a brilliant final summing-up address based on such a grip of the facts and evidence it was hard to believe he had not been present throughout.

Perhaps it was this living a life instead of the lawyer's peripheral intense but fleeting involvement in clients' lives that motivated Gorman's decision to cease the practice of law post war. Then, again, I recall an observation made to me by the late Peter Liddell QC that the pressures of the job meant that few barristers were active after 50.

Chapter 4: The Law, 2, Collins St [1960-1963]

It was 1960. In the course of my solicitor employment with John Don at the relatively inner Melbourne south-eastern suburb of Elsternwick, I had been on my way up Collins Street, headed for the Supreme Court registry. Just west of the intersection with Swanston Street, at number 331, was the now-demolished old bluestone Union Trustees Company Building. You could say it was the very heart of Collins Street. In front of the entrance was a newly erected sign offering a legal practice for sale on easy terms.

The asking price all-up was about 2,500 pounds with a deposit of 500 pounds. There was extra to pay for the value of the unfinished work in hand when it was completed but events were to prove that this was inconsequential.

It was not a lot of money in today's terms but a reasonable house in the eastern suburbs could be had for about that sum at the time. This was before Australia free floated the dollar, after which Australians had to compete for local real estate with an endless line of cashed up potential overseas buyers and Australia's federal parliament made maintenance of high real estate prices a key aspect of government policy. The financial world has been awash with money, little of which has been seen on Main Street except to inflate asset prices.

The seller was executor of the estate of a deceased solicitor who had conducted legal practice from the very building. The executor was upstairs on the fourth floor ready to meet prospects. In and up I went. There I met the deceased's brother–in-law, Mildura solicitor Mr. Duck. The deceased was John B Plant of whom I knew nothing.

The office suite was spacious. It had been shared with Stephen Hayes whose personal professional office was at the rear. A partition at the front of Stephen's office was the dividing line marking the boundary of the front separate office which had been occupied by John Plant. In front of that again was the shared typing pool and the reception desk.

I knew nothing of the backroom machinations of legal practice. Impressed as I was by the office, the price and the terms, I was hooked. With hindsight, that decision and what I was to learn from it, were to stand me in excellent stead when, nine years later, I decided to return to legal practice in Darwin.

The landlord was not prepared to grant a lease. The law practices' tenancies were at will with no security of tenure. The Trustee was prepared to indicate it had no plans for the tenanted space but no more. I derived some sense of tenancy security from that and that the tenancy offered was the same as the deceased had been operating under for some years.

With my father's assistance and his signing up to guarantee a modest bank overdraft with the National Bank, I was able to sign up to Mr. Duck's carefully drawn contract and take possession of my business. The bank arrangement was handled through the Stock Exchange branch under the management of Gordon Nalder.

Given that I found Gordon was so smooth as to give new meaning to the word, as well as so efficient that a film of his example could have been used in bank training, it was no surprise to me that it was not that much later he scaled to the pinnacle of his bank. The last time I fleetingly glimpsed Gordon was from the inner line in a double lined queue of cars lined up from about where the Pratt mansion Raheen is today. All were slowly making their way over Melbourne's Johnson Street bridge connecting Kew to the City. It was about 8,30am one week morning. Gordon's chauffeur driven limousine temporarily drew abreast of my humble self-drive while Gordon luxuriated in the rear reading a newspaper.

Truth to tell, the actual business was more or less moribund. It would have been doing little more than paying its way, if indeed that. The ace in the hole was the St. Vincent's public hospital client. It was run by the Sisters of Charity. The big questions was whether it chose to remain as a client and whether any other legal work might flow from the connection. Time alone would tell.

John Plant had died suddenly. Up to his death there had been sporadic adoption matters flowing from securing, from single mothers in the hospital maternity section, written consents to adoption of their babies. His secretary and his legal clerk brother were kept on, at least for the transition. Accountant Geoff Brennan was engaged to look after the books and trust account.

I owe a great debt of gratitude for the friendship and assistance I received from Stephen Hayes, with whom the space was shared. Stephen was in his sixties and I in my late twenties. Of all the people I have met over the years, to me Stephen only yields for charm to my late Rotary mate Nicholas Paspaley (on whom see below). I would often be brought into friendly conversation with his client Norman

Putt. Norman had a boating connection. Stephen's most celebrated client was Mario of Melbourne restaurant fame.

As the months went by, we often lunched together at little coffee shops around the area. One of our favourites was on the northern side of Bourke Street just west of Queen Street. Over these lunches, Stephen was to introduce me to his senior legal figure mates like Taxing Master Cyril Fyffe, County Court Judge Grattan Gunson and then silk John Nimmo. Solicitor John Wilder was often good company.

Nothing was held back. There was no pomposity. The talk was always energetic and free flowing. We could have been a bunch of young students. Although we were all lawyers, no gnomes sat at our table. Really it was a bit like my final term student days at Melbourne's Public Library. After shared laughter, grumbling, ideas and legal gossip, we could return to our respective treadmills mentally refreshed.

When we were among solicitors the grumble was always about the unrelenting difficulties with legal practice. Cyril Fyffe had been a senior solicitor/partner when he jumped ship for a quieter less demanding more regular life supported by a predictable and regular income. His predecessor had left under something of a cloud of unsustained accusations of predatory behaviour towards young women. Cyril breathed nothing of this.

At the time, assessing legal bills was far more in the nature of a black art than it is today, as least in the NT. Among many arcane things, it involved word counts and counting of the number of 72-word folios in a document before computers did this automatically. Unless you were familiar with the quirks of the Taxing Master and had worked your file under taxation with precision so that all work had been recorded with some detail, the strong probability was you were likely to receive much less than your due. I think legal costing consultants looked after much of the heavy lifting. Mind you, this was well before the John Grisham novel "The Firm" purported to reveal how bigger US law firms had the potential to hide criminal behaviour in the logging of and charging for, hours worked.

The last time I saw Stephen was during a visit from Andamooka to Melbourne. It was about 18 months after I had cut free. I had been told he was not well. As far as I knew little was known generally in the community about Alzheimers Disease and this is what I was told had brought Stephen into care. He looked much the same as when I had seen him last and he recognised me, but his conversation, if you could call it that, was disjointed. Phrases we had used in our lunches were brought out in a mixed-up, jocose way. I realise now that he was aware of and acknowledging his mental debilitation as a measure of the toll legal practice had taken over the years. Had we but known it, he was close to the end of life.

The two staff I inherited when I took over were problematic to me. The typist/secretary was extraordinarily slow. When it came to typing a Will, it had to be on expensive paper with no alterations. Her waste basket would be full of pages of this barely used paper. The deceased's brother was a carefree soul with highly limited, if any, legal skills counterbalanced by some reputation as a solo singing concert performer. And he knew where to find things in the massive near office sized bank style combination locked vault abutting the typing area. When, for example, a client died the brother might spend hours in the vault before emerging triumphant with the will held aloft.

Staffing matters were brought to somewhat of a head when I advertised for a junior typist secretary intended at the time of advertising as a back-up. Such was the quality of the applicants that rather, than selecting the one, I decided to select three and put off the two I had. This transformed the office. The new staff were bright and anxious to learn. For example I was able to train them to prepare the affidavits by adoptive parents in support of their adoption applications as well as all supporting documentation. I would take the details and hand them to the girls.

These days it is more or less fashionable to decry adoption or more particularly securing the consents from the mothers. Why, the contention is, should any mother give up her child? The answer lies partly in the different nature of society at that time and partly in the attitude to marriage today. And critics forget, or choose to ignore, that any consent was easily and instantly revocable within 28 days of having been given. This last was a matter I stressed to the signatories at the time of signing. As required by law, they were also given a copy of the consent which included the short form of revocation. No consent I took was revoked.

Back in the sixties, divorce law was spelled out in the Matrimonial Causes Act of 1959. It was founded on the necessity for a petitioner to establish one of 14 matrimonial faults. Such offences included adultery, habitual drunkenness, desertion, cruelty, insanity and imprisonment.

To prove marital fault a spouse would often hire a solicitor or private detective to collect evidence to support the claim. This process was often expensive which made it difficult for the less wealthy to get a divorce.

There was only one 'no-fault' ground that was accepted. That was if the couple had been separated for more than 5 years. Moreover, except with leave of the court, a spouse could not apply for a divorce unless the couple had been married for at least 3 years.

In 1975, the Family Law Act was passed by the Australian Parliament. It had been sponsored by Lionel Murphy. The greatest change was the introduction of no-fault divorce across the board. One spouse had only to show that their relationship had suffered irreconcilable breakdown. This was evidenced by a 2-year separation. The time required for a decree nisi to become absolute was reduced from 3 months to 1. This resulted in a large number of Australian divorces recorded in 1976.

According to the Australian Bureau of Statistics, since the 1980s the divorce rate in Australia has increased steadily, whilst the number of de facto relationships continues to increase. The number of marriages has also steadily decreased.

It is not difficult to extrapolate from this data that 1960 presented very different social and economic circumstances for an unmarried mother than 2019. Add to this the Centrelink entitlements, including rent assistance, for a single mother available today that were not available in the sixties. Albeit with considerable difficulty and subject to her availing herself of the full spectrum of available social welfare payments, an unmarried mother could live independently today where she could not have done so in 1960.

The sixties was also a time when there was considerable social stigma attached to unmarried motherhood. With the larger family with children spread over a wide age group it would not be uncommon to pass off and raise a child produced by an older unmarried daughter as a younger sibling.

Modern application of adoption law in Victoria can yield surprising results. A friend from my old school had retired to Darwin after spending most of his working life overseas. Years earlier he had mentioned to me the considerable age differential of something like 20 years with his older sibling.

In his retirement he had cause to get a copy of his birth certificate. Unlike on previous occasions over the years, he was ushered into a back room where he was told to his astonishment he had been raised by adoptive parents. He managed to piece together the story over ensuing months.

His natural father, a wine and spirit merchant, had been something of a financial celebrity teamed up over the years in business transactions with a onetime Federal Treasurer and a celebrity illegal bookmaker [in the world brought to life by Frank Hardy's 1950 classic, *Power Without Glory*]. The father had been widowed. He secured the services of a housekeeper. The housekeeper fell pregnant and gave birth to my friend. The father's sister ran a foundling home where my friend remained for over 12 months. The sister was moved on whereupon some urgency arose for adoption of the child. The selected adoptive parents lived proximate to the natural father.

My friend contacted and was welcomed into the family of the legitimate descendants of the natural father. It came to be generally acknowledged by the family that he bore a closer physical resemblance to the late father than any of his newfound siblings.

The rejuvenated office was a more productive and happier one. The adoptions continued. The final stage of the applications involved the adoptive couples presenting themselves with the child and the guardian ad litem, invariably a clergyman, to a County Court judge in his private chambers rather than open court. The party would assemble at my office from where we would wend our way on foot to the court. One day I had 10 such applications so as you can imagine I lead quite a large contingent. The guardianship ad litem procedure was designed to have someone formally looking after the interests of the child pending the making of the adoption Order by the Court.

One time there was a minor hiccup. The mother giving up the baby was in a stable marriage with previous children. The Judge wanted a further affidavit from that couple to verify that the child was being given up solely in the interest of domestic economics.

For a brief period, I took on a debt collection agency, It was through this client I became acquainted with E.O [Ted] Moodie Heddle QC. The son of a sea captain, Ted was a highly competent barrister and respected jury advocate [most civil damages cases then were determined by juries] and a man's man who enjoyed a drink. His afternoon court appearances were said to have been diminished by the effect of liquid lunches. One way or another the stress of the job must have so got to him. In his early fifties the alcohol got the better of him. His story did not end well.

My meeting with Ted was unusual. I was acting for a bookmaker over a claimed 35,000-pound debt. The matter shot through to the top of the Court list. A date was fixed. I had spent no time in preparation relying on an undertaking from Ted to pay me the claim before trial. The trial date came. McCormack was hopelessly unready. The client was waiting in the wings. At 9.30 in came Ted - with a cheque.

A fall from legal grace occurred one morning when he was on circuit, I think at Geelong, shortly after he was appointed as a County Court judge. Obviously the worse for alcoholic excess of the preceding evening, it came time to empanel a jury for a drink driving offence. Arthur Adams appeared for the defence.

Arthur was an always impeccably dressed [morning suited, black jacket, Prince of Wales double-breasted waistcoat, striped trousers and Homburg] mature-aged barrister of no special note who as a person was the antithesis of Ted. In his chambers, when any knotty legal problem arose, Arthur commonly and openly would consult with textbook writer Lou Voumard QC [author of a landmark text on the sale of land] in an adjacent room.

In deference to Ted's obvious disability, Arthur had sought adjournment. This was in front of the yet to be empanelled jury. Ted rejected the application. In doing so, he told Arthur it was obvious his client was "guilty as hell." I have no knowledge of the result but I assume a conviction because of what happened next. Arthur lodged a complaint with the AG and one way or another Ted's bench appointment had been terminated.

He took up some kind of directorial appointment with Bourke Appliances, a white goods retailer, behind which was the late Bob Hawke's mate retired silk Lionel Revelman. I met Ted in the street one day and he took me up to show me his office - a tiny dogbox high up above the retail floor below.

The last part of this sad tale was given to me by my old debating partner, the late Peter Liddell QC. Peter was drinking in a Richmond pub. A derelict sat in one corner. He was pointed out to Peter as one who claimed to have been a Judge. Peter looked closer. He recognised Ted. Peter rallied a bunch of barristers to contribute. Ted was close to the end. Peter's team organised accommodation and an eventual hospital bed. Ted slipped life's moorings soon after.

The debt collection agency began to take over the office. We parted company. It was not so easy to prevent the spirit of John Plant from taking me over. John had been president of the silver-tail Old Xavierians Association. While his former clients were by and large good people with whom I could relate, I could sense a pressure to conform to their world that I never saw myself as ready to accept. It would have been all too easy to have stumbled into an "acceptable" marriage to a virtual stranger. There was so much of the world I thought I had to explore before I succumbed to suburban banality.

So while I applied myself unstintingly to the grindstone, as I needed to if I was to survive economically, my heart was divided by my longing for what you might describe as adventure. It became apparent to me that the further I went down the JB Plant road the less likely the chance to live in what I considered any real sense. Meantime, if a phone call I had received in my office late one morning from a young lady meant anything, there was someone at large falsely identifying himself as a rich prosperous single me engaging in a hectic Melbourne social whirl. Whoever that might have been, he must have been well aware that his deception had no chance of being unraveled by my personal appearance.

The practice work saw me in the office 7 days a week. For exercise, I often walked from the family home at Wolseley Street Mont Albert to the office—a distance of about 8 miles in the old money. Over the three years I spent there, I believe the hardest yards had been done in any long-haul perspective. But ...

I mentioned the tenancy. Almost inevitably and after about 12 months, the Union Trustee Company decided it needed the space Stephen and I occupied. Fortuitously, about then, Arnold Bloch, of later Bloch Liebler fame, had upgraded from what Stephen and I found was an ideally partitioned space about midway up the Prudential Assurance Building at corner of Bourke and Queen Streets. Arnold had decided he needed more space. The building was heated for winter but not air conditioned. No parking either although this never was of any concern to me. It was considerably closer to the Courts and registries than had been 331 Collins Street. The price Arnold asked for the partitioning and furniture he was leaving behind was modest.

Prudential's Hector McColl Jones welcomed us. Along the way, with Hector ever the salesman, he sold me a term life insurance policy which I never fully embraced at the time but was grateful for the cash I was able to release from it not that much later on.

I think it must have been Hector who convinced me to take on an adjacent tenanted [in a semi abstract way] space to allow for convenient future expansion. The sub-tenant was a Mr. Weinawa Dlugosowski who was believed to run a building company. Rent receipts from this source were erratic and later ceased altogether. The office was rarely occupied. After payments ceased, I got word his enterprise had collapsed. By a stroke of combined legal skill and luck, I was able to lay valid claim to ownership of the internal partitioning and later to divest myself entirely of this expensive incubus.

Clients and associated personalities from those days I call to mind as I write nearly 60 years later include Frank Reinehr and his father Bert, couple Reg and Sylvia and John Galvin. The solicitor son of one of the trust officers with the Union Trustee Company was to come into my employ in Darwin years later with this provenance unbeknown to me until well after the event.

The Reinehrs were chattel lease brokers. They were involved with the lease of road trains to the NT's Noel

Buntine for his fledgling cattle transport business. Frank, ever the enthusiastic amateur aviator, was to take me for my first light aircraft flight in a Chipmunk [Harvard Trainer]. I was to host his brief visit, in the course of an aerial safari, to Andamooka Opal Field not that many years later. He was a smoker. Lung cancer extinguished his life in his sixties.

Which brings me to Zdnek Kempney. He was closely linked to the International Vending Machine [IVM] scandal the Melbourne media of the early sixties were baying for blood over. At the height of the furore, a client came to me wanting to buy securely a very reasonably priced block of land from none other than man of the moment Kempney. I was to invoke an unusual but simple procedure under the Land Titles Act whereby a purchaser can freeze or injunct a title until a transfer to him is registered. All went well for my client. During the course of this maneuvering, I met Kempney. It wasn't long after that Kempney was on board a cruising yacht, heading out to the open sea from the Brisbane River, when he was arrested.

I was to meet him many years later at my office in Darwin. I had the advantage in that I made no mention of our previous meeting. I could see puzzlement in Kempney's eyes as he tried to place me. All I am able to recall now is that he had just arrived from Jakarta in Indonesia. Nothing came of that one meeting.

Reg and Sylvia were an unusual couple. Reg had gone to school in Adelaide with NT Assistant Administrator-to be Martyn Finger [1922-2011]. His father was believed by Martyn to be a senior official behind the iron curtain. Sylvia came from a prosperous Sydney middle class background.

Sylvia's widowed mother owned property at Balwyn in Melbourne for which the late John Plant had drawn a lease on her behalf. It was through that connection I was to meet Reg and Sylvia. Although I never undertook legal work directly for them, through Sylvia's mother's business affairs I became involved on the periphery of their world.

Reg was to maintain the connection post the sale of my Melbourne law practice. He visited me in Andamooka. During his brief stay, he was successful in finding modest but valuable opal. In earlier days I had visited from Melbourne the couple at their lovely home in suburban Mosman in Sydney.

Reg was dominant and was prepared to bet all on what he believed to be a business masterplan. "All" was money that came from Sylvia's side of the family. His plan was founded on successfully marketing a clip, usually a casting, for quickly safely and easily securing ends of load bearing wire lifting equipment. With hindsight, I don't recall any mention of a patent.

Absent such, that may have been the reason for his commercial preoccupation with getting the product listed with the Australian Army. It was an article of his faith, perhaps encouraged from within the Army, that the fact of such a listing would open the door to considerable wealth. A high-ranking military engineering officer encouraged him to believe such a listing was not only feasible but, over far too long a time, reasonably imminent. When the end of this chancy road came, as reported to me by an independent source, cashiering of the military officer was little balm to Reg as the business had folded with consequent disastrous personal economic consequences. There was unsuccessful litigation in New South Wales.

It wasn't as if the clip economic failure was isolated. Midway through my opal prospecting days, Reg somehow prevailed on to travel to Sydney to troubleshoot his monetary problems. It was midsummer, my work partner and I were not having any luck. Separate flat accommodation was offered at Mosman Wharf together with a modest wage. I was able to get a 3 month leave pass from mining partner Gert.

Not least of the demanding problems was a small factory in the Mascot area manufacturing and marketing automotive tow-bars and windscreen protectors. So far as I could judge the products were excellent but just not selling. The factory was hemorrhaging money. The obvious solution, reluctantly accepted by Reg, was to cull staff at least until there were more sales. Closing down altogether was a better option. Prospects for the clip getting listed with the Army dominated Reg's conversation. There were meetings and banquets with bankers and other advisers.

To cap it all off, Reg introduced into the equation a racehorse that never won races it was supposed to win. The upshot for me was a return to Andamooka in a position worse financially than when I had left and with a temporary infection with racehorse gambling disease. My life in Sydney had been circumscribed by the resultant poverty indirectly caused by this horse.

I am uncertain how John Galvin and I met up. He had not long returned from a post-graduation and admission

European trip. Both trips to and from were typically sea voyages at the time. In my Union Trustee days, he worked for me for a short time. He was an only child and his father, who I was to meet, worried about the large inheritance he would leave based on land in the outer suburban Werribee area. John married a girl he had met shipboard on the return trip to Australia. I may have been the best man.

It was John who convinced me to sign up for 2 vacant blocks of land at Philip Island about an hour's run from to the southeast from Melbourne. It was at an auction of an entire subdivision. I still recall a number of $1250 but not whether this was for one block or the 2. The price was on 10% deposit with the balance due over something like 5 years. Before my departure for the South Australian opal fields these contracts had to be assigned. It would have been futile to attempt to meet the obligations under the contract with no reliable income source.

I lost touch with John. A law reported decision he had made many years later as a Deputy Vice President of the Administrative Appeals Tribunal was relied upon by my adversary in my last case argued before the Full NT Supreme Court.

As I write, I am reminded of the unfortunate result of a jury trial where my client had sued for damages for personal injuries consequent on being struck by a car. There was a serious complication involving the lack of insurance of the driver but that issue could not be addressed until my client had secured a judgment. The media were interested.

My client's counsel was John Galbally. The jury empanelment procedure allowed for a number of challenges after a juryman's name was called and as he rose to his feet and made his way to the jury box. A challenged juror no longer played a part in the proceeding. The jury panel for this kind of civil damages action was made up of 4. Counsel on both sides were provided by the court with a list of the jurors' names, addresses and occupations. One well-dressed juror with some kind of management occupation struck me as one who should be challenged. John resisted telling me the man was a mate. The client was an almost prototypical working class ocker. It was the determination of that jury that my client was 100% responsible for being struck by the car. The result was no damages. The case had been 100% financed by me with no contribution from the client. The unfortunate client's dream of a payday was smashed, let alone mine. The assemblage of media waiting outside the court poised to hear my address on the inequity of a judgment that was meaningless quietly dispersed. There was no sustainable ground of appeal in such a case. John never presented an account.

Back in those days, there was no compulsory professional indemnity insurance. If a solicitor was negligent and uninsured any claim against him had to be met from his own pocket. I came perilously close to becoming liable in another motor accident case. It involved service of the writ.

In Victoria at the time any legal action for damages had to be issued within 6 years of the date of the event, If a writ was issued it had to be served within 12 months. Failing that, provided application for extension for 6 months was made before the writ expired it could easily be extended. Any further extension required a court application backed up by proof of attempts at service, the logic being an application for substituted service should have been made. If there was no story to tell of attempts the application was likely to fail.

In my case the writ may have been issued by John Plant. Certainly, it remained unserved, whereby I managed a 6-month extension. Other office business had prevented me from progressing the service issue. The last day for valid service came up. It was do or die time. There was no reasonable prospect of engaging a process server. Foolishly, I had let myself worry about service without forcing the time to resolve it.

Out I sallied in my ancient Pontiac. It was morning, probably a Saturday. Miraculously I was successful. When the door was opened at the address, upon my inquiry for the named defendant, the lady of the house, probably his mother, led me to a heavily curtained murkily lit bedroom and left. It was difficult to see a body in the much-rumpled bed. I got an affirmative grunt from the shape when I inquired if it belonged to the name I needed. The service copy was quickly given to the shape together with advice to take it to his third-party insurer. Off I went with a great sense of relief. I had come within a hair's breadth of potentially expensive legal disaster. An appearance to the writ was served at my office within 8 days. That action was up and running.

That story reminds me of a better one from my Darwin process server. There were seven Greek named defendants to an action I had commenced. He knew all by sight. He served the one who had seemed to him to be dominant. Then he sat in his car outside the home. Within 15 minutes all of the remaining 6 had converged on that home. He knocked on the door again and served them all.

There were clients who did not pay. This was not because of my generosity but basically because of lack of efficient follow-up from my embryonic office. I suppose I was subconsciously taking in all-comers with a medium-term view of weeding out the non-payers over time. Two that come to mind are George and Wally.

George ran a restaurant dedicated to Can-Can at the bayside suburb of Mentone. In those days, Mentone was about as far a cry from any Melbourne entertainment hub as the Sahara Desert. He invited me to drop in for a complimentary meal. Although I was the only customer, 10 can-can dancers exuberantly displayed their skills. I had the answer to George's cash flow problems. When I left Melbourne, George, miraculously, was still afloat and seeming to be enjoying himself immensely.

Wally was different. He was a grade A hustler. In some respects, he might have been described as a low rent Reg. He was commercially partnered with conservative, feet on the ground, Percy who seemed to be mildly confused by Wally's razzle-dazzle. If Percy had been asked the reasoning behind his link to Wally he very likely would have said it might lead him to wealth. Wally seemed to need a Percy to give to customers, perhaps even to himself, some flavor of stability as well as carry out routine administration. The business was a suburban real estate agency. Wally was consumed by lust to have it all now. He acquired a brand new Mercedes. After

I left Melbourne, I heard he had been arrested and charged with trust account defalcation. After he had been granted bail pending trial, he was charged again with re-offending in much the same way. I was to hear no more of his antics or fate.

During my three years battling against a John Plant takeover, together with Ananda Krishnan and the now deceased Peter Lidell, I had been active in regular Debating Association of Victoria (DAV) events (on which see above). Occasionally our "New Australia Democratic League" locked horns with the Pentridge Gaol debating team headed by convicted [after 3 trials] murderer John Bryan Kerr. Kerr had been a public schoolboy who grew up at a Toorak address next door to that of later Prime Minister Harold Holt. Cricket writer Gideon Haigh has written a book about the trials and Kerr's post gaol life entitled *Certain Admissions: a Beach, a Body & a Lifetime of Secrets* (Viking, 2015).

At the time of the murder with which Kerr had been charged, he was employed as a radio announcer. His three trials had been extensively and sensationally reported in the Melbourne media of the day. Kerr was tall, dark and handsome.

My provisional view of Haigh's ultimate conclusion - that Kerr really was guilty - is that the onus of proof in a criminal trial is "beyond reasonable doubt". Haigh's equivocaton about his conclusion establishes that he is far from convinced to the required criminal standard. Nonetheless, the book and its conclusion almost certainly will preclude a pardon based on an end-of-life confession to the Kerr murder, as well as two others, to his carer from a mentally unstable patient.

Kerr was unlucky with the third trial. The first two had seen their juries unable to agree. This was after the respective judges had given them scrupulously fair charges especially concerning an unsigned record of interview of confession. Crown Solicitor Winneke was close to entering, but never did, a *nolli prosequi* [notice of intention not to proceed] on the basis Kerr was unlikely to get a fair trial because of the prior publicity.

The third trial was presided over by Sir Charles ["Cool Charlie"] Lowe and introduced new prosecution evidence from Kerr's psychiatrist. Charlie pre-empted the jury by eliminating from the panel any who might be worried about the death penalty following a conviction. The psychiatrist disclosed that there was insanity in the Kerr family tree and that Kerr had sought treatment for an ungovernable temper. As to an unsigned record of interview admitting guilt, Lowe put it to the jury that it was "inconceivable" that four senior detectives who had sworn to its truth might be lying.

There was the odd criminal matter. In one case the client was on bail for a moderately serious charge the exact nature of which is beyond my recall. I was travelling to my city office on the train. It was fortunate I had bought a newspaper at the rail station kiosk. Idly glancing through the day's law list, I was astonished to see the name of my client among those listed for that day. There had been none of the required communication to my office from the County Court registry to this effect. So it was off to the court to confront the presiding judge who had a fearsome reputation for the way he dealt with those who incurred his displeasure. There was no requirement for wig and gown for this purpose. I had a rock-solid excuse and could see no reason to concede any ground. I forcefully explained how my first intimation of the proposed trial came about. The judge was eminently reasonable and accepted my unreadiness for trial was attributable to failure of the lines of communication from the court. If I had not casually glanced at the newspaper it could have been a far more troubling event.

Even the Chatham rail station kiosk provided grist to the legal mill. It was operated by a grizzled old timer by the name of Charlie. My arrivals tended to be just about the time he was locking up. We often had time for a chat. He knew my occupation. One day he asked to come into the office with his wife to give instructions for me to draw wills. There were no children. I was mildly surprised to find the wife was considerably younger and quite handsome. Were she not so much better looking, she could have been Charlie's daughter. The accents of both made obvious England was their country of origin. To my considerable surprise both he and the wife wanted to make mutual wills leaving all each to the other whereby I became the sole beneficiary in the will of the survivor.

I did my best to dissuade them from including me, but so their minds were made up. Then the only proper course of professional action was to refer them to another solicitor. This brought Stephen Hayes into the picture. Instructions were given to him. The wills were drawn and duly executed and witnessed. This was not long before I took to the opal fields. It is wildly improbable either is still alive. I had no real contact with either subsequent to the will making.

Since my train travel was immediately after the rush hour, it was comfortable. I even indulged in travelling first class for the more comfortable seating. At the first stop on the way at Canterbury station I would often see a gaggle of County and Supreme Court judges climbing aboard, often as a chatting group. I remember thinking at the time of how odd this seemed. Until I witnessed it, I had imagined quite different transportation for the State's judicial officers - more along the lines of that provided for Gordon Nalder. Nonetheless, the sociable judges gave every indication they were enjoying their travel.

And still the call to adventure kept working against my practice development. I needed to burn out the stresses of 7-day weeks and uneasy nights against a background of very limited finances. There was also the matter of my father's guarantee of my bank overdraft for my legal business. Had I stumbled seriously with that business or my health, the family house would have been in jeopardy.

The alternative life would have no rents or wages to pay. All that would be needed was hard physical work, money for food, explosives and fuel for, and maintenance of, machinery.

Not altogether unsurprisingly, my three years as a self-employed lawyer had left me far from flush. In that time abnormal expenses like an office shift and the cost of the practice purchase let alone bank interest had drained my income. To cap that off, I had committed to buy on terms and was learning to sail a 28-foot timber yacht which would have to be sold as well as the practice if I was to break free.

I had taken over the practice of a deceased older lawyer which had kept me busy. In the course of that business, I had learned that practice was not me. The deceased had even been president of the silvertail Old Xavierians Association. I might have taken over the practice, but simultaneously I was slowly being taken over by the spirit of the dead previous owner. I even had s a client who was a Dame of the British Empire.

Basically, I had laid the foundations for what augured well for my professional work future, but, as I saw it, at the cost of not living a real life. Later, in Darwin that prior experience made opening of my own practice rather than seeking employment with an established law firm an obvious, indeed simple, choice.

Looking back now, I realise my world view then had been hugely influenced by the adventure books I had read during my 15-week confinement to bed with rheumatic fever. This was when I was aged about 11. Then, I had been fortunate to be correctly diagnosed at the outset by family doctor Dan Crotty. The guilty party was Mrs O'Sullivan the matriarch of a family of 12 children mostly by then grown up. Mr O'Sullivan had been employed in a lucrative government position whereby he had been able to keep premier older children's reading in front of his family. Mrs O'S, who lived not more than 200 metres away, brought the books 5 or more at a time. I was a fast reader. When I had devoured them, no more than a few days later, those books would be replaced by another selection. Authors like RM Ballantyne come to mind. This way I must have read about 150 or so of the O'Sullivan books for which I was truly grateful. Also guilty was a 1930s vintage Chums Annual of over 800 coffee-table sized densely printed pages acquired at a church jumble sale.

Bed limited [not ridden] I may have been but, for much of my bed bound 15 weeks, my book freed and fired spirit roamed over the great plains and mountains of Canada and the United States, the wilds of Africa and through the great English public schools.

Sure, I had good elements amidst the dross. There was my yacht which I was learning to sail. My commute to Sandringham Yacht Club from Surrey Hills and later Aspendale was solved by a 20-pound purchase price wonderful 1929 Nash sedan after my lovely uninsured 1938 Oldsmobile had been stolen. And I could look forward to my monthly Debaters Association of Victoria debates.

Cy Cater at Sandringham Yacht Club was convinced my ancient Nash with the roped up rotten timber framing at the roof line on the mid-point of the left side was a matter of deliberate rejection of modernity. So, I would find my Nash sharing parking space with the latest Jags and Mercs at trendy and intensely enjoyable private dinners.

Included were my never dull visits to Dougald and Juliette Maxwell's long gone Coq au Vin restaurant at Aspendale for such marvellous meals it caused me to rent cheaply a house condemned as unfit for human habitation just around the corner. Vigorous night manoeuvres by rats in the walls there were a downside. My mate, electrical goods retailer Alex Encel, supplied me with antique but operational refrigerator, radiogram and washing machine for an all-up price of 15 pounds.

The restaurant was at one end of a short street the beach at the other. The rail station was on the opposite side of the Nepean Highway to the restaurant. The new address enabled a healthy beach run to Edithvale before breakfast. There was even client George Paul's "Can Can" restaurant at nearby Mentone.

But, if I was to be imprisoned eventually by serious professional work, at least I wanted adventure first. The more the work-related pressure escalated, the more I saw the need to release that pressure completely. I suppose in a sense what I was telling myself was much the same as more affluent university graduates who were taking gap years to travel after graduating from university. It was just that I had complicated my life more than most gap year takers.

Thus, while I was building my law practice, I was also thinking about getting out. I even engaged the services of a practice broker. What I was offering was a far better deal than I had signed up to including security of tenure. The great unknown of St. Vincents was still there. I had been engaged to prepare an advice concerning the law relating to abortion. The right disciplined hard-working person, such as the likes of me returning as a married man after a multi-year break, would have had all the opportunity in the world. But that is what I write now, 55 years after the event. And it ignores what I have learned over years of unusual law practice in Darwin.

One day I took a call from Barry. It was an inquiry whether the practice was for sale. Within a month I was a free man. Within only a few more, I was storm-bound aboard a sailboat fighting for my life at the eastern end of Bass Strait. Read on to learn how I handled freedom.

PART THREE—Opals

Chapter 5: Andamooka 1, Opals [1963-1968]

<Opal is a hydrated amorphous form of silica ($SiO_2 \cdot nH_2O$), formed in underground fissures by very gradual build-up over aeons of time. It is deposited at a relatively low temperature and may occur in the fissures of almost any kind of rock, being most commonly found with limonite, sandstone, rhyolite, marl, and basalt.

… Depending on the conditions in which it formed, opal may be transparent, translucent, or opaque, and the background color may be white, black, or nearly any color of the visual spectrum. Black opal is considered the rarest, while white, grey, and green opals are the most common.> (Wikipedia, July 2023)

In Australia, opal is to be fund at multiple sites in South Australia, including Coober Pedy, Andamooka, Welborne Hill/Lambina (a vast, 3,395 square kilometres station), Mintabie [otherwise "Anangu Pitjantjatjara Yankunytjtjara" or APY], and Lake Hart, all in South Australia, at Lightning Ridge in New South Wales, and across a broad sweep of western Queensland (the Winton Formation).>

I arrived at Coober Pedy in about August 1963, and was to spend the next five years between there and Andamooka, mostly the latter.

To say the mining community at Andamooka was polyglot would be an under-statement. German and Yugoslav communities, almost entirely male, predominated. My partner, Gert [Gerhardt Hutterer], of Austrian origin, socialised principally with German speakers. Apart from the Germans and Austrians, I call to mind Greeks, French,

Scandinavians, Italians, Russians, the odd New Zealander, Czechs, Belgians, English, Poles, Romanians and Dutch; native Australians were rare, and it is necessary to recall that this was a time of almost full employment Australia-wide. Members of the mining community was there because they wanted to be and wanted to try their luck. Population then was about 5,000 but already declining as opal was getting to be just too hard to find. People talked of better prospects in the Queensland opal fields.

Apart from a few jobs associated with the Co-op and Johnny Lyons store, the aboriginal welfare office and the nurses at the inland mission, the only industry was mining and dealing in opal. Self-sufficiency was the order of the day, welfare was unknown and there was no doctor or dentist. There was a swamp close by the township to the Northwest, where those who fancied themselves with a shotgun stalked duck. Old-timers dreamed of a holiday at Coopers Creek in the corner country. Ex-ship stewards Max and Gunter, from Hamburg, even attempted to grow potatoes in the sand hills.

Australian naturalisation was popular during my time as chairman of the Progress Association. It was a festive event, with a full hall and concert items from local talent. I made a speech laying into Adolf Hitler and the dark forces that were promoting the government of the day to apply the Gold Buyers Act to the opal industry. After the formal ceremony, I was taken to task by Hans Herr, a miner originally from Austria whose family he believed had been freed from grinding, degrading poverty by the Hitler regime.

Regular visits to the Post Office were not on my schedule. Postmaster Gordon Bohlin was never one to stand on ceremony. On the occasion that Opal Air dropped off at the airfield a brown paper-wrapped $50,000 brick of banknotes for an opal buyer agent, it was Gordon who made sure the parcel was delivered to the right hands.

Opal prospecting was physically demanding. There was no rent or wages to pay. All that was needed was hard physical work, money for food, explosives, fuel and maintenance of machinery. It was also dangerous work, mainly for the risk associated with falling earth. The deeper the shaft the greater the potential for falling material to reach terminal velocity speed and strike the shaft sinker at the bottom in the combined space of the shaft. Hence the need for a hard hat. Also, the deeper the shaft the greater the likelihood of encountering layers of rock or jasper, which would then have to be cut through. Working in a two-man team greatly increased efficiency and safety. One man down in the shaft would break the earth while the other waited on the windlass above, ready to lower the bucket for filling and windlassing up, the two taking turn-about with the tasks. Blasting involved gelignite or dynamite. In my time a case of gelly cost about $13. Of late the price has hugely escalated so an alternative as become common: rolling a thick slurry mixture of ammonium nitrate and diesel fuel into sausage-shaped newspaper wrapping to be triggered by detonators.

We set up camp, erected our army ridge pole tent an unloaded our windlass and compressor, the latter a Broomwade 120 cubic feet per minute [cfm] powered by a Lister JP3 diesel. There were no frills such as generator or starter motor and it had seen better days. I bought it from the plant hire people, Wreckair, in Melbourne for around 300 pounds. It included a light jackhammer known as a clay spade, several steel picks for the jackhammer, hoses and a rock drill. I had a working knowledge of petrol-engine cars and motor cycles but till then none of diesel.

The original opal prospectors used sink shafts laboriously by hand with pick, shovel and windlass. Once bottomed, lying prone they would use pick to excavate or gauge under the opal level, relying on a carbide lamp to see in the gloom. My preference was to work in standing position in drives excavated so that the opal level was at a height of about five foot six. Our unit was basically 1930s in design. My equipment was the ancient diesel-powered compressor generating about 120 cfm, jack hammers to break the dirt, windlass for use in sinking the shaft, a York scaffold hoist to haul the dirt above ground, a length of pipe upon which the scaffold hoist could be set, and lengths of timber to collar any shaft. My partner at this time, Gert Hutterer, and I were both fit from hard work but towards the end of the engine's life on a cold winter's morning would both be exhausted by having to crank vigorously for over an hour to get things moving. When it eventually started, we gave it one or two minutes to warm up before putting it under load with the compressor. Over time we found our Lister diesel could power without apparent stress two pneumatic hammers running at almost full capacity. It was reliable.

We began by putting put down one wildcat hole to a depth of about fifty feet. But the outcome was: Nix. Nada. Nothing. And we were fortunate, or lucky, to have no serious accident. So, we kept on digging and searching.

About 18 months into my life as miner, my tent was blown away in a heatwave windstorm. I was able to replace it with basic but comfortable digs in a not-congested part of town, at a cost of about 350 pounds. My new home was a dugout with modest Euro-Alpine style above-ground attachment, of floor dimensions roughly 12′ by 12′, with two horizontal red-curtained slit-type windows on the south-side (the north being underground), and a fine wire mesh-enclosed porch at the front. There was a drop toilet appended to the north side of the porch. The toilet was also the location of my truck tyre mounted Southern Cross 32v diesel generator. With its open and unsilenced exhaust, I could hear when a visitor entered, and the area was so draughty as to make it safe from carbon monoxide poisoning.

The tent was home for a year and a half; then it blew away in a sandstorm

In about 1965, the opal industry, free-wheeling way of life as we knew it came under threat when out of the blue, the South Australian government let it be known that it intended to gazette opal under, of all things, the Gold Buyers Act.

Presumably some interested party was pushing this cause in anticipation of profiting from the amendment.

The best effect of the gazettal would have been a bureaucratisation of the industry, the worst its destruction, with opal open to legal possession only of registered miners or dealers. The requirement of registration of miners and payment of a fee called to mind the circumstances of the Eureka rebellion of 1854. It was put to me that with my background in the law I should be prepared to lead the attack to preserve the opal fields way of life. I would travel to Adelaide to research the proposed Act and then prepare a draft constitution for a new body to be known as the Australian Opal Miners Association (AOMA). I would address meetings in Adelaide, Coober Pedy and Andamooka. Out-of-pocket expenses (transport by Cessna and accommodation) were to be met by Andamooka opal buyer Dag Johnson.

The last few miles of return in the Cessna were enlivened by a very low-lecel swoop from the rear over the bald head of a Hungarian miner known only as Kruschev. Had he been wearing a hat we would have blown it off. At the time of our over-flight he had been on the last leg of a delivery trip with a new backhoe.

Public meetings on gazetting the opal matter went ahead as planned, with copies of the documents I had gathered in Adelaide posted on the Post Office notice-board. Facing the proposal that would have led to imposition of registration fees on impecunious miners before ground could be broken legally, miners remembered, or learned, of Eureka.

Eventually the government dropped the idea. The Gold Buyers Act was repealed in its entirety in 1976.

Involvement in the public life of the community had its downside. I had no warrior woman guarding my threshold. There are always desperate souls who think that pubic life means those involved think of nothing else. They like to drop in of an evening. Many is the occasion when I went to bed in the dugout below leaving them rambling on in the kitchen-dining room just steps above.

I call to mind one other occasion. Lord [Richard] Casey [1890-1976, Governor-General of Australia 1965-1969] was in town. He was democratically inclined in his habit of meeting personally with those who wanted to meet him. He then sat at a table, facing the plebs. When I made a plea for the extension of the Murray River water pipe at Woomera to Andamooka he jolted as if shot. But he made no comment. On to the next petitioner.

One great advantage of Andamooka was the willingness of top chefs like the Romanian George Pascu ("Fat George") to act as chef for a meal for two or three guests with his only price being the placing of his own legs under the table. George would present the hoped-for list. I would do the shopping and George then get on with preparing a sumptuous meal. This, mind you, in a tiny room where those sitting on the south side of the table couldn't sit up straight because of the slope of the roof.

There was also the option of dining out at Andamooka. Steve's "Tucker Box" operated seven nights a week serving simple but affordable dishes, a sort of working man's club.

Unlike Umberto's restaurant attached to the Coro underground hotel at Coober Pedy, a workingman in work attire would never feel uncomfortable here. By contrast the only night I dined at Umberto's I was grateful I was wearing a jacket. It was the minimum standard of the males I saw there. The food was elaborate, the ambience five star.

Another neighbour was Johnny Buzza from—I think—Hungary. He lived with his family about 100 metres to the northeast, in a conventional suburban home. He had some luck. Passing a used aircraft lot near Mascot with money in his pocket, he agreed to buy a plane if the vendor could get him a license to fly. That led to Johnny overflying Andamooka one Sunday. Watching him wobble about in the sky at what must have been virtual stall speed, I felt uneasy.

Not long afterwards, when staying in Adelaide, my host woke me with the day's Adelaide *Advertiser*. There on the front page was photograph of the wreckage of the Buzza plane. Descending to try to get beneath a fog, Johnny had flown into the only hillside around, Snowtown, killing instantly he and his Australian-born wife, orphaning three children and scattering opal among the debris.

Maybe Gert and I had become too preoccupied with excavating unproductive ground. Just a little before this time, we had been offered for $200 an opal tenement in shallow ground that had never been open cut by bulldozer. We had turned it down. A friend originally from Germany, Werner Wilschke, had no such doubt. Werner was an ex-Berliner who had, at the age of 15, been captured on the Russian front and shipped as a prisoner to Siberia, assigned to timber cutting. Not released till the early 50s, he then made his way to Australia, where he found fortune that day at Andamooka. He paid the $200, called in a bulldozer and produced over $35,000-worth of opal on his first day. He later took on a farm in the South Australian southeast for a short while before returning a year or two later as an opal buyer. A heart attack, all too soon, finished his life not too long after.

One day in 1968, a chance encounter in Sydney with my former university and National Service friend, Keith Gale (on whom see further below) transformed my life. The outcome was my recruitment as Australian head of a joint Australian-Japanese fisheries venture and my transfer to Darwin. That fishing industry position included a clause that I should give three months-notice if I wanted to resign. So, I took the last salary man's position in my life, and after 3 months I gave notice.

Selling up from Andamooka was no easy task. My share of the partnership mining equipment aggregated so painstakingly over the years had to be capitalised. In the end, whatever was unsold and never fitted into one suitcase or the boot of my 1937 Oldsmobile had to be abandoned in the residence I was selling. Prices were generally depressed at Andamooka. Keith became concerned about when he could expect to see me in Sydney for two weeks orientation with Gollin. While I was in liquidation mode, I arranged for Gert to have full use of my share of our mining gear. He continued to call each morning on his way to our claim.

It was not easy to confirm that my mining days were over but confirm it I did. I found a buyer for my hacienda, a young schoolteacher originally from Poland. The sale was for about $300. It was complete with 32-volt diesel generator. I arranged to pack just one suitcase. I can't recall now what became of my opal cutting plant. Excess possessions were stuffed into the boot of the Olds.

My car by then needed a rebore and the complicated knee action front shock absorbers had effectively long since ceased to do their job. My next-door neighbour and good friend ex-Berliner and Russian POW from Siberia Manfred Wilschke wanted his Karnan Ghia VW delivered to Adelaide to a buyer. The rear mounted engine put weight over the rear wheels which would assist on the greasy dirt road. Manfred and his ex-nurse wife were planning to quit Andamooka not long after me. He offered me the VW for the delivery trip. His offer accepted, the Olds was driven to a block owned by another mate, Geoff Watson, and carefully locked up.

Then it was on the road with my one suitcase. It was 1968. I was not to revisit Andamooka until an overnight visit in 1997.

Chapter 6: Andamooka, 2, The Blitz Buggy and Woomera

I called it my blitz buggy. I spotted it in the side yard of Postmaster Gordon Bohlin's private residence after I had been in Andamooka for several months (in 1963). It was never in usage and unregistered. Later when I was in the rare position of having spare cash, I inquired about it. It was for sale.

It was a long wheelbase, forward control 3-ton 4x4 ex-military truck. Forward control minimised front overhang and was incorporated for efficient transport of maximum numbers by sea. Doors were cloth around metal frames leaving open space where one might have expected to find windows. Brakes were hydraulic with vacuum assistance via the carburettor. And it was of massive construction. No elegantly curved thin sheet metal here. Metal sheathing of the cabin was of heavy gauge straight material. Any bending was made up by hard angles. Wheels of heavy steel were a massive 20." Punctures were repaired by undoing 5 large bolts so splitting the wheel and the spare, clad with a 14 or more-ply rating tyre of a considerable all up weight was mounted high up behind the passenger seat. It took all of the combined effort of Gert and me to mount an assembled wheel there. Up front there were 2 cloth covered basic seats one each side of the removable engine cover. Power, modest by today's standards, came from a 3.5 litre [216 cubic inch] straight 6, 63.4 Kw [85 bhp] overhead valve Chevrolet petrol engine. Mounted on the chassis behind the cabin was a very solid very heavily constructed and quite long steel tray upon which was mounted an easily removable steel framed canopy under which one could comfortably walk about without bending. The tailgate at the rear was easily lowered. The tray base was over 4 feet off the ground—a serious matter when Gert and I had to haul up a 44-gallon drum of fuel.

I estimate the wheelbase at 158 inches. If correct this would have constituted it as a Chevrolet model C60L CMP [Canadian Military Pattern] truck. Chassis and production were licensed to Australia during World War 11 allowing local production. It is almost certain at least the engine and ancillaries as well as gearboxes and differentials were imported. The operating lever for the four speed gearbox sat beside another smaller lever which was intended to engage four wheel drive.

Almost primitively simple as it was, with suspension so harsh as to make one wonder if the wheels were indeed round, under my ownership it traversed much extreme country with no problems apart from [quite expensive] tyre replacements until it settled down. The engine and gearing meant it was no highway cruiser, but that gearing could enable the Blitz to go up the steepest grades with a heavy load.

Sure there were matters I had to work around or spend a lot of money on. The universal joints on the drive shaft to the front differential were so badly worn I drove with this shaft removed unless and until I needed 4-wheel drive. This was somewhat incongruous in that the rear drive shaft was in perfect condition. It was inconvenient to go underneath to do the job when needed but the truck was so high off the roadway this was not the hardship it could otherwise have been. The tyres when I bought were very ordinary so that in the early days of my ownership it was not uncommon for me to find myself by the roadside with two jacks propping up the fully laden truck changing a wheel. The two conventional car type jacks had to be worked in tandem together with stones to get the height required off the ground.

The 4-wheel drive selector lever mechanism was badly gummed up and I usually needed a tyre lever to actuate the selector the lever was unable to move. A similar reverse procedure was needed to de-activate the 4-wheel drive, The overall condition of the truck and the jammed-up selector suggested that before I came along 4-wheel drive had never been deployed. The odometer tended to confirm quite a low mileage. Top speed for that design was supposed to 50 miles per hour but my cruising speed was no more than 35 miles per hour on a bitumen highway. The motor seemed to be busy enough for me at that speed.

About the time I bought her—as buy her I did—the Woomera hut craze was just underway. It may have been the reason for me buying. The powers that be at the Woomera rocket range had decided their old then unused single men's quarters were surplus to their requirements. They were available for sale for removal at 5 pounds each. Delivered on site to Andamooka the going price was 35 pounds. Like triffids these huts could be found scattered all about Andamooka when I last visited.

These were no flimsy lightweight things. Dimensioned at 12x12 or 12x15 feet they were timber framed with a plywood-type lining and painted corrugated black iron sheathed with one door, no windows, a modest two-piece gabled roof devoid of guttering and a timber floor. Each hut broke down into 4 sections for the walls 2 for the roof and I think 2 for the floor. It seemed the sections were put together to a set pattern off-site so that assembly was quite straightforward. Reassembly at Andamooka was similarly straight forward. The task of a trucker was to dismantle, load and deliver.

On occasion a hut would be balky and resist giving up its connecting wall corner joins. The reason was usually a surfeit of nails as if a madman had attacked with a nail gun. A jemmy might be inadequate, and a sledgehammer have to be brought into play. Of course, the roof had to come off first, but this was relatively straight forward.

To embark on the exercise, I needed to get leave of absence from our mining from my partner Gert. I was somewhat grudgingly given 2 weeks to attempt to rehabilitate my finances.

Then the nightmare began. It was mid-winter. The first run established the basic pattern. I needed 2 assistants to help demolition and loading. That meant an uncomfortable trip both ways for one given the layout of the cabin of 2 seats only with the engine cover occupying the middle ground. No machinery was available to assist loading. Placement of the load along the length of the tray as for my first trip was too limiting as well as the load being too high. This was even using the tray floor as the base instead of the tops of the tray sides as was the case for the super wide cross loads.

Eventually I learned cross loading, so the load, was either 12 or 15 feet wide, was easier and enabled three huts. The assistants were paid 2 pounds 10 shillings per hut loaded, whether that was two or three, so it meant three huts for practical purposes. On the road, the extra width and wire tie down bracing made crossing cattle grids problematic. Often the load fixing wires had to be loosened off to get through. And if the police had been in town I had to pull off the road at about the halfway point in the middle of the night to wait for their Land Rover to whiz through. This was to avoid any embarrassing meeting with my grossly over-width and unpermitted load. Once fortunately during daylight, I met an armoured car but as I recall it was able to pass under the right side of my load. That was nothing compared to Australia's fleet of sold Mystere fighter jets on route from storage at Woomera to Pakistan via Port Augusta. I was north bound on the Port Augusta-Woomera Road in my 1938 DeSoto at that time.

In the initial flurry of the Woomera huts invasion, bizarre events worked out on the road. Early on driving my blitz there was a completely upside-down truck resting mid road supported only by its load of huts. The truck had a flat top tray and a destabilizing high load, longways as it was, was too high for the speed being driven. The driver complained a speed wobble converted to total uncontrollability on a straight section of road. Fortunately, the capsize happened near a station homestead and a tractor was available to roll that truck upright. If the huts thus transported had any subsequent structural problems that news never reached my ears.

I found many opal field people tended to drive flat out over barely graded virtual tracks usually overloaded and with barely adequate ply rating tyres. In the case of the upended truck, I suspect the load had ended to float the front wheels. Furthermore, unlike my Blitz, it was a conventional light weight truck of the same rated 3-ton capacity.

To illustrate one trip as an example, we set out about 8 am one winter morn. My 2 assistants were Yugoslavs who needed the money. Like many Andamooka males very likely they were tradesmen. The trip over about 130 kilometres took about 3 to 4 hours over a barely graded track. Then the work began. One benefit at Woomera was our unquestioned - or more precisely unchallenged - acceptance in the mess hall at meal-times. Likewise for the showers. For me the food was brilliant and plentiful, and I went back on numerous occasions for seconds or even thirds. The cooks looked approvingly on at their ragged hungry guests and beamed. So, another break for tea excluded, it was demolition and loading to about 2.30 am the next day. Then it was a freezing trip back home not helped by the open airy nature of the cabin and the pretzel like shape one of my assistants had to adopt to work around the solitary passenger seat and centrally positioned engine. Opening the rear door on the engine cover in hopes of a blast of warm air was no help. Even the engine was feeling the cold.

Wearing as I was an insulated jacket over rolls of newspaper about my trunk I was still freezing. Back at Andamooka well after daybreak it was necessary to help my unfortunate unseated assistant out of the cabin gently untangle him and lay him in the sun out of any breeze to thaw out. He and his mate had been good intelligent workers but after they were paid the unseated one's last words to me were "Never again." I wish I could have said the same but my leave from my partner Gert was not yet up and I needed the pittance I was earning. The huts had to be delivered that day and another run undertaken the next. My profit margin was virtually non-existent, but my market was destitute and desperate prospectors. Amazingly, I find now one photograph of my wide-loaded blitz buggy from this time, taken from my tent.

The tent is another story. I am surprised I never took up a hut for myself. Circumstances forced my hand somewhat not long after. We were shaft sinking in a sand hill. It was summer during a heatwave and windstorm. Initially, for every shovelful of sand removed another half would fall in from the sides. Eventually we reached a level of hard compacted sand which we were able to use as a base. Shaft timbers in about 4-ft lengths that we normally used to collar a shaft as our spoil increased were deployed with cardboard backing to keep out invading loose sand. Then the windlass was

Sinking a shaft

mounted on the collar and it was back to normal shaft sinking.

It was a desperate day made even more desperate by the discovery, when I returned to camp, that my tent had blown away. One of my mates, Len Zimmerman, [Zim] kindly offered to share his erected Woomera hut with me so the immediate problem was solved. Eventually this led me to the purchase of my final Andamooka accommodation off to the

The underground house. (Walkabout Magazine, July 1970; photo by Geoffrey Harris)

northern side of the hospital road and just below the opal level. This was a dugout cum above ground accommodation. It was the original digs of my new neighbour opal buyer Manfred Wilschke who lived next door with his wife in a conventional house.

New owners of the huts for a time virtually stopped prospecting while concentrating, as tradesmen, on erecting their new residences. Hammering and sawing went on all over town. Wives and girlfriends were imported, and domesticity reigned. Prospecting was forgotten by midday. For some months opal production collapsed. Gradually the imperative to earn bit and slowly the field returned to productive normalcy. Then the talk turned to the potential of the Queensland opal country.

About 12 months after the Woomera Hut craze had settled down my partner Gert and old timer Jack Hillman and I decided to look for Jack's old copper mine workings near Boorthanna also in far north South Australia. Work there had been brought to a halt for practical purposes by World War 1. The ore had been transported by camel to the rail siding at Boorthanna and shipped to Germany through Port Augusta. Prohibition on trading with the enemy put paid to the enterprise. Jack moved on to Coober Pedy to prospect for opal, an occupation that took up the rest of his life. He had never returned to Boorthanna.

Jack had discovered the mine when he was a relative youngster working with the railways out of Boorthanna. At week-ends he roamed the countryside prospecting. He had picked up copper sheddings in a creek bed and followed those until he arrived at what he thought was the source. A few shafts were sunk and were confirmatory. Coincidentally an Englishman with a team of camels came wandering through the area. A deal was done whereby for a share of the profits the camels would be used to move the excavated ore cross country to the railhead about 10 or 15 miles distant. Shafts were sunk and the ore stoped out and bagged. The ore was very rich right down to blocks of pure or native copper as big as a human being. The final destination was Germany. After the war the customer who had been unable to make payments for all the ore delivered brought its account right up to date.

So off we set one bright morning to Boorthanna rail head—hardly a bustling scene. I drove the blitz and Gert drove his Land Rover ute. Jack preferred the Rover for its comparatively softer ride. We needed the two vehicles because of two only seats in the Blitz. Our route led north from Andamooka on the rarely travelled sand hill track to Charlies Swamp and eventually linked up with the Oodnadatta Track. This track ran alongside the old railway line to Alice Springs. Gert was able to hit the sand hills with some speed but not so in my case. Four-wheel drive had to be engaged, which meant connecting the drive shaft to the front differential. Then it was a case of just ploughing through.

We made Boorthanna and with Jack directing made off cross country approximately due east. And there was the old mine. Jack was able to quickly assess that the area had been worked since he left in 1914. All about were old drink bottles which I am aware now are valuable collector's items. Looking back now it is easy to conclude these were left by the last operators which given the age of the bottles would suggest the works post Jack were undertaken not long after World War 1 in perhaps 1918. Scattered about were plenty of rocks in the form of copper sulphides. I had one assayed and from memory it graded 27% copper. Gert, to fill in his time smashed all bottles within his range.

Then it was back to Boorthanna and up the highway to the junction point of the track to Coober Pedy which I think was William Creek. This track traverses some of the lowest lying land on the continent and of course lies in an east/west direction.

Blitz carrying Woomera huts, 1960s;
Author facing camera

As an illustration of how rain can obstruct passage Jack cited an example in his experience, Back in 1914, well before the Stuart Highway passed through Coober Pedy the William Creek railway station was the drop off point for those travelling to Coober Pedy. There they had the choice of making their own independent way or by paying a fee to the operator of a horse and camel drawn drag place their gear on the drag and walk alongside to Coober Pedy. The distance is about 167 kilometres. On this occasion one traveller had a bicycle. Jack did a deal and bought the bike. Off he set. Somewhere along the track in the reasonably early stages heavy rain fell. Jack could have turned back in the interest of caution. Instead he elected to press on. Eventually, the conditions made use of the bike impossible. It was abandoned. Jack now no longer had any option but to get to Coober Pedy if he was to survive. This urgency precluded sleep and meals. It needed an all- out effort on his part. Clothing was ripped off his body as he battled the terrain. He dared not stop. He made it to his shared camp and collapsed into his bunk. When he was woken up the next morning by the elderly camp cook, he was so spent he had to struggle to move out of the bed. The other unhappy walking group arrived 6 weeks later.

So we set out on the track to Coober. The terrain was super rough. I was bounced about in my cabin, Jack travelled with Gert. I am unable to remember now if 4-wheel drive was necessary, but it almost certainly was. Back in the post-World War 1 days Jack was able to recall Coober Pedy as quite active with a population around 5,000. A camel racing track had been set up and hosted many events.

Then it was back down the highway to Woomera and Andamooka. On the highway the corrugations were the worst I have experienced. My slow rate of progress made getting on top of them with speed out of the question. It became a matter of rolling over each one individually. That part of the trip was a nightmare. By comparison the Andamooka track was like a billiard table.

I cannot remember now why I decided to part with the Blitz. I had investigated a possible sale for some time. The model was not in demand at the time. These days, as an antique, large sums are common. I do recall a rather impersonal delivery to a mineral exploration associated operation in Adelaide. Nobody even came out to look at it. I parked in the yard presented to the office left the ignition key and registration papers collected somewhere about $300 and that was that.

John at his mine site, Andamooka, 1964

It may have been that at the time I was en route to Melbourne. Certainly, about then I visited the Disposals Yard of the State Electricity Commission [SEC] in Melbourne where the man in charge was most helpful. I bought for $300 an almost new condition replica of our worn out Broomwade compressor. On a freezing winter day it started readily and filled up the air receiver in the twinkling of an eye. Then to get it to Andamooka and for about the same money I bought a Dodge three-ton truck with a canopy.

This was at a time when Gert and I had spent a considerable sum rebuilding the 3-cylinder Lister diesel motor on our ex-Wreckair Broomwade at Andamooka. Like grandfather's clock, it had stopped dead with one last gasp, never to go again without a major rebuild. The rebuild was only of the engine block. We had to fit the 3 separate cylinder heads—no easy task. Were it not for the invaluable assistance of Zim we would never have got it right. We learned the purpose of the copper head shims. We learned later, after having sold the recon ex-Wreckair unit, that the extra time taken to fill the receiver was the fault of the compressor - it broke down soon after in the hands of the new owners. Retrospectively and in a perfect objective sense there was an almost perfect mechanical symmetry when the 2 units each constructed by different manufacturers wore out at almost the same time after prodigious service over a very long period.

The return trip with the new Broomwade was marked by one incident on the rather good, unsurfaced section of roadway between Port Augusta and Woomera. I had pulled up to check all was well with my tow. It was not. A central pin locking the turntable in the correct central position relative to the front axle had fallen out and the compressor trailer front axle was far out of position. Continuation would have been a risky business especially given the much worse road surface from Woomera to Andamooka.

The compressor was unhitched. I went back to search for the missing pin. It was quite large and sure enough, about 20 kilos back, there it quite obviously was—contrasting black against the reddish yellow tinged road surface. Breathing a silent tribute to lightly travelled unsurfaced roads, I was able to re-install the pin in its rightful place and proceed home albeit with more frequent stops to check. The compressor trailer was designed for smooth English roads. Running our two compressors side by side the new import was a hands down winner. The fate of the old but reliable was sealed. All things considered it had given remarkable service in its last days.

For a while when Gert and I were compressor-less Len Zimmerman [Zim] generously loaned us his petrol engine wartime model Ingersoll Rand rated at 100 cfm. It was a fine looking all yellow thing on a two-wheel trailer with the compressor deploying 3 cylinders in a semi radial formation, reminiscent of an older radial aeroplane engine. Zim was a skilful man with machinery and it had to be right. We were both working underground with it at White Dam. The day was hot. Our hammers were at full blast as had been the case with the worn out Broomwade. Air supply stopped. When we climbed up to investigate there was Zim. His loan had been boiling. He had turned it off. Looking back, I suppose we should have been more careful until we had tested Zim's machine in action. We had wrongly assumed it was delivering the 100 cfm as its label claimed. As it was, it had been working flat out to match our hammers with a combined usage of 70 cfm. So, it was a case of using it with one hammer or not at all. Maybe our hammers were using more compressed air than their specification suggested. Fortunately, no permanent damage was done.

Returning to the Blitz for the last word. Up until I bought it overnight rain never concerned me. The stores truck from the Andamooka Co-operative store made I think two trips from Adelaide per week rain hail or shine, owing a large trailer. In skilled hands like those of Ladi Hartmann it took a lot of stopping. But Ladi left the job, and an Englishman took over. From what little I saw of his driving skill, I was not impressed. And it was none of my business or at least I thought so. That was until the powers that be at be at the Co-op decided to involve me. At the time I was chairman of the town Progress Association. I had also formed the Australian Opal Miners Association [AOMA] for the purpose of fighting the plan of the South Australian government to gazette opal under the Gold Buyers Act. Of which more elsewhere in this memoir.

Late one evening after rain a deputation knocked on my door. It represented the Co-Op. The stores truck was bogged. Could I help with the Blitz? Caught somewhat by surprise out I went to find, as I saw it, a self-made bog situation, contrived by the new panicked English driver from sheer lack of skill. Then it was a matter of hooking up and with assistance from the towee's power train pull him out. This was a no charge service. It was repeated so many times that I began to dread the patter of rain on my tin roof dugout annexure. Maybe the Co-op driver became so reliant on my tows he never tried enough. I saw it as part of the town political infighting in the wake of my takeover of the Progress Association. I should have charged but my political response was to choose not to do so. I suspected Frank Schulton, the former town maker and shaker, as being behind my discomfort as well as being responsible for the ill-advised consideration by the South Australian government of gazettal of opal.

The sale of the Blitz terminated my free, public-spirited community service.

PART FOUR—Darwin and the North

Chapter 7: Transition to Darwin, 1968

Encounter with Old Mate

In 1968 I was still basically a desperate prospector. But from time to time while at Andamooka I found myself in Sydney, on route to or from elsewhere. Apart from hawking opal at jewellers along Castlereagh St., I had on this occasion been in Sydney on a mission to help a friend with his business affairs. In due course, mission completed, I was remunerated but my mate had a racehorse that kept draining our collective pockets. I needed money for fuel for the return trip to Andamooka.

One day, when crossing a city intersection, a large, black, chauffeured car, executing a left hand turn through the pedestrian flow, stopped in front of me. The rear door opened. All six-foot six of the impressive vision of my old university mate, Keith Gale, resplendent in striped trousers, morning coat and homburg was framed in the doorway.[8] He

---

[8] Ed Note: The text refers often – always warmly – to John's friend and sometime colleague, Keith Compton Gale (1932-2013). It makes only the briefest mention of Gale's extraordinary business record over decades. In 1976 Gale's Gollin Trading House dramatically collapsed, less than a decade after their Sydney meeting and John's acceptance of an executive position in its fisheries subsidiary. Gollin's losses, when liquidated, were reckoned at about $120 million. It was the largest corporate collapse in Australia's history to that time. Found guilty in 1977 on multiple counts of fraud and conspiracy, Gale was sentenced to 13 years penal servitude, of which in due course he served about four and a half, the longest prison term for a white-collar crime in Australia to that time. Released from prison in 1983, he was in 1984 appointed financial adviser to the Brian

must have had some doubt because his first words were "Is that you, John?" The assurance given, the next words were "Jump in" which I did.

I think the last time I had seen Keith the bachelor was from a seat in a tram in Collins St Melbourne around 1962, when I was still enslaved by my Melbourne law practice. While I was idly watching the world go by, and the tram was stationary at a red traffic light, a large black car pulled alongside, festooned with white wedding-style ribbons. My idle gaze took in the back seat occupant. In the instant it dawned on me it was Keith. The lights changed. The black wedding car pulled away.

The newspapers of the time recorded the marriage and that the newly-weds were off to Tokyo where Keith was to take up an appointment as Australian Trade Commissioner

During my compulsory military training at Puckapunyal near Seymour in central Victoria I had struck up an unlikely friendship with Keith. Likewise with ex-Melbourne

---

Burke (premier 1983-88) government of Western Australia, asked to advise on the establishment of a state government trading arm (WA Exim Corporation). The Burke government plans turned to dust, however, with the change of government and the opening from 1990 of the WA Inc Royal Commission, a 1980s scandal no less momentous than had been the 1970s Gollan collapse. Gale cut his links with EXIM in February 1986 and seems not to have figured in the WA collapse and criminal proceedings. As of 1990, however, he was reported to be again on the verge of bankruptcy, pursued by Westpac and other banking groups [Tony Kaye, "Gale on verge of bankruptcy," *Australian Financial Review*, 31 May 1990, and Jenni Hewett, "Close business links between Gale, Symons," *Australian Financial Review*, 18 May 1992]. He appears to have moved to London in 2002 and died there in 2013.

["Wellborn"] Grammarian Barry Humphries [1934-2023]. In Keith's case I say unlikely because he was a Jesuit product from exclusive Xavier College in Melbourne, while I was from the working-class Parade College conducted by the Christian Brothers, and a scholarship had covered all my secondary education school fees. Whereas Keith's father was a high-flying company executive and the family lived in a grand home on a one-acre corner site abutting Mont Albert Road in Canterbury, my father was a tram driver and the McCormack residence was a comfortable but modest three bedroom weatherboard home in Wolseley St [now Wolseley Close] Mont Albert. Keith, a florid but highly competent public speaker, and I had crossed swords in occasional multi-school debating contests.

At university [Melbourne] for a time Keith had been a fellow law student. He persevered at the law longer than Barry Humphries but not long or hard enough to earn a degree. He became too distracted by the pomp and pleasures available to a rich young man in Melbourne at the time. We had attended some of the same lectures. Because of his considerable height expensive dress and highbrow accent, Keith initially seemed to me the face of flatulent and brutal capitalism and as such a person one I should dislike. To make matters worse, I learned later he received from his father a generous weekly allowance. This without ever really meeting the guy and talking with him. It was so easy to so act when I had around me former fellow pupils from my old school from much the same backgrounds as I. So the attitude had been to greet Keith civilly but have no more to do with him than was necessary.

It was only on completion of my second year of my law degree study when I had to serve my National Military Service 3-month basic training camp that I found Keith was so engaging and genuine as a person that he was impossible to dislike. This was despite his handicaps [as I saw them] of wealth, accent and birth. We lived in the same 24-bed marquee type tent. At the end of the confusion of the first day receiving our kit from the Q store, I found Keith on the adjacent bed and his old Xaverian mate and fellow law student [later Judge] Michael [WMR] Kelly on the other side. Of medium to light very slim build Kelly's attire as a law student was a heavy medium grey cloth three-piece suit complete with steel watch fob and pocket watch. It meant little to me at the time, but his father was the Chief Justice of the Federal Arbitration Court. But as a person to get to know he was beyond me. But years later, when I was undertaking my articles of clerkship, I found myself sharing an office with Michael.

When we talked it was apparent to me Keith saw me as an embodiment, albeit friendly, of forces endeavouring to wrest wealth and power from his governing Liberal Party class - a kind of proxy for Vladimir Ilyich [Lenin]. I learned of his father's stressful contribution to the merged entity Dalgety New Zealand Loan Limited, his pride in that and his almost desperate ambition to make a better mark in the world than his father.

So it was that post my compulsory military service it became not uncommon for me to occasionally drop by the Gale home. I met Keith's mother—his father was never there - and his two much younger brothers Tony and Kevin.

Intermittently a sheep on a long lead affixed to a central post was deployed on the front lawn to keep the grass down. When I was embarking on my articles of clerkship it was Keith who prevailed on me to commission a tailor-made suit from Alby Bennet - as it turned out the best suit I ever owned - lost all too soon to the machinations of the Mont Albert branch of the Lyke Nu Dry Cleaning Company. I learned of his concern that one of his Old Xaverian schoolmates Philip Lynch [Sir Philip, 1933-1984] was dickering with joining the ALP [in preference to the Liberal Party] as a political career move. An alumni from the same college currently [Bill Shorten, b. 1967] was leading the parliamentary Labour Party in 2018. When Philip served as Deputy Prime Minister near the end of his political career and, as it turned out, life, his principal staff member was a former Parade classmate of mine from Footscray Brian Buckley (1935-2013).[9] Like Philip, Brian was a Melbourne University Arts graduate. His primary occupation was journalist. He had put in a stint as a teacher at Xavier College where his students had included prominent politician Tim Fischer.

In his later corporate life Keith became such a generous donor to the Fraser Liberal government through the company he then headed that he personally attracted the ire of the Labour opposition in the form of questions incorporating allegations in the Parliament. Yet when Keith's personal and business fortunes took a disastrous and ultimately terminal turn and in desperation, he tried to speak

---

[9] Further on Buckley, see Amanda Buckley, "From journalism to politics to football, a man of many colours." The Sydney Morning Herald. 9 July 2013.

to Philip he was denied audience - on the strong advice of Brian Buckley. I had that from Brian himself who it seemed to me never passed seeing Keith as an odious symbol of rapacious capitalism rather than a fellow human who tried too hard in a field of human activity to which he may not have been best suited. So much for the generous donations. After Philip's death not so long after Keith's fall from grace, Brian wrote a book entitled *Lynched* about his political adventures with Philip.[10]

Having greeted Keith in his limousine that day in Sydney, we lunched, and I learned that Keith's company Gollin and Japanese company Kyokuyo Hogei [literally Polar Ocean Fisheries] were planning joint operations for the Gulf of Carpentaria. The Gollin company GKFC had a Northern Australian Prawn Fishing Licence, conditioned inter alia upon its building within a set time frame a prawn processing plant on Groote Eylandt A support office was to be established in Darwin, run by one Australian and one Japanese national both equal. GKFC had conducted a highly successful preliminary prawning survey and I was told the prawns were so plentiful in the Gulf they were close to being a hazard to shipping. Keith was looking to the Australian component of the shore-based office. Did I want the job?

This was 1968, at a time when apart from the respites noted I had been doing very hard physical work, sinking shafts and tunnelling most of six days a week nine hours a

---

[10] Brian Buckley, Lynched: the life of Sir Phillip Lynch, mastermind of the ambush that ended Gough's run, Frankston, Salzburg Pub, 1991.

day since late 1963 without any real break-through. It had become a hand-to-mouth existence, the yield from opal finds inconsequential when weighed against the cost of maintaining and operating the partnership. I had worked together with my partner Gerhardt Hutterer [Gert] for most of that time. By the nature of the work each entrusted our lives to the other every workday. I had bought a simple but comfortable semi-dugout. I aspired to nothing more grand on the local real estate front. Life was hard but good. I had good friends, occasional interesting visitors and no health problem. But, despite everything, perhaps Gert and I had become too preoccupied with our un-productive grind, so I responded to Keith's importuning by saying, yes.

I arrived in Darwin in mid-1968. It was towards the last days of the central city cinema. The Star Cinema, for that was its name, offered more-or-- less Spartan accommodation for all its patrons. The "more" applied to those seated in the front unroofed part when it rained. It would be surprising if heavy rain did not fall most nights during the monsoonal "wet" season from about Christmas to Easter. The skeleton of the same structure forms the bones of the Star Village adjunct to Darwin's latter-day Mall. That Village displays an ancient movie projector as a tribute to its past.

I was sent from Andamooka Opal Field via a few weeks' orientation at the Gollin and Co Ltd Sydney office. I was to take up a land-based position with joint venture prawning company GKFC. Involved first were finding office accommodation and setting up an office. These were the days of the telex machine. Initially my base was the Michael Paspalis-owned Darwin Hotel. Unbeknown to me at the time, I later learned that while I resided there for my first few weeks a Dutch waitress in the hotel dining room who was accommodated on the premises was found dead in her room impaled by a spear from an underwater spear fishing gun. I am told the police still have an open file concerning the death.

By then the drive in at Nightcliff had all but taken over from the Star Cinema. The same Michael Paspalis was at the helm of that later enterprise. Tom Harris, Michael's erstwhile partner in the Star Cinema, was left to take it over. His son, also Tom, took over the reins and set up the Village after Tom Snr's death. Bagot Road, the then only artery from Darwin to Nightcliff was becoming a separated 2 lane road. Much of its length was unsurfaced. Martina's Restaurant at Nightcliff was regarded as the lead restaurant in Darwin. It was not until after I had been in town for about 8 or 9 months that I was dragged, unwillingly at the time, to what was then known as Alceo [Charlie] Cagnetti's Olympic Restaurant, later simply Charlies. Over the ensuing years I was to lunch there at least two or three times a week as well as, in earlier days, often an evening meal. A few years later, when Charlie bought his restaurant building, I handled the title transfer. More of Charlie and his famous restaurant below.

About 6 months after my arrival Michael Paspalis was to become my landlord for a shop-front law office in Herbert St opposite what is now known as the old Supreme Court building. My office was a bare, open, undecorated space with one separate partitioned off area at the front. No air-conditioning and precious few fans. Then, the old Supreme

Coat building opposite housed both the Supreme Court and the magistrates court. There was one resident Judge, Richard Blackburn, assisted by his Associate Tony Ryall and one resident magistrate Haynes Leader. The Judge was helped out intermittently by visiting elderly Federal industrial jurisdiction judges of the likes of Edward A. Dunphy [1907-1989] and Percy Joske [1885-1981]. There was no compulsory retiring age for these judges. I am told that prior to the arrival of Justice Blackburn the complex intersecting jurisdictional arrangements of the time could see the resident Judge determine a Workers Compensation claim—a Local Court jurisdictional matter - to have his decision, to his chagrin, reviewed by a visiting Dunphy sitting as a Supreme Court judge on an appeal. Justice Dunphy was known to the profession to be unpredictable in his decisions in civil matters. If his arrival was pending, most if not all civil cases in his list would be quickly settled before trial.

It was not always easy to make things work from a small office, whether at the government registries and decision-making process or with other lawyers in private practice. It was a time before practising certificates and professional indemnity insurance became compulsory for lawyers. My Gollin mate Keith Gale had married Justice Dunphy's daughter Jenny, as a result of which, while I was a GKFC man, I gave his honour a guided tour of such operations as were able to be seen about the waterfront. This was largely introducing him to the Perth based Hunt brothers who happily showed him over their lovely timber hulled Rottnest Island ferry which they had temporally converted for prawning. At the time, the cost of a Northern Prawn fishing licence was $5. Well before I left Darwin, such a licence was valued at over $1M. Justice Dunphy's lawyer son, John, made one visit to Darwin. He appeared as a very able visiting counsel in a civil action. Healthy as he appeared, he told us his days were so seriously numbered that he did not expect to see out another 12 months.

When I commenced legal practice about 6 months after my arrival it was sufficient to produce a copy of my certificate of admission to the Victorian Supreme Court and proof of my signature to the High Court roll. The latter I signed on to at the old High Court Registry building in Little Lonsdale Street on the same date as my Victorian admission. On the advice of Tony Ryall and as a courtesy to the Court, in early 1969 I made formal application to Justice Blackburn for admission to the Supreme Court of the Northern Territory. I was to learn my choice of professional rooms had an unfortunate legal history. Shortly before my arrival in Darwin, their previous lawyer occupant had been sentenced to a term of imprisonment. He was from Victoria and had taken up a legal job I had vacated before I took over a deceased lawyer's Collins Street city practice in Melbourne.

All of this pre-dated the Darwin Mall. That section of Smith Street that became the Mall was trafficked. It was the background to one extraordinary New Year celebrations emblematic photograph in which the only newspaper, the Murdoch owned NT News, depicted on page 1 four nude males on a motorcycle. Crusading Editor Jim Bowditch was at the helm in those days.

Towards the southern part of the commercial section of Smith Street there was a modest building owned by the original Nick Paspaley [he of the pearls].[11] Nick and Michael Paspalis were brothers. As you can well imagine, especially with two such entrepreneurial types it could and did lead to confusion especially with such little difference in the Christian names initial. Nick had resolved any problem by varying the family name.

John at his Office in Darwin in the 1980s

These days his son, also Nick [b. 1948], has taken over. The Paspaley-owned building was almost opposite Cashman's Newsagency. When betting shops were legal in the NT, Nick Paspaley ran one from there. This preceded the wealth explosion inside Paspaley Pearls. Nick's Japanese partner had withdrawn from its joint venture pearling operation with him in Northern Australia leaving that bailiwick entirely to the Paspaley interests. The Japanese ex-

---

[11] On Nicholas Paspaley and the story of the family's expansion from arrival in Australia from Greece in 1913 to become a global pearl business: https://www.paspaley.com/our-story/ See also "Paspaley," in Wikipedia: https://en.wikipedia.org/wiki/Paspaley/

partner had offered Nick participation in a planned new venture in the eastern Indonesian islands. Nick had refused instead concentrating his energies in Australia. Soon afterwards, pollution in Japanese waters seriously reduced pearl production there. Production and prices of Paspaley pearls soared.

Nick was a longstanding member in the Darwin Rotary club with the unusual classification of Master Pearler. He loved good conversation. Many were the times I was privileged to enjoy his company when the Rotary meeting formalities were completed. Nick was Mr. Charm himself except when he saw a threat to his commercial interests. If in a bar he was to strike up a conversation with a stranger, he always described himself as a public servant. As for putting a pretty girl in front of him I can only compare his enlivenment then as akin to a dead neon sign suddenly connected to electricity.

John bewigged for Court, Darwin, 1980s

Young Nick recounted to me an episode when the Paspaley pearling operation had elected for economic reasons to scuttle a larger imported vessel used in the industry. It was an option under the terms it had been brought into Australia. The period had expired when it could continue to be used. At the scuttling destination the doomed vessel was abandoned. The observers and participants were standing off. The seacocks had been opened. The foundering vessel was ablaze with its electric lights Nick had fame inside his family for watching the electricity meter. Power was never wasted when he was about. A pensive Nick watched. Suddenly he was heard to cry out about the waste of electricity on the fast settling vessel. A man was sent to board and extinguish all its lights. A way to alleviate grief at the murder of a good ship?

Nick could be a stubborn man. At a ladies' night Rotary function he was displaying some pearls. Peg McGregor wife of Ian another long-standing member who could be cantankerous was especially taken with one particular pearl. Nick gave it to her. Now husband Ian saw the relationship between the sexes in black and white terms. If a man especially of Mediterranean origin gifted a lady a valuable gem it must be for a fell purpose. At his insistence, Peg returned the pearl to Nick. Nick became possessed of a cold rage at what he saw as a calculated insult. The pearl was put in a drawer. Wars have been fought over less. From that time any Rotarian who never knew of the reason could but wonder at the ferocious attacks Nick launched at the weekly Club meetings questioning Ian's integrity. Ian's chairmanship of the then operating Darwin Cyclone Relief Trust Fund contributed to by Rotary clubs Australia wide became the attack vehicle. What was happening to the money? How was it being distributed? Why was any distribution taking so long? Was the account audited? It was not a matter I ever spoke to Nick about. But, after some months, peace broke out. Nick was able to take the pearl out of the drawer. With Ian's blessing the pearl was regifted. Peace broke out over the Cyclone Relief fund accounting.

Nick hated debt. Perhaps he had seen too many come undone in the north through the vagaries of climate and economics. I had posted him a small bill. Like me I think Nick collected his mail from a post office box. One of my office window overlooked the public car park and the post office the other side. Glancing out this window the next morning I noticed Nick making his way on the footpath from the post office in the direction of my office building. He seemed to be in a great hurry. I returned to my work. I learned later from staff that Nick had called in to pay my account. The reason for his haste became apparent. It was his hatred of debt.

Unlike Ray McHenry's Rotary talk, [see below] Ian McGregor's was highly emotional. He was adopted. He knew nothing of this until he was in his late teens. It was a hammer blow. Tears in his eyes, he implored his audience to inform any child they might adopt of that fact at an early age. Another club member Stan Miller had to help him back to his chair after his talk. Ian was laid low by a stroke. He got back on his feet and was able to re-attend meetings. There was a problem. Ian was never slow to speak up at meetings. Post stroke he continued to do so, but his speech was all but unintelligible. Mystified we may have been but no club member complained. His funeral service was majestic. As the coffin was led out of the church, a solitary piper played a lament. The cleric leading loudly invoked the biblical words: "I am the resurrection and the light."

It was while I was with GKFC [1968] that Martyn Finger, a friend of a former Melbourne client, arrived in town to take up a position as one of two Assistant Administrators. The Administrator as the Queen's representative occupied the role of a State Governor in the Territory. His role was more ceremonial and statutory. The real work was done by the two assistant Administrators. In earlier days it had been customary for one of these to reside in Alice Springs. The government of that day comprised a Legislative Council [Legco] made up of a majority of Commonwealth nominees balanced against a minority of elected members. You could say it was a "guided" democracy. Canberra controlled the NT and the minority was at one level a fractious noisy group made up of the likes of my next door Darwin flat neighbour Harold [Tiger] Brennan as well as Dick Ward and Ron Withnall baying at what they saw as the dead hand of the Commonwealth stifling independent and better ideas.

Early on in my Darwin law practice days, while the war in Vietnam was at its height, charter outfit World Airlines ran R and R charter flights to Sydney for American servicemen. Darwin was selected for crew basing. It was a convenient halfway staging post. From there crew would do the 8 hours or so return trip to Vietnam or Sydney. The airport was convenient to town and the tropical climate lent itself to easy informality off duty. I got to meet some of the flight attendants. I could drop the girl off at their hotel the Capricornia before midnight and by 8am or so the next day they were back after an 8-hour shift north or south. I recall taking what I assumed to be an American girl to the home of Martyn Finger on one Christmas day. Her voice had no trace of accent other than of the US. Martyn had his aged German mother living with his family. The widow of a German speaking Lutheran missionary, she had never developed any real command of English. To my surprise my escort started singing Christmas carols in German with Martyn's mother. It turned out she was a German speaking Swiss national. She had gone to the US as a Swiss consulate secretary. From there she had made her way to World Airlines. No sooner had we met than the local baggage handlers went on strike and forthwith World Airlines withdrew from Darwin altogether.

Some weeks earlier I had been dragging my off the beach catamaran to the water over the mudflats by the sailing club at low tide. It was January. The wet season was underway. As I was to learn later, nobody went sailing that time of year. Two delightful young ladies came up and asked if they could "have a ride on your boat." One was an extraordinarily personable Hispanic from California named Ophelia. Hosts at barbecues I attended with her about this time still remember Ophelia. You guessed it. She was from World Airlines.

I recall being puzzled during my National Service days about a fellow conscript named Conway telling me his father was the Alice Springs-based Assistant Administrator of the Northern Territory. As it turned out his father was Dan Conway, a fellow Rotarian with my Darwin Club.

Legco to LA

A word here on the constitutional background of the NT. Legco came into being from 1947 until its replacement by the fully elected NT Legislative Assembly in 1974. Limited self-government had to wait until mid-1978. The original Legco comprised 13 members. Six were elected and seven nominated by the federal government, including the NT Administrator, who held both deliberative and casting votes. Legco could "make Ordinances for the peace, order and good government of the Territory," although these could be vetoed by the federal government. The NT had no authority over money matters. The longest-serving member of Legco (Legislative Council) was government appointee Harry Giese from 1954 to 1973.

Over the years Legco elected members consistently opposed the federal government's reluctance to grant them more power. The Commonwealth believed that the NT needed to be self-supporting before greater powers were given. A stand-off in 1958 saw the elected members resigning their seats *en masse* in protest. They were all re-elected at by elections. After, a new structure was put in place - eight elected members, six government appointees and three nominees to be drawn from outside the public service. Further reforms were made in 1965, when for parliamentary purpose the Administrator was replaced by an elected Council President, and in 1968 when the three non-government nominees were replaced by thee further elected members. The Commonwealth still retained the right of veto.

In 1973, the Whitlam government abolished Legco to create a fully elected Legislative Assembly. This body held its first election in 1974. Self-government had to wait until 1978. That self-government was still limited. The federal government retained and still retains control of Aboriginal land, industrial relations, national parks and uranium mining. For inter-governmental financial purposes, the

Northern Territory has been regarded by the Commonwealth as a State since 1 July 1988.

Legislation passed by the Assembly requires assent by the Administrator, acting on the advice of the Government. The federal government also retains power to legislate for the Territory in all matters. Included was the right to override legislation passed by the Assembly. Thus was overturned the NT Assisted Dying legislation of 1995.

Sad to say the standard of debate in the pre-1974 guided semi-parliament was well ahead of the best the post self- governing parliament in the Legislative Assembly has been able to manage. The clerk to the old Legislative Council produced a booklet under the auspices of the government of the day in which he, arguably not wisely so far as his personal interests were concerned, discussed very frankly and in schoolmaster report mode the oratorical powers and parliamentary skills of all the members both government and private.

Through my duties over 6 months with GKFC I worked alongside my Japanese opposite number, Hiroshi Amemiya, better known as Amemiya-san. We met up with staff from other joint prawn ventures especially the American owned Tipperary, whose lead figures were Geoff Samuelsen of Tipperary and Gary Nielson, an MG Kailis Gulf Fisheries consultant.

It was Geoff [Samuelson] who convinced me to set up law practice in Darwin after the expiration of the 3 months' notice that had been agreed between Gollin and me in 1968. Unlike Geoff and the Amemiya-san of that time, I was not a company man. Amemiya-san has long since become a successful self-employed Australian citizen. While I mostly enjoyed the company of visiting corporates both from Japan and Sydney, I found it increasingly difficult to lead an independent non-work-related life because of their visits—invariably over week-ends. Amemiya-san and I lived above the office we had found on the edge of town. This building was later purchased by Gollin.

Before Geoff's advice I had a vague notion to try my luck at the Melbourne Bar. Years later Melbourne barrister as he was then Bob Brooking QC told me if I had done that I would have been fitted into a narrow work slot to maximise economic advantage to law firms and barristers clerks. It was my pleasure to recently thank Geoff for his advice. This was by phone not long before my voice had been destroyed but after I had been laid up at my Scottsdale nursing home. Time had not dulled Geoff's unique voice—always serious and measured but with an undercurrent of wonderment an almost musical style lilt bespeaking humour was never far away. Maybe it was a fusion of his father's Sweden with his mother's Ireland. We had not made contact for long and Amemiya-san another long-term contact of mine had visited him at his last home at Yamba at the south side of the mouth of the Clarence River in Northern NSW. Soon after I left GKFC Geoff had taken himself to Saudi Arabia where he was engaged in operating super-markets. There had been a period living in the US. Three wives later and only a few years ago he had returned to Aus alone, wiser and in indifferent health from heart disease, but with little money to show for his troubles. It was not long after the visit from Amemiya-san less than 18 months ago [about 2016] that he was found dead sitting up in bed with a book in his hands. May he rest in peace.

Fisheries

My time with GKFC gave me some insight to the Japanese way of doing things. Amemiya-san took in good part Gary Nielsen's exaggerated bowing and hissing. After this, I was able to observe Amemiya-san's mild embarrassment at his consciousness of his disrespectful onlooking Australian mates as in our presence he bowed to visiting Japanese superiors. With Amemiya-san acting as interpreter, it was possible to have a boisterous friendly chat over a wine lubricated meal with for example the likes of the Kyokuyo fleet engineer Kawakami-san. After such an encounter both Kawakami-san and I were reduced to embarrassing friendly grunts to each other when we met without any interpreter.

Amemiya-san had been married to Kazuko only weeks before his departure for Australia. It had been a traditional Japanese courtship. Some 6 months or so after his arrival in Australia, his employer sent out the wife. Apart from his rambunctious Australian mates and his part Australianisation, his life was additionally complicated in that he had to fit into his already busy life a hardly-known traditional Japanese wife. Unlike her spouse, Kazuko was not an easy or early adaptor to the Australian way of life.

Geoff Samuelsen took a special interest in all things Japanese, involved as his employer was with marketing Tipperary's sorghum production to Japan. Geoff loved insider stories. He it was who recounted to me the behind closed doors soul searching of executive of the hard drinking Darwin Club when it came to consider the membership application of Amemiya-san. The application approved, Amemiya-san never attended.

Post my GKFC employment and my discovery of Charlie's, I recall lunching there with Gary when he introduced me to a travelling French Canadian, Cathy. Coming from a family of 9 children as she had, it was not altogether surprising that she more than held her own albeit charmingly in the cut and thrust of conversation. It was only recently that I learned post Darwin Cathy had worked in the Michael Kailis office in Perth and later married Gary. Together they had created a family and sponsored a successful public company. But Gary was never one to let his right hand know what the left was doing.

The Australian/Japanese prawning joint ventures apart, the local vessels played an important role. So far as I could make out most of those in Darwin came from Western Australia. Presumably the east coasters had sufficient pickings closer to home. During the wet season some Australian vessels returned to Perth to refit. That was a lengthy voyage. Most seemed to get by with local input. For example, Amemiya-san struck up a rapport with a local outfit specialising in marine diesel engines. Many of the staff were of German origin. I was told the annual refit could cost up to $200,000.

Particular fishermen became glamorous figures. All seemed to be doing well but some spectacularly so. Johnny Wheeler was the top gun. One season's catch was over 1 million pounds. Sam de Sousa was another top catcher. Crew were not salarymen but rather percentage participants. Successful skippers were never wanting for top crew. Gary Neilsen looked on, missing nothing. The prawn potential seemed unlimited. Lessees of financed boats committed to more leased vessels to be constructed in WA. Inevitably a lean season that came found them wanting. The connection was made between a good wet season as a precursor of a prosperous prawn season. The inverse applied equally. The financial conservatism of the likes of seagoing marine engineer New Zealander Reg [Bones] Doherty seemed to pay off.

Bones liked motorcycles. He seemed to change regularly. All of his bikes were the latest most powerful and best Japan produced. As a former keen motorcyclist when England had ruled that roost I was pleased to accept his invitations to try out his rides. The last, a Honda Gold Wing flat 4 large capacity water cooled bike had me bamboozled. It was quite unresponsive to ordinary handling when changing direction. The rider had to lean to the point of leaving the saddle to get response. It was dramatically different to my briefly-owned Triumph 650 Thunderbird of another era. That bike steered itself. After a few seasons Bones loaded his vehicles, his Burmese wife and himself and perhaps a sack of gold on a plane back to the Land of the Long White Cloud.

Soviet Visitor

During my time at GKFC, in1968, Darwin was visited by the legendry eastern Russian Commodore Solyanik with his super-sized trawler Van Goth.[12] It was soon after his visit to the Gulf of Carpentaria. That visit had provoked a storm. Abuse had been hurled and shots fired by Australian fishermen at the Van Goth as it sailed the Gulf of Carpentaria. Allegations of vacuuming up all that moved through the sea were made. The visit coincided with the opening of a prawn processing plant at Karumba by Craig Mostyn. Deputy PM Doug Anthony who did the official opening was greeted with stony silence when he put into perspective what was happening in the Gulf prawn fishery. Until not long before, foreign fishers had enjoyed carte blanche in the Gulf because Australia had not been interested. How things changed.

One Saturday, as lunch was being served at the Capricornia Motel on East Point Road at Fannie Bay, somehow or other Amemiya-san and I had invited the Commodore to lunch. He accepted. The Commodore was accompanied by two heavy dark suited males who said nothing. I assumed they were KGB. The Commodore gave no indication he was fazed by their presence. He appeared relaxed and talkative. He spoke excellent English which I suspect was beyond the comprehension of the suits. The suits tucked in with no less gusto than the Commodore. All I remember of that conversation now is that the Commodore had a terrible spare parts problem with his Packard Clipper

---

[12] On this incident, Georgy Zaytsev, "Unexpected Soviet Visitor: the trawler 'Van Gogh' in the Gulf of Carpentaria," *The Great Circle*, 37, 2 (2015). https://www.jstor.org/stable/24583100/

back home in Vladivostock. And when he saw an aborigine driving a Holden car he refused to believe his eyes.

In my time, Tipperary was American owned and controlled. Apart from the prawning joint venture, it was engaged in agricultural development on Tipperary Station south of Darwin. The Americans had adopted the long-held station name. The station comprised about 209,000 hectares in area. To that may have been added the areas of Litchfield and Elizabeth Downs Stations—the combined area being known as the aggregated station. As I understood the concept, it was clearing land by tractor 24 hours a day with a view to turning off 72 separately titled paddocks each of about 30 square kilometres. To do this it had to establish that each paddock was an economically viable unit for growing sorghum. Many employed in the land clearing had hopes of purchasing one of the paddocks. But the venture failed and Tipperary withdrew. I was present at the Darwin Hotel when visiting American chairman Bill Neely delivered its last hurrah.

In more recent times the aggregated stations have been owned by developer Warren Anderson who in turn sold to lawyer Alan Myers. Alan was investing a windfall profit from a fee paid in Polish shares of little value but which had an astronomical rise. Anderson had undertaken a massive building programme including an airstrip which could handle a Boeing 727 and a zoo of exotic wild animals. His departure created issues on disposition of the animals. When a station-hand out hunting shot what he thought was a wild pig, closer examination of the corpse, and consultation with experts, determined that it was a highly endangered West

African pygmy hippopotamus - at the time worth over A$100,000.

Throughout my time with Kyokuyo (GKFC) Amemiya-san had very little free time. He was busy looking after all the needs of company vessels in port. Scotch whisky aside, they required engineering repairs and to take on fuel. He had spent some time at sea on a Kyokuyo vessel. Luminaries of Kyokuyo who passed through Darwin included fleet master Iwasaki-san christened "Mudguts" by crusty, outspoken fellow Rotarian Harbour Master Carl Allridge. Iwasaki-san was a failed World War 11 Kamikaze (Divine Wind) pilot. Engine troubles had brought him back to base. Amemiya-san was heard to hint darkly of shame when reference was made to the incident. During the same war, Carl had three merchant ships torpedoed from under him by Japanese submarines. He and Amemiya-san nevertheless struck up an unlikely, mutually respectful and long-lived, friendship.

The concept of the joint venture was that it would construct in Australia a fleet of around 6 vessels, to be Australian crewed. Prawn catch was then to be delivered onshore for processing. Pending arrival of the new vessels, the fishery would be worked by a fixed number of Kyokuyo vessels which would process the prawns on board. Crew on these Japanese vessels would be largely if not entirely Japanese. The disposition of the new trawlers was to coincide with construction of a prawn processing plant on Groote Island,

As to Amemiya-san's experience at sea, I learned that when the nets were being put down it was full on 24/7. It was eat, sleep and work. Largely the crew ran on Johnny

Walker Scotch whisky. A bottle was kept by the bunk. There was no nicety like decanting. It was consumed simply to keep going. Harbour Master Allridge was astonished at the massive loadings of duty-free Johnny Walker when the Kyokuyo boats were leaving port. Even Amemiya-san who was at best a very light drinker in Darwin freely admitted he relied on Johnny Walker at sea. In his time the average voyage was for 6 months most of which was relentless 24/7 trawling. He was able to recall an incident where a crewman died at sea from natural causes. The body was placed in the vessel freezer and almost totally forgotten until the fish cargo was unloaded back in Japan. Personally I can understand working under pressure but not that sort of brutal pressure as a salaryman.

Sadly, the GKFC venture failed. Not long afterwards, Gollin itself went into liquidation. The liquidations were preceded by decimation of the newly minted GKFC fleet of Australian built trawlers. Several had been trapped in port when Darwin was ravaged by Cyclone Tracey on Christmas eve and morning 1974. If they had but followed the example of the Paspaley operation they would have steamed into the local mangroves and lived to catch more fish.

Rotary and the Darwin Club

I have a lot to thank Martyn Finger [1922-2011] for. He it was that early in my Darwin legal career sponsored me into Darwin Rotary Club. The post-club Thursday evening meetings fellowship was an important part of my life until I drifted away when I reached 65 years and attendance was no longer compulsory. Rotary clubs are limited to one member per classification. Last I heard, Darwin club was resolutely all male although other Darwin clubs are have included women as members. The meetings got members away from their often-limited work horizons. Membership was fluid in part from the banks and insurance companies transferring their executives to Darwin for shortish 2-year terms. It was there I met up with Ray McHenry, an old Paradian [Melbourne's Parade College was our alma mater] with whom I had shared a desk for a year in Form 11 in 1948. That year was the last I had seen of Ray. He was then about 14-years old, 5'6" in the old money, football mad, slight of build and known colloquially as Chooka. When we met up in Rotary he was so tall, well over 6' and substantially built that I had to ask this figure whether he was one and the same Ray with whom I had shared a desk. This was even after what the club called a "me" introductory talk to the club from Ray as a new member. He gave nothing away in his talk. Or it may have been that Ray in full awareness of who I was wanted to test my reaction. The only thing I could otherwise identify was a vague facial resemblance to the Chooka of bygone years. Ray having arrived in the NT as one of two Assistant Administrators, went on to lead a Territory push to set up a manufacturing hub in a specially set up Trade Development Zone.

Ray was a man of many parts. An accomplished public speaker and of no mean intelligence, in the immediate post Cyclone Tracey aftermath it was not uncommon for him to take the microphone at the damaged Travel Lodge Hotel to croon popular songs to the other cyclone refugees. When he arrived in Darwin, he had never been outside Australia.

Before he left and through government service, he was able to become a devotee of ultra-expensive [US$8,000 return] high speed [3 hours or so] luxury transatlantic flights at Mach 2 speeds [about 1,400 miles per hour] on Concorde.[13] I have been told stories of Ray idling away days if not weeks to wait for a booking on Concorde. By all accounts those favoured 100 or so passengers comprised the international elite. It was possible to take Concorde from London, complete a day's work in New York and return to London for tea. On board atmosphere was said to be ultra-friendly and informal.

Britain and France each took on seven Concordes. Only twenty had been built, six of them used only for testing. The British Concorde story never started well. By around 1981 its future looked bleak. Money had been, and was being, lost operating it. Moves were afoot to cancel the service entirely. A cost projection came back with greatly reduced metallurgical testing costs because the test rig for the wings had built up enough data to last for 30 years and could be shut down. A newly appointed boss of British Air set up a small group inside the airline to turn Concorde's fortunes around. It was do or die time. Research revealed very few Concorde patrons were aware of the cost. Those few who even considered it thought it was much more than it was. The fare was increased. The small sub management group cultivated the image of exclusivity and ultra-luxury so well that Concorde became hugely profitable. Pilots had to complete a special and demanding training course that took

---

[13] "Concorde-Wikipedia," https://en.wikipedia.org/wiki/concorde/

up about 6 months. Only the best of the best wines, spirits, steaks and seafood were served.

In 2001 a French Concorde crashed on take-off with the loss of all including the Caribbean bound German tourists on board. Not long afterwards, there was the terrorist hijacked airliner-based attack on the New York World Trade Centre. Even then, the English passenger loadings were holding up well but the French demand collapsed and there was a slump in air travel generally. Steeply rising maintenance costs contributed. Concorde was technologically advanced when introduced in the 1970s, but, thirty years later, its analogue cockpit was outdated. There had been little commercial pressure to upgrade Concorde due to a lack of competing aircraft, unlike other airliners of the same era such as the Boeing 747. Concorde was seen as an outdated notion of prestige. After 27 years of glittering success the flights were eventually stopped in 2003.The French disaster derived from an unfortunate combination of circumstances none of which could be said to be the fault of the aircraft.

On one occasion Ray had been dispatched to America's Atlantic City to negotiate with casino interests there on behalf of the Northern Territory. At the time the free enterprise Everingham government was busy hosing the Farrell family interests out of the Darwin casino. Ray was well known to the NT racing cognoscenti of the day to have a serious gambling problem. To the astonishment of a Darwinian attending the Royal Ascot race meeting in England then, and to not a little of Ray's chagrin, he found there a top-hatted and tailed Ray escorting a gorgeous American blonde. This, as the good Darwin burgher later interpreted, may have been courtesy of Concorde and the Atlantic City casino interests. As for himself, Ray wasn't talking. Equally likely was the unwitting sponsorship of the NT government. Was it just a day trip? Maybe. If only Ray had written **his** memoir.

It was after I had set up my private law practice that I became involved on behalf of Michael Kailis [1929-1999] as a hastily appointed director of his MG Kailis Gulf Fisheries company in the purchase of the then being liquidated GKFC's prawn processing plant which it had erected on Groote Island. The liquidator, one Warhurst, was in Darwin. I later learned he was seriously if not terminally ill but there was no indication of this in either his appearance or manner. Gary Nielsen was my wingman. We both sat in with Warhurst. As we were to learn later, the negotiations were not exclusively about price but how that price was to be paid. Cash was not necessarily king. This was contrary to the way our principal and my then co-director Michael was thinking. A price to be paid over a term with interest accruing on the unpaid balance would perhaps enable a liquidator to pay more money to the creditors. This message was circuitously conveyed to Gary and me by Warhurst and communicated to Michael in Perth. Michael had another message for me. "Get this deal and next time you are in Perth I will meet you at the airport in my new Jaguar V12 and take you home for tea."

All this was happening after office hours on a Friday evening Michael was not the only prospective buyer. He was very much aware of a keen competing interest from the Raptis family in South Australia.

About 8.30pm there was a lull in negotiations. I was hungry. Over Gary Nielsen's protests, I managed to get him to Charlie's restaurant for a feed. Withal, Gary was distracted. He was feeling chest pain. Half-way through the meal I had to have, a message came from our host Charlie. Gary was wanted on the restaurant phone. Remember all this pre-dated universal mobile phones. It was Michael. Had we abandoned him? Eventually we were given a pass to finish tea before a return to the fray. A half hour was mentioned. Michael had accepted cash was no longer king in this deal and amended his offer accordingly. Return we did. A deal was hammered out. Michael was ecstatic. Gary relaxed. I could look forward to being hosted and chauffeured.

Not long afterwards, I picked up a report of the Warhurst death. And Michael was having trouble with the Jag. It had stopped. All the efforts of the distributors to start it again were in vain. Months later Michael had a call from the distributors. The Jag was running again. How was it fixed? It wasn't. A mechanic had climbed in, pressed the starter. True to his word though Michael met me at the Perth airport. With both of our fingers crossed we got to his home. His charming wife had prepared a marvellous feast. We dined under a wall sized blown up image of the harbour at the small but barren Mediterranean island of Castelhorizon—the ancestral home of the Kailis clan. The Jag even got me to my hotel afterwards.

The Michael Kailis connection led to other things. Michael was the Australian representative of the Taiwanese fishing group Kaoshing Fishing Guild. He had on hs board retired military men like Colonel Ken Murdoch and dedicated anti-Communist Brigadier General Ted Serong. They and their likes cemented the Kailis link with anti-communist Taiwan. I still chuckle to myself recalling over lunch at Charlie's Ken delivering an argument against an Australian President. He recalled an event during World War 11. A desperate struggle was underway. Ken's lines had been overrun by the Germans. His troops were exhausted. The battle was in the balance. A cry went up: "A special effort for the King." It was taken up. Through the ranks the cry went "For the King." "The King." Tired warriors were rejuvenated. The tide was turned. The invaders were repulsed. Ken contended that was wildly improbable that a group of Australian soldiers would rally to a cry where the special effort was "For President Hawke."

Occasionally a Taiwanese fishing trawler was apprehended by the Australian Navy in the 200 nautical mile Australian Exclusive Fishing zone. Arrests usually occurred at night. The Australian patrol boat would douse all lights and sneak up on a radar targeted fishing boat, pop its armed boarding crew into a Z boat and board the suspect before the drew knew they were there. The procedure then was to escort the arrested vessel to Darwin. The crew were expected to live aboard in Darwin Harbour until any charge of illegal fishing was disposed of by the courts. My remit became to undertake legal defence to prosecutions.

It was at a time when a finding of guilt would commonly lead to an order for forfeiture of the vessel and its catch as well as a heavy fine. The master ran the risk of imprisonment. There were language difficulties in obtaining instructions. The invariable legal procedure was for the local Commonwealth Fisheries inspector, Col Mellon, to conduct through an interpreter a recorded interview with the vessel's master. I or an employed lawyer staffer would sit in on the interview and object to impermissible questions. No admission of guilt was ever made. Nonetheless, the prosecution would rely on this record of interview in any prosecution.

These prosecutions came to depend on locating the fisherman's position precisely and within the 200 nautical miles exclusive Australian Fishing Zone [AFZ]. When it became a matter of a vessel being very close to the AFZ boundary the key task of the prosecution became positioning the arrested vessel beyond a reasonable doubt. Incidental but still important matters concerned the nature of activity at the time of arrest. Did the vessel have its trawl nets down? Were fish being processed on deck? Was the vessel moving? These questions arose from it being both legal and permissible for a fishing vessel to traverse the AFZ so long as its fishing gear was stowed.

Especially by night and only if a vessel is well within the AFZ is it possible for a prosecutor to rely on the time proven nautical sextant and navigation tables used to reduce a sextant sight to a position. In the cases I contested [and none were admitted] the prosecutor invariably relied on a position given to it by a electronic navigator backed up by dead reckoning from the last sextant sight. In earlier days the electronic aspect was by Satellite Navigator [Satnav]. This relied on a limited number of satellites and positioning was far from continuous because if at least two satellites weren't available a position couldn't be transmitted, and a sailor would have to wait. Hours could pass. So long as the sailor had adequate sea room this was no problem for him either. As for a prosecutor, identifying a position during such an interlude would have to rely upon dead reckoning from the last satellite pass. Even then, this was no panacea as the Satnav receiver took time to compute position after it locked on to two or more satellites. I compared this with a hen cackling after laying an egg. The GPS would light up and make noise. It could be 20 minutes or more before it announces the result of its labours with more noisy fanfare. As one who had difficulty with sea sickness using a sextant and making the ensuing calculations the Satnav was a marvel. In the Indonesian archipelago between Ambon and Darwin and on the blackest of nights, even with hours long delay it is very comforting to be reassured there is plenty of sea-room.

I am not altogether sure now that the Satnav system is still operational. Some years back and in light of the newer more heavily satellite saturated system of Global Position Satellite [GPS] navigation I read that the Satnav system would not be maintained. It is a few years now since I have ventured on the ocean, and I have lost touch. My Satnav cost me over A$3000 at a time when as I look back it was close to being replaced by GPS. When the first Satnav units became available the cost was 40,000 pounds and looked on as good value for a ship. When I checked last GPS units were around A$300. They are even included in heart rate monitors and cameras.

Both systems rely on regular programming of the satellites relied upon. I think the base that looks after this is in Hawaii. Unless an assumption this is done correctly is enshrined in legislation, it must be a productive area to exploit in disputing GPS positioning. Others must be the installation of the system and its proper initialisation.

The last fisheries case I was involved in presented a curious set of facts. When the trawler was approached by an unlit patrol boat it was motionless and its lights ablaze. At worst it was no more than two nautical miles inside the AFZ if it was at all. The engine on the patrol boat had been turned off and its lights doused for the final approach. Suddenly, the trawler master became aware of its presence. Remember, we are here on the high seas accessible to anyone with a navigable vessel. As the trawler skipper later declared in his interview, he thought pirates were at work. The trawler fired up its main engine and made off at full speed before the navy Z boat could load and land an armed boarding party. The navy took off in pursuit. The Australian flag was raised and spotlighted. As the patrol boat came alongside the trawler swung attempting to collide. The patrol boat easily evaded collision. The chase lasted for over 50 nautical miles outside the AFZ. The navy was engaged in hot pursuit— permissible only if the vessel had been inside the AFZ in the first instance. Radio messages were relayed to and from Canberra. No doubt likewise between the trawler and Taiwan. The navy's oerlikon gun was readied for action. Shots were fired across the trawler bow. The trawler stopped. The boarding party took over.

Personally, I doubt the navy would have sunk the trawler. That would have involved loss of all evidence of what the trawler was up to not to mention a rescue of its crew. On the other hand as I was to learn later, a former Darwinian, John Chadderton, was operating his tuna boat in waters proximate to the remote Kerguelen Islands. These are one of the most remote places on earth located as they are in the Southern Ocean about 450 kilometres northwest of uninhabited Heard Island. They are a French possession. A small group of scientists ranging in number from 50 to 100 are in occupation. One way or another, Chadderton's vessel came to the attention of the French navy. Asked to heave to, he took off. The flight was ended by his vessel being shelled and sunk. An unsympathetic Court at Madagascar sentenced him to a term of imprisonment. The sentence never precluded John taking windsurfer sailing lessons from his championship winning 2IC. One day he and his instructor took off over the horizon—this time successfully - about 200 miles to a non-French rule island. Last I heard, John was running a health food store back in Australia.

During the hearing, I was able to create a doubt about the accuracy of the GPS position. The prosecutor, Terry Gardiner, was baffled and unable to resolve this doubt. Over that night, the magistrate was busy. The next day, he announced he had been reading a surveyor's journal article about the GPS system. He proffered the article for comment. Then, over my objection, he tendered the article as evidence. The article sang the praises of the GPS system.

I mention here another element in this curious case. The Kaoshing Fishing Guild of Taiwan was to be my paymaster.

Mr Woo of the Guild came to see me. He professed no faith in paying a fee where there was no performance incentive. He came up with a formula based largely upon saving the vessel from forfeiture. I listened. He must have taken my listening as agreement.

The magistrate found the trawler was in the AFZ at the time of first contact by the navy. But he also found its presence and activity at that time to be a mystery. The catch was ordered forfeit, but the vessel was not.

A month or so later I had not submitted any account. Pressure of work, I took off for a short break. Singapore was the first port of call. Next, it was to the Philippines. On that second flight who should I meet but Mr Woo. Greetings exchanged; he inquired if I had my money. He had remitted it to the Kailis Perth office with instructions to pass it on to me. A not insignificant sum was mentioned. I told him I would look into the unpaid funds on my return to Darwin. Subject to me getting my hands on the money, the Guild was the perfect client. It was a case of money paid after the event before a bill had even been sent. The quantum was the Guild's assessment of the value of my work to it.

At the time the Kailis fishing business had fallen into financial doldrums. I learned later preparations were in hand for bankruptcy. Newly set up pearling operations in the north might just save the day. In the event they did. At the time though money was tight. Michael's son George was at the helm in Perth. George was a much colder fish than Michael. The money was paid.

As a fellow Darwin sailing club member found to his cost there was an etiquette to be observed when arresting a vessel. It was not a prize of war where the victorious crew could help themselves. My yacht was once peripherally involved in an arrest. Our last port of call had been Saumlaki in the Indonesian Taninbar Islands. The distance to be covered (to Ambon) was about 200 nautical miles. We had left the previous morning. The only noteworthy passage event had been the disruption to lunch on the day of departure because Tom Pauling and Jenny Simondson had served up an exquisite meal. That was the signal for the weather gods to up the ante. Platters of fine food had been trampled underfoot as we set up for the new conditions. It was late in the evening the second day out, maybe early morning the next day. My 30' yacht was rollicking along on a tight reach. We had closed Rocky Point on the unlit northwest point of Bathurst Island. The echo sounder was closely monitored. I was below when a bright light illuminated our deck. The hum of a diesel engine could be heard accompanied by an oath of surprise from my deck crew. It was an Australian navy patrol boat. The patrol boat slipped back into the darkness. We were to learn later it had been following a Taiwanese fishing vessel. As we closed Darwin harbour the navy accompanying an arrested fishing boat arrived likewise there was much noise, deck movement and shouting from the fishing vessel. The arrest had occurred in a small bay at the southwestern corner of Bathurst Island. The patrol boat was commanded by a sailing club member. He was to be cashiered for the events of that evening. His boarding party had appropriated the fishing boat's noodles.

Some years later two mainland Chinese trawlers were arrested when traversing the AFZ in circumstances that appeared to me to be tenuous at best. The confused owner was in Darwin. He discussed with me my possible representation of his interests, but I heard no more from him. This time there was at least one full blown jury trial in the Supreme Court. I looked in briefly. To say matters were proceeding slowly would have been a serious over statement. Questions were being put through an interpreter. Counsel for the Chinese was an import. I suggest if he had no seagoing experience, he would have found the going heavy. The jury returned a finding of guilty.

The second arrested vessel had a seriously chequered post-arrest history. It was anchored in Darwin harbour without crew. No prosecution had been launched. From time to time a government employee on a chartered large dinghy attended to give the main engine a run. The engine would then be left running while the vessel was left unattended. An interval of hours could elapse. On the last occasion some matting had come up against the engine exhaust system. Fire broke out on the unattended vessel. It was gutted. The event was recorded in the NT News. By then I was out of touch, and I never found out what the ultimate wash-up was.

Above, I mentioned the Raptis family.[14] Some years after the Kailis purchase of the prawn processing plant, one morning at my office I received a phone call. As a matter of urgency, I was required to attend on Con Raptis at Karumba a small seaside town located at a river mouth where it met the Gulf of Carpentaria on the southwest of Cape York. The national news over the preceding 24 hours had made me aware there was a major hunt for a trawler suspected of illegal fishing activity in the Karumba vicinity. Aircraft were involved. I had no immediate court obligations to hinder me, so it was off to the airport. There, my secretary Linda Barret took transcription and instructions on client matters while I waited for the passenger loading call. The airline flight went to Mt Isa. Then it was a charter light plane to Karumba. As he bundled me into my light plane connection the pilot soon made me aware how critical time was if we were to land at Karumba before sunset. We just made it. As he left me on the tarmac, darkness closing in, I realised there was nothing more there than the landing strip upon which I stood. I picked up my bag and commenced to walk to the lights of the town about one kilometre away. Halfway I was met by Con in his car. He was far from communicative save to mention he thought he heard my flight come in.

A brief interlude at the Raptis home then it was up the mangrove lined river for something like 2 hours in an outboard powered alloy dinghy. I was put aboard an

---

[14] Further on the Raptis group, see Eleni Bozos, "The Raptis Group ranked as 100 wealthiest companies," *Greek Reporter*, 26 September 2010.
https://greekreporter.com/2010/09/26/the-king-of-shrimp-from-eyboia-to-australia/

obviously oriental designed trawler—about 130' long, all ends with a massive concave sheerline. I was to learn it was of Taiwanese origin, had been seized by the Commonwealth for illegal fishing and sold, to be likewise seized and sold again. The master an affable Queenslander ushered me to the comfortable wheelhouse. Over a few drinks we discoursed pleasantly until a few hours later we kipped. All had been quiet. In the morning we weighed anchor and got underway to Karumba. Our arrival caused no fuss. The Department of Primary Industries [DPI] Inspector there peered into the whistle clean freezer hold. His only comment was how earlier that morning several Raptis vessels had been in to unload. They had boasted remarkable prawn catches.

NT News

Presiding over, and recording as best it could the activity of turbulent Darwin Town, was the NT News, edited between 1955 and 1973 by Jim Bowditch [1920-1996].[15] Jim had been scarred by his service as a Z force World War 11 commando. Especially, he was haunted by remembrance of his killing of a young Japanese soldier whose path he had intersected in a jungle to Australia's north. It was kill or be killed time and he killed. About the time a retired Jim left Darwin for Perth I ran into him over lunch. Tears in his eyes, he relived the episode. Though his killing had been sanctioned by the state, that fact gave him no solace. Another local, retired WW11 hero, RAAF Group Captain Wilf Arthur,

---

[15] Jim Bowditch - The Australian Media Hall of Fame (melbournepressclub.com). See also *Big Jim – Crusading Territory newspaper editor, Jim Bowditch*, Dymocks, 2022.

exhibited no sign of mental distress over the enemy aircraft he had downed as a fighter pilot. Socrates was probably not the first to philosophise about the divine implications of humans from birth being hard-wired with an innate sense of right and wrong.

Despite his outward hardiness, I suspect at heart Jim was a romantic who in different circumstances and time could have been a poet or playwright. Much, if not all, of the record of his legacy of newspaper crusades on behalf of, among others, the mysterious Mrs. X [eventually unmasked as Winifred Ida Lennon], aborigines generally, Carlo Finemore [imprisoned for failing to pay spousal maintenance], was destroyed with all other historic NT News photographs and records on the morning of 25 December 1974 by Cyclone Tracey. Bob Hobman, Englishman, former temporary Territorian and, last I heard, Bali resident and sponsor of the Last Great Jukung Race, is said to have been working for years on a biography of Jim with Jim's assistance.

Chapter 8: The North, Politics, the Future [1968-]

Politics in Australia 2019 has been by most objective measures in serious decline. My measuring instrument is the facts posited against sensible planning for Australia's future.

Perhaps the symptoms are unavoidable with mature, relatively affluent and economically linked, western democracies. Amid the distractions of affluence such as megaphone lobbying and fake news propagated by venal media barons, how is the voter to be able to keep abreast of politically concerning issues so as to prevent power falling by default into the hands of greedy, self-absorbed, inner circle, backroom cliques?

On my first overseas trip, to Singapore in the early 1970s, it took S$3.27 to buy A$1. In 2019 these dollars are about on a par. Singapore has no more than position and sound management to account for this. No mining boom or China boom there.

One example is superannuation. There, compulsory superannuation was mandatorily invested into state housing development and returned a modest interest rate. Lack of housing for the average Singaporean is unknown. Contrast this with the dog's breakfast the Australian government has made of local compulsory superannuation funds where the recent Royal Commission into the Banks has revealed wide scale fraud. As for housing, the less said the better.

Perhaps the economic ascension of Singapore has a connection with the salaries of the politicians there. When I last looked years ago, the salary of a cabinet minister was over S$1M. And while we wring our hands over our highest value A$100 note encouraging a black economy, let alone drug dealers, Singapore has been issuing S$1,000 S$5,000 and S$10,000 banknotes for years.

Still as an Indonesian academic was to remark to me, Australia is a rich country. It can afford bumbling incompetent government. The main political parties seem more pre-occupied with advancing ambitions of party apparatchiks who have no real-life experience and no fall back non-political employable skills if their seat was lost. Former Prime Minister Malcolm Fraser characterised such people who secured election as utterly lacking in independence. As for independent self-employment if their seat be lost, forget it.

It is not unknown for the wives of elected politicians up to the rank of Prime Minister to create and run multi-million-dollar businesses heavily reliant on government subsidies or contracts. Pollsters are engaged to ascertain what voters think because the endorsed candidates, not mixing with the masses. have no idea. Perish the thought that these candidates might have thoughts of their own about how to best advance the national interest consistent with humanity.

Outside consultants run election campaigns for big fees with the sole goal of winning at all costs. In most if not all cases, if the dependent candidates have earned income at all pre political life, the lowliest backbencher's salary of just under A$200,000 in most states, let alone the perks, far exceeds that earlier income. If a seat is lost and the candidate has the reputation of being a safe pair of hands so far as his party's best interests are concerned he can realistically aspire to a princely salaried senior diplomatic or other government representational position. The position of NT Administrator nay not be a peak of ambition for many, but, after a two-year term, it pays a nice life pension.

Once elected, the principal task is to be re-elected at least for enough terms to qualify for a generous life pension. The second is to use as much ingenuity as it takes to convert unspent income plus accommodation and other parliamentary allowances into negatively geared real estate.

One serving politician is the proud owner of 40 separate units of real estate. Good luck to his voters who might need his attention. He of course hides behind the Party to which he belongs and without which membership he might find his real estate business irksome. And the most beautiful thing of all is if the electorate office is located proximate to a local real estate agency with staff including an aspiring politician also with no life experience to deal with inquiries or calls for help from the punters in the electorate who finance the whole shebang.

Professional lobbyists have a large say in setting policy and the legislative agenda. Recently one serving politician was so far into lobbying that he discharged both roles simultaneously. He voted for legislation that he was paid for by his lobbyist co-master. The combination of facts noted above has weakened the hitherto immutable two-party system in that the parties have thrown up in important positions sitting members who have little in common with rank-and-file party members.

So you may ask and without changing the system, what qualities should we look for in a politician? Putting to one side the measure of real estate holdings what might be describes as a truly successful one? I realise now that if I was serious about being an elected politician unbound by party discipline, the trail even then has been blazed uniquely by New South Welshman Ted Mack, whose last seat was for the North Sydney federal electorate. This he held from 1990 to 1996. As he had done with his earlier held State seat for much the same area, he failed to re-nominate at the end of his last term to preclude his eligibility for a parliamentary pension.

The Gove/Yolgnu Land Rights Case

Occasionally the political system seems to get things right. Prior to Darwin's December 1974 cyclone Tracey, while I was endeavouring to balance managing professionally with the financial demands of rapid expansion followed by equally rapid contraction and those of living, a novel and far-reaching challenge was brought for adjudication by the NT Supreme Court's single judge Richard Blackburn (later Sir Richard Arthur Blackburn, 1918-1987).

The matter became known as the Gove Land Rights Case brought by the Yolgnu Aboriginal people (Milirrpum v Nabalco Pty Ltd). The decision was handed down in July 1971. Although I was not personally involved, the issues and the following events were of such importance to the future of the NT, let alone the Australian States as to omit them would be neglectful.

I was given a measure of ongoing insight into the inner workings of that case through occasional meetings in Darwin with Victorian lawyer and old Melbourne mate, Frank

Purcell. Frank, through some connection, possibly Articles of Clerkship, with another Victorian solicitor, Ian Secombe, was in the solicitor team acting on behalf of the plaintiff in that case. Ian's father, Arthur, may have been solicitor for the Methodist Church.

Lead counsel was Ted Woodward (later Sir Albert Edward Woodward, QC, 1928-2010). Ted had been one of the stable of counsel relied upon by my former Master in Articles John Adam. He was backed by two other barristers, John Little and John Fogarty. There was no paymaster for the Yolgnu legal team until the Commonwealth stepped forward.

The action was sponsored by the Methodist Church, which had conducted a Mission at Yirrkala since 1935. Many of the native Yolgnu peoples of eastern Arnhem Land had come to live, mostly about the mission, where they could be assured of supplies. The various Yolgnu clans which had gathered at Yirrkala visited their tribal country intermittently, mainly during the dry season. White men moved about their country and interfered with it as they prospected for minerals. Before Nabalco, they never stayed.

Much of East Arnhem land had been classed as an Aboriginal Reserve in 1931. Nabalco started excavations in the Yirrkala area some of which interfered with sacred sites. The government excised part of the reservation so that mining could be conducted on the excised area. The Yolgnu became concerned. They took a petition drawn up on bark to Federal Parliament. That was when the Methodist Church entered the legal scene.

It sought advice whether there was any way the grant of a mining licence to Nabalco could be prevented. Legal opinion was that there was an arguable case based either on breach of faith in taking the reserved lands away or that Aboriginal people had occupied the land, without significant disturbance, ever since at least 1788. Old overseas cases recognised communal title in Aboriginal peoples. The decision was made to litigate. The NT Supreme Court was selected as the venue rather than a single judge in the High Court in its original jurisdiction.

Roy Marika was the key witness for the Aborigines. He coordinated the evidence of the older men. To get the case trial ready, the witnesses' stories and recollections had to be reduced into the form of evidence which would satisfy a court of law that particular pieces of land had belonged to their direct ancestors for time immemorial. The 1970 trial commenced in Darwin where the Aboriginal evidence was heard. Thence to Canberra for the historical evidence and legal argument.

Judgment was delivered in April 1971. The trial judge had a deep interest in Australian history and in the Aboriginal people. He gave patient and careful consideration to the Yolngu argument. In the event, it was not enough for him to depart from conventional law. He acknowledged the claimants had a system of law that provided for a direct relationship between Aboriginal clans and particular identifiable areas of land. However, he concluded that the Aboriginal people belonged to the land rather than the land to the people whereby there were no proprietary interests which the law could recognise. The doctrine of native title had never formed part of the law of any part of Australia. The claim was dismissed.

No appeal was launched. The reasoning was the finding of close identification between particular groups of people and particular land was sufficient to mount a claim for recognition of Aboriginal title at the political level. There was no confidence that the High Court would produce any better result for the Aboriginal people than had already been achieved. Indeed, quite the contrary. That reasoning was not misplaced. Post judgment, the Australian Labour Party [ALP] announced that, when it was elected, it would recognise aboriginal land rights in the NT. It was elected in 1972. Through Prime Minister Whitlam, it empowered Woodward to conduct a Royal Commission to recommend how to recognise these rights.

Woodward had previous experience with Royal Commissions. These had taken years and cost millions. He believed he could do better. Excluding his Federal Court judicial salary and that of his two assistants, his Associate and an expert anthropologist] and including a trip to look at the problems of the North American Indians and the Eskimo people, the cost of the Commission was an extraordinarily modest $35,800. The task took him about eighteen months. Unusually for a lawyer, the modus operandi was eminently practical.

First, he travelled through much of the Northern Territory. Visits for informal discussions were made to Government settlements and mission stations, as well as Aboriginal communities in Darwin, Alice Springs and some cattle stations. He concluded that all that most Aborigines wanted was a chance to pull back from the government policy of assimilation. He saw the then current movement of some Aborigines to outstations as an attempt to achieve a breathing space. The communities on these settlements appeared to him concerned to maintain health and teaching services.

As this was happening, written submissions came in from interested parties including government departments and the mining and cattle industries. Tentative conclusions were reached and included in an interim report. Northern and Central Land Councils were established to enable Aborigines to be legally represented in the closing stages of the hearing when formal submissions could be made. Post the interim report, time was allowed for the Land Councils to engage legal advisers and arrive at considered submissions. Then the only formal Commission sittings were held in Darwin and Alice Springs. All interested parties were given the opportunity to comment on the tentative proposals and to advance other ideas.

The final Woodward report formed the basis for the Aboriginal Land Rights [NT] Act 1976 [ALRA], eventually passed by the Fraser coalition government. Similar Acts providing for aboriginal land rights were later passed by most of the States. Paradoxically in Australia, until the 1976 ALRA nothing had been done to recognise Aboriginal land rights, unlike in North America there was a clean slate. In North America, the rule is broken treaties which promised much to those Indians who could now claim under one of them, and little or nothing to those whose lands were not the subject of a treaty.

The ALRA constituted massive social reform. Immediately after its passage, all aboriginal reserves in the NT became Aboriginal inalienable titled. The Hawke ALP government passed legislation setting a cut-off date of 30 June 1997 for any Aboriginal land claim. Claims could be made only with respect to un-alienated crown land.

Aboriginal Land Rights Commissioners were appointed with the secondary offices of NT Supreme and Federal Court judges. Their primary role was to hear such evidence as might be put before them both in support of and objection to Aboriginal land claims and then report ensuing recommendations to the Federal Minister for Aboriginal Affairs.

Self-Government and Aboriginal Rights

After NT self-government came into effect in 1978, it became the policy of the prevailing CLP government, which endured until 2001, to resolutely oppose every Aboriginal Land Rights application. Presently, 50% of the NT land including 85% of the coastline is Aboriginal titled. All such land is held by an Aboriginal Land Trust.

Within the severe inalienable limitations of the title, nothing can be done with the land except by direction of a Land Council after an exhaustive procedure whereby the traditional owners approve. The traditional slow aboriginal decision-making process is paramount. Ted Woodward casts a long shadow.

He had taken the long view that, while no change can be expected overnight, there may be a productive generational change as Aborigines come to understand and appreciate their ownership of their land. It also created a nice problem for government in the NT for administration of large swathes of Aboriginal titled land especially if it is not being used for other than living and enjoyment and if the occupants can't speak English.

The former government policy of assimilation being set aside, it also raised a new issue for government services for a dependent distinct ethnic large landholding, at least in the NT, group of Australians, many of whom are non-English speakers, living on community land that is unable to be privatised and where other Australians cannot enter without formal advance permission.

There is no evidence that up to now [2019] any new proposal has been advanced by government to handling housing, health and education services for residents on aboriginal titled land. Or, for that matter, dealing at all with Aboriginal titled enclaves that contribute nothing to the greater economy. As to housing, has any attempt been made to instruct Aborigines in the knowledge established by owner builders in the UK who use local timber they fell and mill to frame and wall and even roof tile their own constructions? What happens to the local timber milled at Millingimbi? Even rammed earth flooring with a final sheen of bees wax and the like can meet any standard of elegance. Opal prospectors at Coober Pedy and Andamooka had adapted to a harsh treeless environment by going underground to construct comfortable heat resistant dug-out or cave dwellings. Old automobile tyres laid horizontally and filled with rammed earth can be used to create a wall. What about mud brick or straw bale construction? Are teachers to be sent out who stubbornly insist on Aboriginal education being conducted in the local dialect?

Money aside, innovation alone offers any prospect of meeting the new challenges raised for government by the ALRA. A useful starting point would be special construction training for teachers who are sent out to the new Aboriginal titled areas. Things like simple timber, mud brick or even straw house construction should be considered.

The watchword surely must be to motivate the aborigines to become self-sufficient as opposed to mendicant in attending to their own needs. Viewing of the relevant extracts from the TV series "Grand Designs" could be used to assist these aims. Given that aborigines comprise about 85% of the NT prison population, a signal opportunity thereby presents itself to provide what could be called "in house" simple and appropriate house construction training. Woodward came to understand even in the Aboriginal outstations the parents were concerned not only for the health of their children but for their education. At least now in the NT they have 50% of the land area for breathing space.

Throughout its lengthy first incumbency [1978 to 2001] the NT CLP government fought unsuccessfully with the Commonwealth to have transferred to it all powers relating to aborigines. Yet, when it came to more funding from Canberra, indigenous disadvantage was the catchcry. That baton has been carried forward by successive governments of whatever stamp.

The reality of cash shortage was mismanagement of a bloated [22,000 for an NT population of 240,000] public service with more executive positions per capita than in Victoria. If and when more money came in, it was spent on anything but aboriginal welfare - if the costs of maintaining the 85% Aboriginal prison population and public service executives overseeing Aboriginal programmes and services are set aside.

Pork barrelling the electoral base in Darwin's northern suburbs with money granted for aboriginal welfare was the real name of the game—described by the Australian newspaper as "the greatest scandal in contemporary Aboriginal affairs." The empire of $3B debt created by successive NT governments has led to a confession by the NT government in late 2018 that it was having to borrow $4M a day to pay salaries and operational expenses. The $3B debt is projected to grow to $35B over the next 10 years. God forbid that there should be any suggestion of government living within its means.

But a plan was announced. A former WA Treasurer was brought in as a consultant. Not surprisingly, job cuts were prescribed and persistent departmental overspend targeted. Sporadic and expensive attempts have been made to increase the population and thereby the NTs share of Commonwealth revenue. There has been no suggestion, as there must be, of structural reform. Essentially, it has just been more of the same. It could be likened to a crash diet and just as ineffective for the long term.

In the immediate post 1978 self-government era it was the Northern Territory Development Corporation [NTDC]. Now it is the Northern Territory Infrastructure Fund [NTIF].

Aborigines make up about 30% of the population and own half the NT land area including 85% of the coastline, but they make up 85% of the prison population. There is no plan to involve them save to keep the gaol industry humming. Surely that is an area that can be developed but only by the aborigines themselves. I find it difficult to believe they would not respond to some form of incentives. New thinking is required. If the prisons pressure could be relieved consider the ongoing saving to government. Yet Chief Minister Gunner talks about a new manufacturing industry in the NT of all places—to attract investment. At the time of writing, breathless assurances are given that work on this initiative is going on behind closed doors.

Obviously, there are no easy answers. But surely some novel approach should be sought to harnessing undeveloped energy of the sleeping aboriginal population.

My Short Career as Politician

When I began to take an interest in local politics and joined the Darwin branch of the Country Liberal Party [CLP], it came about that I saw a lot of Fred Canaris [1934-2016] who had until then been a casual acquaintance. For some reason unbeknown and inexplicable to me, the CLP is no more. With much dramatic fanfare it changed its name to the Country Liberals.

With hindsight my joining a political party was a mistake, for a number of reasons. As one who had stood twice for NT elected office as an Independent, I realise, belatedly as I write this, I was a marked man so far as the party grandees were concerned. Sure, it was not unknown for a political neophyte to swarm a way into the good offices of the party's upper echelon, but I was not that sort of person.

On the second occasion I ran as an independent against the Chief Minister Paul Everingham [1943-, NT head of government 1977-1984]. It was an unforgivable sin. My candidacy was founded solely on a perception I had been wronged professionally by Paul some months before. I am unable to recall the relevant facts now. In fact, I quite liked Paul and over preceding years had enjoyed his company over many lunches at the iconic Charlies Restaurant accompanied by immense infusions of Paul's favourite Ben Ean Moselle.

When I come to think about it at my leisure now, after my joust for his seat and although Paul and I crossed paths many times after, his attitude was always guarded. There was never to be any more mutual breaking of bread. Perhaps my institution of ultimately successful proceedings against him on behalf of Alexander Prus Grzybowski for damages for professional negligence was a factor.

An essentially city and inner suburbs man so far as Darwin went, I did no electorate work in the wilds of the Jingili electorate, ran some TV ads and printed some how-to-vote cards and posters. Then, as election day was a lovely Darwin dry season day, I chose to go sailing. Actually, running as candidate was quite inconvenient, busy as I was with my stressful law practice. But in my mind, I had to make Paul realise I was not to be seen to take his perceived slight, whatever it might have been, lying down.

Post that election and in the aftermath of the Darwin to Ambon yacht race, some wit crewing on a competing yacht took it upon himself to put up several of my surplus posters in the more remote Indonesian islands. Maybe that helped to explain the presence of head of Indonesian internal security, Admiral Sudomo, as part of the Ambon yacht race welcoming committee the following year.

As to the election, not surprisingly I received a modest vote and may have lost my deposit. One vote I was sure of was that of Paul's wife Denise, who was of a strong view politics the way Paul played it was not helping their marriage and family.

The actual final votes notwithstanding, I learned quite some time later the way voting preferences were going early in the count combined with my votes caused Paul to think he had lost his seat when he boarded a flight to Canberra on election evening. Fortunately for both of us, he thought wrongly.

This political maverick joined the CLP a year or two later. In my political innocence I thought then that the CLP was not akin to the national Liberal Party but rather represented free enterprise with a unique Territory slant, courtesy of Paul's Chief Ministership. To exacerbate my ignorance and sin, I nominated for pre-selection for Paul's seat when he resigned it to successfully stand (in 1984) for the position of NT MHR in Canberra.

Looking back now, it should have been no surprise to me that the party faithful for Paul's Jingili branch pre-selected Rick Setter. He won the seat and held it between 1984 and

1997. If, until his retirement, he rocked the boat, I have yet to hear of it.

It was my experience that a fair measure of the Darwin party faithful non-parliamentary members were there for financial gain. This was not especially direct and most of those faithful would not have even been aware of it. But there were issues dear to them that could be brought more forward or to fruition through political administrative power. It was common for branch meetings to be attended by cabinet ministers. Senior public servants got their marching orders from their ministers or, more properly speaking, their political masters.

Up to that time, ever since self- government in 1978, the CLP had utterly dominated NT politics. My misfortune and serious misjudgement was that I joined the party solely to seek out a seat in the legislature.

Parliamentary CLP members were preselected by their branches. The branches in turn were careful to select people who had every reason not to rock the boat. For example, at the first Darwin CLP branch meeting I attended, I asked then Minister and very influential CLP policy-man Jim Robinson, a difficult question. He chose a McCarthyist response unleashing a tirade in the course of which he fulsomely accused me of being a Communist. But I never got the message—or any answer to my question. On I ploughed.

A branch election was in the offing. Over a meal with Fred Canaris, I revealed that I thought the branch needed a shake-up. Unless I was elected the branch chairman, I could see no point in continuing my CLP membership. The decision was made to nominate and try to get more laissez faire members, who were more likely to vote for me, to attend. Fred was exactly the right man and round up the votes he did. I became chairman of a branch which preselected candidates for 3 Darwin electorates including that of the then Chief Minister Marshall Perron [b. 1942] in his pre-euthanasia enthusiasm days.

Then entered Elizabeth Eustance as honorary branch secretary. Elizabeth was the electorate secretary for MLA Shane Stone, her office was in central Darwin in the Star Village, her official duties were not too demanding, and she enthusiastically embraced the idea of livening up meetings.

A marvellous meeting venue was available. This was a special fully fitted out licensed meeting cum dining room for around 50 at the top of the stairs opposite the main dining room at the RSL Club in central Darwin's Cavenagh Street. Seating was in a U-shaped configuration with the top table at the furthest end of the room from the door. There was a lectern and a microphone sound connection to it and the top table. There was no fee for the room so long as we ate and drank there. Quality three course meals as well as drinks were served at very reasonable prices and the branch was able to profit from a small surcharge added to the meal price.

Darwin Rotary Club, of which I was a member, had been meeting there, and I knew it was ideal—in fact better for my plans than Adolph Hitler's beer halls were for his. Elizabeth organised the location so seamlessly all I had to do was float the idea to her. Sadly, and more recently, the RSL board decided to convert this space to offices with the objective of earning more rental income. Elizabeth kept careful meeting minutes and - if they are preserved - they will establish that meetings were far from dull. Offhand I can recall a few highlights.

There were two Mick Palmers in responsible public positions in the NT. Both lived in Darwin. One was the Police Commissioner, the other an elected CLP member of the NT legislature. Both Micks loved public speaking and were good at it. No sooner had I suggested to Elizabeth the possibility of each speaking how they thought the other's job should be done than she had everything in place. A great evening ensued.

One year the parliamentary party was in some disarray about the time of the Party's annual conference at Tennant Creek. At the time, recently appointed Chief Minister Marshall Perron was seen to be fumbling the ball He was pilloried in the pages of John Hogan's NT News. Fred Canaris mooted that the Darwin Branch invite Alastair Heatley, academic and part-time NT News political journo/academic, as part of our team to give a talk on his take on the confusion.

Darwin Branch reps and Alistair flew by light aircraft piloted by member Tony Field. Alistair was brilliantly lucid and pulled no punches. When he got to his feet to give his political diagnosis and prescribed cure, all the parliamentary party walked out. Later, Marshall was in tears as he was responding to questions. Shortly afterwards, Marshall took on board Andrew Coward as his minder and he was not seen to put a foot wrong politically thereafter.

On another occasion an East Timorese cultural group of singers, dancers and musicians was in town. A former East Timorese lady, Ariange Mage, invited them to a Branch meeting at her cost. They gave memorable performances. My later information was that all of this group went underground when it was time to return home.

Another time, the Branch meeting was given over to a debate. All I can recall is that one speaker, Tony Field, a serving NT public service engineer at the time, flirted with the bounds of polite contrarian discourse and embarrassingly heaped vitriolic scorn on Chief Minister Marshall Perron. I doubt if it helped his public service career or indeed any aspiration I might have had for government preferment.

In the late eighties, branch member, surveyor Gary Nairn, was nominated to prepare a report considering whether fixed term NT pastoral leases, some extending over vast areas, should be converted to freehold as the pastoralists were requesting at the time. Thankfully, his firm negative recommendation decided the issue. It saw a close friendship develop between Gary and Marshall.

When I stood down as Branch Chairman after 3 terms, my executive was of the opinion Gary was not suitable to take over the reins. Nevertheless, Gary went on to become the CLP Party President from 1990 to 1994 and later the Federal Member for Eden Monaro from 1999 to 2006 and a Special Federal Minister of State under John Howard. Which just goes to show how on the nose politically my CLP Darwin Branch was.

The last time I ran into Gary was in Darwin when he, as special Minister of State, was all set for a cruise on a Darwin Patrol Boat. Maybe I am wrong but I thought I detected in his manner and eyes as he spoke to me that he was dealing with an irrelevant and insignificant being.

If that be true, he was correct so far as the parliamentary wing of the CLP was concerned. To that body at that time, the sole role of a Branch was to give unmitigated support to whatever, it in its untrammelled wisdom, the parliamentary party came up with. Late in my 3-year stewardship, I was approached by Marshall to see what I could do to expel a former Party President, Graeme Lewis, from the Party. I was aware at the time there were Party members who, regardless of the ins and outs of any situation and in the cause of their personal ambitions, would have moved heaven and earth to please Marshall. Another Party member John Hair had put it to me once that, if a Party cabinet minister wanted a report on anything, all that mattered was to recommend what the minister wanted to hear—a point missed on Mr. Bradley when he delivered his MACA report to then Chief Minister Everingham back in the seventies [see below].

Graeme, an accountant was all but a foundation Party member and had paid a price professionally for his unswerving commitment. He looked after the books of Fred Canaris through whom we had met and broken bread occasionally at Charlies restaurant. Also, Graeme was the accountant for one of my clients, John Grice, who operated a very successful landing barge transport business out of Darwin.

The North, Politics and the Future [1968-]

Fred had made me aware that, for a reason unbeknown to him, Graeme was persona non grata with Marshall. My response to Marshall was that I was unaware of any Party transgression that would justify the action asked for, let alone any action against Graeme. There the matter rested. I can't recall now whether I reported Marshall's request to my executive.

About 1995 the CLP called for nominations for the Federal NT seat. There was consensus that the seat was winnable but not easily. From memory I was the only nominee. No decision was made and after this went on for months I withdrew. Clearly, I was not approved by the Party king-makers. Then followed internal and confusing party machinations involving Bob Liddle of Alice Springs with an ultimately unsuccessful attempt to strike Shane Stone off the Supreme Court roll as a solicitor for unprofessional behaviour for what he was alleged to have said concerning Bob Liddle at, of all things, a CLP meeting.

At the time I never appreciated the depth of feeling against my CLP branch from the party leadership. Perhaps I should have taken more to heart a meeting with Deputy Chief Minister Barry Coulter when he loomed at the doorway of the RSL meeting room in the course of my attendance at a Rotary dinner meeting. He made it plain he wanted to speak with me. Out I went.

Face to face as we became when I stepped out it became apparent Barry was the worse for alcohol. We were in a large empty room. Barry had nothing to say. He manoeuvred me close in front of him so that I was back to a glass door. I was unaware of this positioning until after what happened next.

Then he pushed his chest against mine so that I stumbled back. As I did so I caught at one of his arms to steady myself. Steadiness was bought at the expense of one sleeve of Barry's white shirt which parted company with its shoulder seam. I returned to my Rotary meeting.

Not long afterwards, I deputed Fred to act on my behalf to approach Barry to join me in the boxing ring to give an exhibition bout. Nothing came of this. For the record, I have to say that on all other occasions I had met Barry he had been the soul of uncommunicative hospitality.

There was never to be for me any peaceful party indorsed accession to a chance of a NT political vacancy along the lines of the ascension of a youthful possible forebear Cormac Mac Airt to the hastily vacated High Kingship of Ireland about 200AD. In that case, Mac Conn had been forced to flee in fear of his life after word of his exposure by young Cormac as incompetently unjust spread in a nation that esteemed justice above all. The universal perception of the all-enveloping wisdom of Cormac trumped all.

The NT voters will never know what they might have gained. For the record, Cormac ushered in a forty-year golden era of plenty. The land, it is said, yielded harvests such as never were known, while the forest trees dripped with abundance of honey and the lakes and rivers were alive with fish. Game was so plentiful that the inhabitants could have lived on that alone without need to farm. Autumn was not wet; Spring not plagued with icy winds; Summer was devoid of extreme heat and Winter of extreme snows.

Legislation of Note

There are several fundamental areas of the law in place in the NT pre-cyclone which were dramatically altered after 1978—post cyclone and post self-government. These included Workmen's Compensation, Workmen's Liens and Criminal Law. Up until self-government, the first was roughly comparable to the law applicable in the Australian States. Its initial replacement in 1986 was an exquisitely incompetently drafted mishmash labelled the Work Health Act. The legal profession and the courts had to struggle to make sense of it.

The applicable Act now is the Return to Work Act. The 2018 consolidation of this Act bears the hallmarks of similar legislation Australia wide. There is no monopoly insurer. The second, which enabled a worker to take security by registered lien over the title to real estate improvements he had worked on, was abolished post 1978 self-government. It was not easy to apply but its repeal could only have been to the benefit of landowners. The third the Criminal Law Consolidation Act of South Australia of the 19th century was largely the same as the English legislation at the time it came into effect, whereby the Standard English Archbold textbook was most helpful for interpretation. It was repealed and replaced in 1983 by a new Criminal Code based largely on the code drafted by Sir Samuel Griffith in 1899 and then in force in Queensland and Western Australia. This code was tweaked by Queensland lawyer Des Sturgess in an attempt to bring the question of criminal liability, especially as concerned drunkenness and intent, up to late 20th century community expectations and standards.

It was introduced to the NT in 1983 as the NT Criminal Code. It was supplanted in 2003 by Chapter 2 of the Commonwealth Criminal Code 1995. While it lasted it had a far from easy ride. A former High Court Chief Justice was to describe the principal criminal responsibility section as "astonishing." A former Prime Minister had cause to write to the NT Chief Minister of the day to request changes under threat of direct Commonwealth intervention.

Until the Motor Accidents Compensation Act [MACA], which became effective from July 1979, a large percentage of the work of the Supreme Court had been taken up by common law personal injuries damages claims for negligence arising out of motor accidents. My then professional office had been averaging trial or other completion of 4 or 5 such cases per month. The MACA abolished the right to make such claims.

Under the new legislation, everyone, except those excluded, injured in a motor accident was compensated but in a dramatically lower measure and under the all-seeing eye, demands and decisions of a rehabilitator and decision maker in the office of Territory Insurance Office [TIO]. Persons over the age of eligibility for the age pension [67 as I write] were not to be compensated for pain and suffering, loss of enjoyment of life, loss of earnings or earning capacity. Their claims are now limited to medical costs, attendant care and medical aids. TIO manages the MACA scheme. The only clue as to where it might have come from is the interest in the concept displayed beforehand by Chief Minister Everingham's buddy Ian Barker QC.

Quintessential salaryman lawyer and behind the scenes associate of the ultimately collapsed Loopholes Loftus' legal practice, Bill Raby, was given, in his post pensionable age years, to riding a motorcycle. Whilst so engaged, according to reports riding furiously, he came to grief. The administrator of the "fake" Crown Law legal aid was dumbfounded to be told he had been denied all but his medical expenses because of the combination of his age and a "fake" government motor accident compensation scheme.

The story is the Australian third-party insurance industry has always been unable to show a profit. It always relied on its other general insurance business for that. Very likely and on a per capita basis, the NT showed the greatest shortfall of premium paid against money paid out. Passage of MACA must have been a source of great jubilation to the industry. Perish the thought that it may have been, from the shadows, a secret driver of the abolition of common law damages, with the Everingham government its unwitting dupe.

That the NT government through MACA has been able to show considerable profit to take off the table speaks volumes for the low compensation level in the NT. No scope here for dissipation by the injured. The lesson to learn here is that, if government has anything to do with it, only government is allowed to squander money in the NT.

The introduction of euthanasia legislation in 1995 was in many respects analogous to how the MACA came into being. It never comprised any part of either major party election policy. The electorate were not demonstrating in support of it. The only political link was with the prevailing CLP government through its sponsorship by then Chief Minister Marshall Perron.

"It" was the Rights of the Terminally Ill Act [ROTIA] passed by the NT legislature in 1995 by a majority of one on a free vote. Subject to compliance with strict and quite complex conditions involving the medical profession, it legalized euthanasia [mercy killing] and assisted suicide i.e. doctors killing or helping to kill patients. It put to naught the Hippocratic oath.

Assisted Suicide

By September 1996, Darwin medico Dr. Philip Nitschke [1947-] had become an enthusiastic NT promoter of assisted suicide.[16] To this end, he had designed what was a do-it-yourself death machine—that is if the candidate was able to obtain Nembutal and was capable of inserting a needle into a vein. The machine comprised a laptop computer connected to a length of rubber hose with a pump at one end and an injection needle at the other. The candidate was 66-year-old Darwin carpenter Bob Dent, who was suffering from terminal prostate cancer.

I assume the comprehensive medical preliminaries required under the legislation had been completed. Nitschke hooked up the aspiring suicide to his device by inserting the needle into his arm and loading the hose with appropriate poison such as the otherwise illegal Nembutal. All that remained for Mr. Dent was to answer a series of computer questions designed to create assurance he wanted to die,

---

[16] See https://www.en.wikipedia.org/wiki_Philip_Nitschke

then press a computer key which activated the pump. Mr Dent became the first person in the world to take his own life under this legal voluntary euthanasia scheme.

It was about this time Dr. Nitschke reported theft, from his semi-rural block on the Darwin outskirts, of his store of Nembutal. Dent was the first of four terminally ill people to undertake voluntary euthanasia before the Federal Government stepped in. As it was constitutionally entitled, it overturned the Northern Territory law. All four deaths were assisted by Dr. Nitschke.

Dr Nitschke no longer practises as a doctor in Australia. He burned his medical registration documents in protest after the Australian Medical Association imposed restrictions on him in 2015, so he could not promote suicide as well as practise medicine.

These days Mr Nitschke, has founded Exit International and calls Europe home. He came to Australia-in 2019 to promote his latest suicide contraption which relies on release of s nitrogen gas into a sealed coffin like structure resting on an inclined base so the candidate can clamber inside unassisted and pull down the lid before pressing a button to release the gas stored in the base. He talked about replicating his machine by 3D printing to the home at a cost of about A$5,000. He described death by nitrogen in his then untested device as peaceful and elegant. Apparently a Swiss national was standing by to prove it. Not for Mr. Nitschke the simplicity and economy of a motor vehicle and a length of hose.

During his 2019 visit, a woman confronted Mr. Nitschke at a pro-euthanasia forum in Perth. She demanded he apologise for what had happened in the case of her father. Aged in his 60s and suffering from no more than depression, he had taken his own life two years previously. This was after getting advice from Mr Nitschke's Exit International group. She asserted her belief the information Nitschke distributed caused people who were not in a rational state of mind to decide to kill themselves. This is all against an Australian national background of suicide being acknowledged as a serious social problem.

At the height of Darwin controversy pre the passage of ROTIA a section of the Darwin northern suburbs representing the CLP branches there became eager proponents of the bill. Perhaps it was their first time to be involved in any way with the political process further than manning the polling stations on election days. When an information evening came up, they seemed to have so packed the venue with enthusiastic euthanasia supporters I was lucky to get in.

The Nitschke complications associated with suicide devices puzzle me, I was impressed with the economy and simplicity of the scene in the film "House of Sand and Fog" where the protagonist, the ex-Iranian colonel acted by Ben Kingsley, simply pulled over his head a plastic bag and closed the top drawstring.

There had been a very clever humorous take on the organised euthanasia movement quite some years ago now in a BBC TV one hour play screened on the ABC. George Cole acted the role of a travelling representative of an outfit with a name that could even have been Exit International. He had called on a member to deliver a poison draft. This was poured into a glass. As Cole spoke the glass was moved about in such a manner as to be easily confused with another glass containing a non- lethal beverage. Amidst the confusion the wrong person exited, after mistakenly downing the poison for the innocuous drink.

As for Marshall Perron, his enthusiasm for his cause remains undiminished. Latterly he has conceded he was mistaken to have left the legislation open to non-Territorians. The feature film "Last Cab to Darwin" played this theme the cab being from Sydney. He believes this caused its repeal from Canberra.

As for the idea, the promoters won't have it that there is any possibility it may go amiss so that the disabled or aged of no means might find themselves for reasons of cost being quietly euthanased. They will not concede that hostel palliative care nursing of the terminally ill in severe pain is a valid answer even though it may result in prescription of pain killing drugs which incidentally may lead to legally permissible death caused by a doctor without any need for euthanasia enabling legislation.

Statehood and Its Issues

The Federal Government's illegalisation of euthanasia was the flashpoint for an attempt by the CLP to move to Statehood through a preliminary referendum. The then Chief Minister was Shane Stone. A failed referendum was conducted on 3 October 1998. Stone was to resign the following February.

For some years prior to October 1998, a bipartisan NT Legislative Assembly Legal and Constitutional Affairs Committee [LALCAC] had been working towards having popularly elected delegates to a Statehood Convention to recommend a Constitution for the Northern Territory. A draft constitution had been prepared.

Preliminary to the planned referendum, much of the previous work by this bi-partisan LALCAC was put at naught. Fifty-three delegates were appointed to a Constitutional Convention. In the event, 52 delegates attended initially. Twenty-five of these were elected from government nominated organizations. The remainder were appointed.

Pre-convention the government failed to adequately consult with Aboriginal people and paid scant regard to their aspirations. As one leader expressed it, Aboriginal people were fed up with the abuse, intimidation and insults to their intelligence, integrity and cultures from the CLP government.

The ATSIC delegation withdrew about a week into the Convention and the trade Unions followed in sympathy. Stacked as it may have been, that convention recommended the issue be put to the electorate as three separate questions:

That the following questions be put to a vote of the electorate of the Northern Territory:

whether the Northern Territory should become a State;

what the name of the new State should be;

whether the proposed Constitution be adopted as the Constitution of the new State of the Northern Territory.

The referendum question put was simple, but loaded:

> Now that a constitution for a state of the Northern Territory has been recommended by the statehood convention and endorsed by the Northern Territory parliament, do you agree that we should become a state?

Voting 'yes' implicitly meant accepting the draft constitution that had been recommended by the non-independent convention to the CLP controlled Northern Territory Legislative Assembly. That draft could never have been taken seriously in that it incorporated a section whereby the Premier could dismiss the Governor, effectively making the constitutional role irrelevant and putting the NT State at odds with all other Australian States. The electorate was called upon to vote when it had neither the terms of the errant Constitution nor all other relevant terms and conditions before it. Essentially government had been asking for a signed blank cheque.

Aboriginal people voted in a strong bloc against the referendum question. There were also concern about the process. An official post-mortem examination conducted by a parliamentary Standing Committee concluded that most people who voted 'no' in the referendum were not opposed to statehood *per se*. Their concerns were about the process: The clear implication was that if the voters had been given a fair shake there probably would have been a yes answer. In 2014 there were two sales by the NT government involving TIO for a gross $424M. The first was of its banking business to People's Choice Credit Union. The second was of its insurance business to German group Allianz Insurance. The

NT excluded from the sale what had become the very profitable MACA scheme insurer arm.

MACA soldiers on courtesy of an unaware or unconcerned highly transient electorate and government with priorities elsewhere other than collecting and dissipating the profits. The figure of $424M quoted by government included $140M capital drawdown on the MAC division [government speak for taking off the table profit in the books of TIO from operating its "fault free" third party insurance scheme]. If the MAC arm had been included, the government claimed total value would have been $609M - an extra $185M. TIO chair Bruce Carter categorised the $140M as "excess capital."

For many years now, Paul Everingham, the MACA architect, has called his Queensland State of origin home. I have no knowledge of Paul agitating for introduction of his scheme to Queensland. Nor does Queensland have any plan to emulate the NT scheme.

The sale of TIO was accompanied by assurances there would be no job redundancies. Within 5 months, 43 staff were cast adrift. In September 2016 it was announced all 4 of its branches would close over the next 6 months. All contact would be limited to phone or internet. Maybe this decision was made to prevent a repeat of a dissatisfied work health claimant firebombing the Darwin TIO office in 2010.

In July 2016 Matthew Littlejohn, then of Maurice Blackburn Lawyers [MBL], reported 1/3 of his 82 pending TIO insurance claims were contested. His complaint - bad decisions founded upon bad law. Cases not resolved within

12 months were met with a policy of them being dragged out until the claimant ran out of money or energy or died.

The scope of the MACA has been progressively narrowed over the years by legislative amendment. As a former lawyer who had extensive experience pre-MACA with common law damages claims, I find the nibbling exclusions and presumptions against claimants quite sickening—all designed to maximise the gap in favour of TIO between premiums paid and "benefits" paid out—whence the $140M profit. And cynically designed by lawyers to pre-empt legal intervention on behalf of a claimant.

Neither NT political party of today seems even remotely concerned about its impact. Perhaps more blood than that of motor accident victims will have to be shed ere MACA gets serious or indeed any political consideration. The dual catchcry of the NT promoters of the no fault scheme were it was just that and it was less costly than the usual third party insurance which basically preserved common law damages rights.

Common law damages had been marginally more difficult to achieve but exponentially greater than TIO "benefits" for the same disability. These damages mandated allowing for pain and suffering, loss of enjoyment of life, loss of earnings and reduced future earning capacity to which was added the cost of past and estimated future medical and hospital expenses.

The government thinking behind the Everingham scheme was the belief that prior to its introduction, successful litigants for third party damages tended to squander their awards. If any reader is interested to learn the case against "no fault" as it was proposed for the NT, he need look no further than the pages of the Bradley Report commissioned by the Everingham government. Rather than seeking truth the commission was given on the assumption the ensuing report would sustain the government position. Lawyer Mr. Bradley came down heavily negative in his report. The government went ahead with its new plan anyway.

By 30 June 1989, TIO was able to report considerable profit, that the same Mr. Bradley was Deputy Chairman of its board and that the TIO flagship real estate investment, NT House, was expected to be completed in October of that year. Mr. Bradley's law firm became a NT House tenant soon after.

The way the draft MACA was released to the public was confusing. Unbeknown to me at the time I prepared a detailed letter canvassing the proposed changes, a new draft was released. That draft altered the section numbers so that my comments, measured by the new draft, were rendered nonsensical. Well after the event, I learned the Labour Opposition leader Jon Isaacs relied on my critique letter in his opposition speech to the Legislative Assembly. Perhaps the transient nature of the white NT population and the comical incompetence of the NT self-governing parliament and its desperate need for endless money, have combined to enable the pernicious MACA to stand.

At the time of writing [2019], I have attempted to find out the relative cost of compulsory third party insurance [TPI] across the Australian States and Territories. The best information I have found up is total cost for registration including compulsory third-party insurance [TPI]. There is no breakup to enable any quick comparison between what the NT driver pays for dramatically less cover than drivers in the states.

However, the all-inclusive 12 months registration cost, including compulsory TPI, of all the States and Territories has been tabulated as at 1 August 2018 by Queensland. I cite only the figure for a 4-cylinder car. The NT comes in at $748.30. Lesser charges apply in Queensland $727.60, Western Australia $747, Tasmania $562.16. The charge in South Australia is 95c higher at $749.25. These States offer the sort of compulsory third party insurance cover against common law damages claims the NT had before it went down the TIO road.

You can imagine the profit the TIO must continue to make with its business model—selling a product without which no motor vehicle can be registered in the NT; no office open to the public; no competition; a quiescent parliament and stonewalling, let alone reducing by legislative amendment, payment of such very limited "benefits" as it might have to pay out.

When the States listed above are offering common law damages for third party insurance claims for the same or less charge than the NT backed TIO charges for miniscule, albeit fault free, cover, one is left to wonder why not a peep comes from the NT parliament. One conclusion that can be argued is that the NT governments from both sides of the political fence is in such desperate need of the ill-gotten profit to finance its errant ways, that it is prepared to have no concern about the unnecessary misery occasioned to its citizens.

What became of the $140M "excess capital" taken off the table and shovelled into the greedy financial maws of the NT? Firstly, the shovelling had well taken place and the $140M most likely had been already well spent. For what it is worth, then Chief Minister Adam Giles placed on record a denial that it would be used as part of a pork-barrelling exercise for the imminent 2016 NT election. A government spokesman said it planned to invest $215M in an infrastructure fund, pay $9M for the costs of the sale and use $200M for "community development."

The $404M had been augmented by another $506M from the sale by the Northern Territory government of the Darwin port to Chinese based interests in late 2015. In addition that buyer paid the NT government A$23M in stamp duty on the transaction. The deal gave the Landbridge Group 100% operational control of the port and 80% ownership of the Darwin Port land, facilities of East Arm wharf including the marine supply base, and Fort Hill wharf.

The remaining 20% is held by the Northern Territory government until late 2020 when that 20% is transferred to another Australian entity to ensure some local ownership is retained. Should port revenue rise above 130% of initial modelling, the government will receive 15% of those profits. Of the gross proceeds, A$27M in fees was charged to the NT to broker the deal including A$13M paid to Melbourne based financial firm Flagstaff Partners for helping select Landbridge. That left around $14M for payment of the seller's legal and other incidental expenses.

The numbers suggest the relevant privileged Darwin legal firm or firms has taken to heart and learned from the embarrassing earlier yokelish objection of the NT to the Hong Kong legal account associated with financing the Yulara Village.

Although the proposition is arguable, the port acquisition was said to have been under the Chinese government Belt and Road policy. The sale has deeply disturbed Australia's traditional allies let alone the Federal Government. Forget that the sale was blunderingly bypassed and thence in a very broad sense impliedly approved by the federal Foreign Investments Review Board [FIRB]. Like what was left of the TIO money the net port purchase money has to all intents and purposes disappeared as a comically mismanaged NT hurtles to bankruptcy.

Whatever was claimed by government, it is improbable that any of the $424M or net of the $500M was spent on aboriginal welfare, at least if that term excludes the cost of incarceration of the 85% aboriginal NT gaol prisoners.

But wait. A move to set aside the transaction has been floated in Canberra. The idea floated bypassed any suggestion of repayment. Which, dare I suggest, is exactly how the NT government would prefer. Mere incidentals such as the $23M stamp duty paid to the NT and $27M paid by if for commissions and charges are not mentioned.

Timber Creek

More recently in a High Court decision on what has been called the Timber Creek case the NT government had been ordered to pay compensation of $2.5M to aboriginal residents of Timber Creek for failing in the 1980s and 1990s to legally acquire the Timber Creek town area site before it proceeded to lay out the town and sell development sites.[17]

The claim by Ngaliwurru and Nungali native title holders was about rights that were extinguished through the building of roads and infrastructure by the Northern Territory Government in the 1980s and 1990s. The dispute had been about how to calculate compensation for extinguishment of native title rights. The Timber Creek claimants were awarded $2.5 million, down from the $3.3 million originally awarded. The High Court rejected claims that $1.3 million for "spiritual harm" was excessive.

The case brought the High Court to sit in the Northern Territory in September 2018 for the first time in its history. It was also the first time the High Court had examined the Native Title Act's compensation provisions, including how to put a price on intangible harm caused by disconnection with country.

The final amount of $2.5 million in compensation settled on by the High Court was divided into three components — economic loss, interest and non-economic loss related to the "spiritual" harm caused by disconnection. It included $1.3 million for non-economic loss. The court rejected the argument from the NT and Federal Governments that this amount was "manifestly excessive".

Northern Territory Media Moguls

---

[17] AIATSIS, "The Timber Creek Compensation Case," n.d. (2019?). https://AIATSIS iatsis.gov.au/explore/timber-creek-compensation-case/

It is impossible to properly review Darwin politics from the 80s until the end of his tenure as managing editor of the *NT News* without paying tribute to John Hogan (1945-2009). Under him as managing editor from 1975 to 1988, succeeding the redoubtable Jim Bowditch (editor between 1955 and 1973) a Murdoch newspaper became in effect John's glorious private newspaper. He held to the fire the feet of both ALP and CLP political parties.

Equally as impressive was the calibre of the coterie of writers he attracted, most of whom were not professional journalists. The names of Alistair Heatley, Frank Alcorta,[18] and the anonymous Nirwad correspondent stand out. The column of the last named was headed by an inverted outline of the map of the NT. And try spelling Nirwad back to front.

Equally impressive were the ideas people behind the newspaper. The name of public servant Col Fuller comes to mind. While John was from the New Zealand South Island, and Fuller and Heatley were also Kiwis, Frank Alcorta came from Spain's Basque country and had enjoyed previous Australian careers as a cane cutter, a New Guinea patrol officer or Kiap and an [eventually] highly decorated Australian Army soldier for his part in the celebrated Vietnam War battle of Long Tan.

Heatley and Alcorta were lecturers at Darwin University, the former in politics, the latter in Australian history. I think Frank joined the NT News journalist staff in the later Hogan

---

[18] On Frank Alcorta, Rob Parer, "The many splendid lives of the legendary Frank Alcorta," http://www.pngattitude.com/2013/01/the-many-lives-of-the-legendary-frank-alcorta-at-last-recognition-of-australia-png-hero-.html/

years. Along the way, John introduced a Sunday newspaper. Nirwad Man's pieces were run in the Sunday Territorian, as was also a column by the anonymous Bushranger.

If one was up to the not so difficult identification of the real personalities named by the former [eg Tuxworth became "Cheap Shirt"] much could be learned from the colourful coded orientalised descriptions about local undercurrent unpublicised political activity. Bushranger worked on a far simpler plane as more of a conventional but well-informed gossip columnist.

The Heatley/Alcorta duo wrote feature articles concerning political issues of the moment. Their literary styles were so utterly unalike that John was to comment to me his input was that the latter was found much easier to read.

For a time there was even a full time NT News Political Editor, a position which fell into disfavour after John dismissed the last of that title for personal misbehaviour. More to the point was that John brought the only public critical eye the CLP government had to withstand during its unchallenged reign from 1978 to when it lost government only in the new century.

I have no doubt that the many locals offended by Darwin press commentary of that time did their best to have John removed from Darwin. They were backed by numerous legal threats of libel action.

An observation to the effect the bull had vacated the China shop was printed when Chief Minister Paul Everingham left on a northern foray for one of several political visits to the Malaysian Borneo State of Sabah. In some respect, it could have been argued the NT was developing its own foreign policy at least as regarded NT inward investment. Malaysian Hishamudden Koh became for a while a maker and shaker on the Darwin property scene.

Perhaps fired by the local political example, John was to essay a unique foreign correspondent role for his paper. Local journo Dave Naismith was dispatched to Vietnam as a war correspondent at the height of the hostilities. Dave became attached to a small group and was wounded early in his assignment. He spent some time stretchered with that group and compiled the best notes he was capable of. It was a very worrying time for John. Last I heard of Dave he was comfortably ensconced in New York as foreign correspondent for the Australian News organisation.

Ex NT News journo Peter Murphy was Paul's "minder" or confidential political adviser. He went on to be retained by all CLP parliamentary leaders until Marshall Perron introduced Andrew Coward. Frank was an admirer of NT senior politico Barry Coulter. He esteemed him as a visionary. It was perhaps my contrary view, communicated incidentally to Frank, that led to my physical encounter with Barry at Darwin's RSL Club. Barry came from a technical educational lecturing background.

Frank was an industrious penman. Before I met him, I had been asked by fellow Rotarian John Hogan to review for publication Frank's just-published book *Darwin Rebellion*.[19] It concerned the rise of the North Australian trade union movement to such power it was able to have expelled from Darwin an unpopular Administrator, one Gilruth. The writing style owed much to Michener. In his research for the book Frank had been delighted to find a Basque, Parer by name, playing a part in the Darwin of a bygone age. Post publication of my review, I was to enjoy breaking bread with Frank. He even published a review of my review. That was Darwin - and Hogan.

Years later, John asked me to review Xavier Herbert's mammoth (1,463 page) work *Poor Fellow my Country*.[20] Reading took several months, necessarily interspersed with much other reading to preserve a perspective. I was not to meet with that author. I gather at least as much had been edited out from Herbert's acclaimed earlier work "Capricornia" as was included. I suspect much of this excess found its way into a more indulgently edited *Poor Fellow*.

John's enemies succeeded in having him transferred to Townville to serve out his pre-retirement days. The NT News reverted to such a bland admixture I once heard the incoming editor apologise to Chief Minister Stone for publication of a piece vaguely critical of the CLP Hogan perceived loyalists of eccentric bent within the local newspaper organisation became marked men.

---

[19] Frank Alcorta, *Darwin Rebellion 1911-1919*, Print Book, 1984.
[20] Xavier Herbert, *Poor Fellow My Country*, Collins, 1975.

John's new journal I think was under the mast head "Townsville Bulletin." Sadly, the farm property he bought on final retirement was discovered to have been in an area somehow isolated from whatever rain might fall around the vicinity. It just never saw rain. Pre purchase John had seen it extraordinarily lushly well-presented just after an all too rare downpour. I don't think it rained again during his tenure.

What remained of his generous superannuation began to be dissipated with a parcel of slow racehorses he became given to travelling the North Queensland racing circuit with, accompanied by his mate, one Butts. Until one day he had thrust into his hands a sheaf of legal, including divorce documents from his wife, Denise. All assets had been frozen. His relationship with alcohol, always on the dangerous side, became terminal. It was said of him when he died at Townsville Hospital that he never possessed more than the clothes he wore. Of money not one cent. Rest in Peace John.

Auditing must be a difficult profession. Unlike the mills of God, grinding exceeding small is costly and likely to lose the client.

Chapter 9: Charlie's of Darwin

In about 1970, Alceo Cagnetti [1927-2010], later to become known as "Charlie," arrived in Darwin from a Woomera Rocket Range facility located on Mt. Eba cattle station in the far north of South Australia. Mt. Eba is about midway between Woomera Township and Coober Pedy, with Woomera Township itself about 130 kilometers to the west of Andamooka Opal Field and Coober Pedy about 640 kilometers to the north of Woomera. Mt. Eba was and is still remote by any standard.

I had the opportunity intermittently to sample and enjoy immensely the meals provided to the workers at the Woomera mess. Once was after a visit to the Woomera dentist. Other occasions related to my demolition and removal to Andamooka of Woomera workmen's huts that had become surplus to the needs of the rocket range (See above chapter 6].

There was nothing formal to my visits. I was close by and hungry. It was usually a middle of the day mealtime. Apart from the first instance, where I was guided to the workers' cafeteria, for that is what it was, bearded, unkempt and raggedly dressed as I tended to be in those days, I just walked in, selected my food, sat down and gobbled it up. That food was always sensationally good and plentiful. It was my wont to go back for seconds, even thirds, as the cooking staff smiled approvingly behind the food counter. Like with the dental services, admittedly limited to one extraction, I was never challenged.

So, I had some experience of the quality of meals provided to the masses at Woomera. The likely explanation is that during the sixties and earlier, new immigrants had been required to spend at least two years rural living immediately after their arrival. Manfred, my neighbor at Andamooka, had spent his two years trapping possum in Tasmania for their pelts. There were worse ways for a chef to notch up his two years and save money than as a salaried cook at a remote government establishment. The meals I ate were beyond the skill of mere cooks.

At Mt. Eba, Charlie saved his wages. He asked his older brother John, who had settled in Darwin, to look out for a restaurant business that might be for sale. Maria Donatelli's Olympic restaurant was then on the market. It fronted Austin laneway behind and in the same building as a sports store that fronted Knuckey Street, a short distance from what is now the Smith Street mall.

By the time Charlie arrived in Darwin, the purchase had been completed. He was able to step into gear immediately. Thus commenced an application of such steadfastness of purpose that saw him reach the pinnacle of the Darwin dining scene and ultimately, because of his unawareness or intransigence in the face of later changes in the town's eating out habits, to became an irrelevancy.

I had been in Darwin the best part of 12 months before I heard mention of the Olympic. During my first six months, while employed by the Australian/Japanese joint prawning venture Gollin Kyokuyo Fishing Company P/L, with my Darwin office Japanese counterpart Hiroshi Amemiya I had done much entertaining of visiting executive staff from Tokyo and Sydney, commonly over meals at Martina's Restaurant at Nightcliff or another restaurant located about where

Macdonalds is now in Smith Street, just north of the intersection with Knuckey Street.

Incongruously, given Darwin's climate, Martina's food was of the heavy European winter style, which we washed down with generous infusions of 1963 Yalumba Galway claret. The cost was charged to the office account.

I think it was Harry Smith, an itinerant businessman from Sydney, who guided my initially reluctant steps through the very modest Austin Lane entrance to what was then still called the Olympic Restaurant. In those days Charlie kept to the kitchen assisted by the no less able Luigi. Wife Loretta controlled the dining room including recruitment of waitresses. Over time, many meals later I got to know the staff as well as Charlie and Loretta. Loretta, in Italy, had been planning to enter a convent. Not long after setting up in Darwin, Charlie had travelled back to Italy in search of a bride.

A less than enthusiastic Loretta was chosen, duly led to the altar by Charlie and brought back to Darwin. This had all happened not long before I came on the scene. So far as I was able to discern over the years and apart from rostered honorary shifts with a team of her choosing to clean St. Mary's cathedral in Darwin, Loretta' life was to be consumed by the triple demands of family, the restaurant and various tenancies on the Stuart Park land Charlie was to acquire. Charlie's was similar, although he might not have been the easiest of spouses to get along with, Loretta was an old-fashioned bride, apparently accepting, not with any apparent joy, her husband's primacy. This in no way detracted from her individuality as a strong, even violently, opinionated person outside the loyalties implicit in the marriage bond as I was to learn when I made to her a joking reference to the "evil eye."

The toll was apparent. Of an evening, during the later days of the restaurant, it became not uncommon to see Loretta in the kitchen, sitting bolt upright and fast asleep on a standard domestic dining chair.

There were 3 children of the marriage, Roberto, Carlo, and the youngest, a daughter. Robbie was born after I had become a regular. When he had reached a sufficient age to manage the restaurant during Charlie's solo annual vacations to Italy, he refused to come aboard until Charlie had departed. Likewise, the day Charlie returned was the day Roberto departed. His intermittent management stints were breaks from his regular public service job.

After Charlie had assumed the dining room and departed, as was his wont, on his annual solo vacation odyssey and Loretta had been banished to the kitchen, it was Roberto's whim to employ his own waitress staff. So it came about one January, new in town and originally from Holland via Sydney, budding aviatrix Esther Veldstra donned a Charlie's waitress apron.

From her mention of her father's barge business, I was able to infer the possibility, later confirmed by Esther, that her father was owner of the very same barge whose errant Sydney dredging activities had led to a landmark High Court decision extending the law of tort damages from personal injuries to property damage.

Tony Field was another aviator who, at that time had possession of the keys of a light twin-engine aircraft. So it was that he took Esther on a night joy flight.

Carlo was more of a wild child. He seemed less directed than his younger brother. He consorted with dubious people and had brushes with the law. Last I heard, he apparently had settled in regular employment as a cook in a Cullen Bay waterfront restaurant. So far as I was able to judge, his meals lacked the magic of his father's.

The daughter spent some time waitressing at the restaurant but displeased Charlie for some reason and disappeared beyond my ken. Charlie paid a price for exiling Loretta to the kitchen. Always generous to the needy, she would have long grass dwellers calling for charity at the kitchen back door. When the pressure to keep food up to the dining room eased, it was not unusual for them to be unofficially gifted Charlie's premium dishes.

When Loretta decided she wanted a car, her need was quite specific. It had to be a soft top 4-wheel drive Jeep. With some initial reluctance, Charlie gave in.

Back in the early days, the waitresses selected by Loretta were an efficient, charming and unusual group. Two, Sandy from Hawaii and Frances from the former Yugoslavia, were wives of oil-rig helium-supported free divers, working offshore from Darwin. Frances could be of fiery disposition, and it was not unknown for her to lose control of a bowl of soup in close proximity to a diner who had upset her. Julie came from Melbourne and was to marry local Chinese restaurateur Frank Lam (whose businesses were to consume them both). Teresa from Mexico was very Hispanic. Julie alone was to commit to Darwin for the long term.

As time went by and my work-related needs of the moment became known to the staff, come lunchtime I would be asked the preliminary question whether I wanted a fast meal so I could return to work. They knew how much I enjoyed a leisurely meal with good company. Sure enough, if I answered fast, the meal would be there almost immediately - probably snatched from the order of an earlier diner.

I developed a penchant for a heavy application of chopped raw garlic on my salads. My enthusiasm for garlic meant that one of the town's magistrates familiar with my eating habit was able to identify my garlic aura from his rear without even looking around. These invariably accompanied my favorite lunchtime orders of a small well-done steak, an entree serving of garlic prawns or a similar serving of bugs. Often the salad and a bowl of crisp potato chips would be served almost immediately I sat down. Many a time I was so pleasantly sated by the chips, salad and garlic and a glass of white wine it was something of an effort to deal properly with the entree modest as it may have been.

In my early days I mistakenly assumed I could enjoyably put away a Charlie's three course meal. The minestrone soup could have made a good meal with no more ... but then came the cordon bleu with salad and chips side serves. Before I was half-way through the cordon bleu, I had reached my limit.

About this time, I asked Charlie how he made any money on his cordon bleus. His response: "Must show can do." As to his Moreton Bay bugs, Leo Venturin, a former north Italian and an even more regular customer than I, as well as one who frequently travelled to his former home country, was of the firm view that such a dish, if it was to be found at all in Italy, would cost 10 times more than Charlie's.

Not only was Leo a super regular he was allowed into the kitchen where pre-meal he often conferred with Loretta about having prepared for him traditional Italian dishes not on the menu. Contradictorily, he affected to hold Charlie in low esteem because of his perception that Charlie's was overly pre occupied with accumulating money. Leo had accumulated far more through investments in Darwin land.

I have never been an adventurous eater. In my pre-Darwin years prawns had never been on my menu, let alone bugs - a kind of mini lobster. Yet many times I found myself eating not only the meat but the crisp bug shell. A garlic prawn entrée would often suffice for a meal.

Charlie prospered. Lunch times he usually catered to a full house and, if the trade was there, continuing through until late at night. The phrase "long lunch" took on a new dimension—it could go to midnight or even later.

From about 7pm the restaurant was usually at close to capacity, sometimes with a queue at the entrance. Reasonably priced, top class, meticulously prepared food was the lure. Simple Darwinians were introduced to the delights of classic dishes - Cordon Bleu, filet mignons, Moreton Bay bugs, prawns any which way and *Saltimbocca a la Romana*. The *piece de resistance* was the lobster. This was at a time when the Don Hotel restaurant in Cavenagh Street was offering what the menu modestly described as fish and chips (amounting in fact to barramundi and black bean sauce with chips and salad, at the unbelievable cost of one dollar).

When Loretta ruled the dining room in the earlier days white tablecloths were *de rigueur*. If an outside queue was building up, a lone diner or a couple might be asked to share a 4-man table with strangers. The potential awkwardness of this haphazard system in some instances led to enduring friendships.

Over time, Charlie came to purchase the land upon which the restaurant was built. Then he waited impatiently for the sports store and Lee Transport leases to expire so he could occupy the whole building. He installed a cool-room at the rear of his premises. He also bought a large improved residential block at Stuart Park.

As for sourcing his vegetables, Charlie was out and about at the fresh food Darwin markets at 6 am, selecting none but the best. The original restaurant was quite small. Until he was pulled up by the Fire Brigade, he deployed as many tables as could be fitted into the space. After a Fire Brigade inspection, he would reduce the intensity. My guess is the original restaurant accommodated no more than about 60 diners.

The kitchen was so small it was a mystery how it was able to produce, in such quantities, the marvels that it did. Extensive preparatory treatment was the key. Then Lee Transport, a hole in the wall business with its doorway adjacent to Charlie's but in the same building, ceased to trade. Bill Lee, the proprietor had been the long-time right-hand man for well-established Darwin lawyer John [Tiger] Lyons. Lyons' business around the corner in Cavenagh Street was shut down about this time [in the early seventies] because of Tiger's age and infirmity.

Charlie took up this space with one large circular dining table. By my guess, it accommodated about 20 diners. It was open to the dining room and gave him the opportunity to cater for smallish functions. That table was never left vacant if it was not booked to a group. If the restaurant was otherwise crowded out, potential diners would be offered a seat there as an alternative to a [relatively] more private smaller table. At the later stages of one of my meals a stripper performed her art to a full table in the tiny clear space left there, apparently as a performance for a buck's party.

As to atmosphere, the original dining room, even as configured with the Lee Transport addition, had it all. I could be dining at one table with a client who had just been acquitted by a Supreme Court criminal jury, while two tables away the presiding trial judge might be dining with Crown Prosecutor Bill Raby. Prawn fishermen would be thick on the ground in the off-season while they were maintaining their boats. Wool Board chairman Sir William Gunn might be seen later of an evening waving his hand in the air to attract waitress attention. I would often meet up there with other lawyers, my bank manager or a client. NT News editor Jim Bowditch might be seen at his table ostentatiously chewing a banknote in front of his protesting wife preparatory to proffering it to Charlie as part of the payment for a meal.

Even Cam Cooper, later of the Negri River company float,[21] was there waiting for me lunchtime one day with no prearrangement. On route to Western Australia, his plane had

---

[21] On the controversy surrounding the Negri River Corporation float of 1980, see the debate in the Australian Senate in 1981:

https://parlinfo.aph.gov.au/parlInfo/search/display/display.w3p;db=CHAMBER;id=chamber/hansards/1981-03-03/0057;query=Id:%22chamber/hansards/1981-03-03/0050%22 delivered him for a transit wait in Darwin. He had induced a fellow transiting traveler to accompany him. Thus did I meet a charming Japanese wife returning to Koolen Island off the northwest coast of Western Australia. With hindsight, as I write this it has become apparent to me that Cam was then in the course of laying the foundations for the Negri float.

Pre and post NT self-government it was a commonplace to rub shoulders with Chief Minister Everingham and other senior CLP [Country and Liberal Party] government ministers or Federal politicians. Most everyone knew everybody else. The air crackled with the electricity of animated conversation backgrounded by muted music and the clatter of cutlery and serving dishes, with diners moving from table to table. If the outside temperature was low, Charlie might adjust the air-conditioning temperature to attempt to have the diners drink more. Over lunch my friend Fred Canaris might be heard calling for more wine.

Charlie's had been discovered by fellow Rotarian and Anglican Bishop Ken Mason. As a bachelor he chose to visit often for lunch. Often if I arrived for a quick lunch, we would join forces. In an earlier life I had dined occasionally at Melbourne University's Trinity College where the same Ken, then rector, had recited grace in Latin.

As time went by, the Sports Store tenancy at the front of the building expired. Charlie for the first time had the opportunity for his restaurant to occupy the entire building. When he did so, the dining room space was more than doubled and the kitchen enlarged. But it was never the same thereafter. Instead of the one dining room there were three. This was at a time of vastly increased quality competition.

Nonetheless, the southernmost back room became the haunt of the post self CLP government. It came to be described, by those not in attendance, as the Silver Circle Room.

Once diners passed through the entrance to this room, for all practical purposes they became invisible to diners in the front room or, indeed, the other back room. Excluding the Silver Circle room, the remainder of the restaurant was never more than half full. The old atmosphere was gone. No longer the boisterous crackle and buzz of conversation. If any other place replicated Charlie's glory days, I was yet to discover it when I left Darwin in 2013. As for the Silver Circle room, in its heyday anyone not close to government - in the sense of money - would have felt uncomfortable there.

When the CLP government was toppled in 2001 that room became the almost exclusive preserve of ghosts of times past. I am unable to say whether the new government was interested in regular dining out *en masse* at some other favored location.

As for the glory days of the Silver Circle room, as 5pm drew nigh cabinet ministers closeted there would phone for their drivers rather than walk little more than the approximately 200-meter length of the near adjacent mall back to their offices.

Charlie was a staunch CLP government supporter, so much so that one day, after the CLP had lost government in 2001 and during the incumbency of Tom Pauling as Administrator, Charlie complained to me, as I was leaving his restaurant, that Tom should sack the Labor government of the day and appoint the CLP. Who should I walk into in the street outside but Tom. Frivolously, I passed on Charlie's complaint. Tom chose to treat the issue seriously. He explained that what Charlie wanted was not within his power.

Over the years all manner of conniving restaurant customers attempted to involve Charlie, or more accurately his perceived wealth, in their projects. One such undertook construction of a dwelling on Charlie's Stuart Park land with no written agreement in hand. Charlie had stood by aloof, apparently reasoning he had much to win and little to lose. The builder was far from a benefactor. A reckoning came for Charlie in the form of a writ.

The legal process was one thing; the young woman lawyer who initiated it was another matter altogether. Early in the action, there was a minor interlocutory application. I was unable to attend in person. I engaged the service of then barrister Martin Carter. His sole task was to consent to an interlocutory Order. That Order was duly made.

The next day, to my astonishment, I received a letter from the builder's solicitor "confirming" an overall settlement of the entire action concluded at the bar table with Martin. The terms were very generous to her client. It was thus a blatant "try-on." Martin confirmed that no such agreement had been discussed, let alone concluded. A very clear letter of denial was sent by way of reply. Tedious as it might have seemed, I was on notice that nothing oral was to be entertained with the opposing lawyer.

Protracted applications were brought on before the Master [Assistant Judge]. Lengthy affidavits annexing calculations were filed for both sides. Those for Charlie were done by a qualified expert. The builder's were done by his solicitor. The Master of the Supreme Court, my erstwhile deep-sea yacht race navigator, was heard to expostulate, hours into his hearing one dreary Friday afternoon session devoted to argument concerning Charlie's matter, about what we were all doing in the courtroom and why.

Meantime, although in two successive separate December/January holiday terms my preference would have been to visit my family in Melbourne, while the opposing solicitor remained in town, I was not prepared to take what I considered to be the risk of leaving Darwin for fear there might be another "try on." Loyalty to Charlie exacted a toll, which he could never have been aware of. The war of attrition, for that is what it became, went on. All my communications were in writing and carefully worded. I can only imagine the billing my adversary had been rendering.

Eventually there came a resolution. At last, I was free to leave town during Christmas vacation. But this roughly coincided with the onset of the preliminary lack of balance and need to use a walking frame associated with the early stages of my Parkinsonian central nervous system disorder.

The falloff in trade ate into Charlie's spirit. In his seventies, the can-do enthusiasm was no more. Old customers were heard to murmur things were not as they had been. There were insufficient lunchtime diners to necessitate Loretta's presence - in fact Charlie could manage easily on his own. There was no family member with the capacity or desire to step into his shoes.

The sale of the building became inevitable as a prelude to retirement for both Charlie and Loretta. After an auction of the cooking utensils and equipment, the building itself was sold.

In his early eighties, however, and not long into retirement, late in 2010 Charlie was assailed with chest pain. As Loretta was driving him to the Darwin hospital, he drew his last breath. Son Robbie delivered the eulogy to a crowded St. Mary's Cathedral, praising his father's unstinting devotion to hard work. Loretta was to die about 6 months later.

Editor Note: As of 2023, "Charlie's of Darwin" still exists, in the same city site, described as a "relaxed, fun, funky and casual" cocktail lounge and distillery.

Chapter 10: Meeting Mother Teresa

By the nature of their work, lawyers have all sorts of people as clients, but few get to be consulted by saints. The name Mother Teresa [1910-1997] evokes images of the tiny [five-foot or 1.52 meters] nun who, against formidable odds, established a hospice in the slums of Calcutta to alleviate the last days of life of the poorest of the poor in that city and was later canonized by the Catholic Church as a saint.[22]

Agnes Bojaxhiu, her pre-convent name, was born in 1910 in Skopje, Albania. Her father, a businessman, politician, and charity donor, died in 1918. At age 18 she left home to join the Sisters of Loreto order of Irish nuns. She did not see her family again. In Ireland she took the name Teresa after Saint Teresa of Lisieux. In 1929, she was sent to Calcutta to teach geography and catechism at a school that catered for orphans and poor children as well as more affluent boarders. She developed proficiency in Hindi and Bengali, as well as English. In 1946, after daily observation of the poverty and misery around her she received what she described as "a call within the call" to

---

[22] Edit Note: The encounter with Mother Teresa described in this chapter is undated, but may be presumed to have taken place on Teresa's visit to Australia in 1985. By then, she had already been awarded the Nobel Peace Prize (1979) and the Missionaries of Charity order she had founded had grown to include 4,000 nuns and many more lay workers in more than 90 countries (including "more than a dozen" houses in Australia, one of them in Darwin). She was beatified in 2003, just six years after her death, after what *Encyclopedia Britannica* calculated might have been the fastest such process in the history of the Catholic Church. She was then canonized by Pope Francis 1 on 4 September 2016. In the Church calendar, 4 September came thereafter to be known as the Feast Day of Saint Teresa of Kolkota.

follow Jesus into the poorest slums in the city, live among the poor and do his work there. That call was an inner voice saying, as she recorded it:

> "I want Indian nuns victims of my love who would be Martha and Mary, who would be so united to me as to radiate my love on souls. I want free nuns covered by the poverty of the Cross. I want obedient nuns covered with my obedience of the Cross. I want full of love nuns covered with the charity of the Cross. Wilt thou refuse to do this for me?"

In 1947 she wrote to Archbishop Perier of what God had put in her heart:

> "These words or rather this voice frightened me. The thought of eating sleeping living like the Indians filled me with fear. I prayed long. I prayed so much ... The more I prayed the clearer grew the voice in my heart."

When first she made application to her Archbishop to be released from her convent to go into the streets she was told to go back and pray. As she prayed, the outline of what she was to attempt became clearer. Many humble, prayer-backed applications were unsuccessfully made to her Church superiors to this end.

Eventually she succeeded. Permission was granted also to live outside her convent and on the streets whilst remaining in her Order of nuns. Then came the test of whether she was physically capable of carrying out the mission she had set herself. She had doubts. But she got on with it. By and large, her religious peers were generally not encouraging. One convent where she came to lunch ordered that she eat under the back stairs like a beggar. One Yugoslav Jesuit in Calcutta observed at the time: "We thought she was cracked."

Getting on with it meant outreach to the most destitute living in conditions of indescribable squalor, lepers, untouchables. She founded a home to where she transported the dying, picking them up on the streets. She did her best to nurse back to life infants and babies abandoned in the garbage heaps and rubbish bins almost as soon as they were born.

She explained she served Christ in the distressing disguise of the poorest of the poor. She warned that it was not possible to do her kind of work "without being a soul of prayer." And so she labored, in obscurity, until English magazine editor, BBC host, libertine and bon vivant, Malcolm Muggeridge, "discovered" her in the course of making a TV program. Later, he made her work the subject of a book. She featured on the cover of *Time* magazine in 1975 and in 1979 was awarded the Nobel peace prize. The respect for her saintliness spread. Her Order, the Missionaries of Charity, grew to be active in 139 countries, including some in the west, as for example Darwin. It came to number over 5,000, including two orders of brothers and one of priests.

At least two black clouds overshadowed her work. The first was in the form of Australia's Northern Territory Town Planning Board, the second, hostile writings, best known of which being those of the late English journalist and polemicist Christopher Hitchens.

As to the former, her order had been expressly invited to Darwin by Catholic bishop John O'Loughlin [1911-1985, Bishop from 1949 to 1985]. A hostel/convent had been established in the upper crust Darwin suburb of Fannie Bay. There came the need for expansion of the building. Plans were drawn up and the necessary submission made to the Town Planning Board. Objection was raised by some neighboring residents. The substance was largely that the drunken and abusive aboriginal husbands of the women being given refuge by the nuns were creating not only disturbance in the street outside the refuge but also vomiting, defecating, and urinating there. In the event the Board upheld the objection and rejected the application.[23] To this point I had no personal involvement.

Then, in the late seventies. I received instructions to appeal the decision of the Board. It was a Friday. Late that afternoon I was at the Darwin Sailing Club. So too was John Hogan, managing editor of the local newspaper the NT News. We talked. I told him of the Board's dismissal of the application. To get away from the noise and bustle we walked along the beach. He wanted as much fact as I could give about the dismissal.

What followed were the largest headlines I have seen in any newspaper at any time which includes those for war victory (VE and VP Day) of 1945. In unambiguous terms NT News told the world that it had taken the Northern Territory government through its Planning Board to offer a living saint an effective slap in the face.[24] Hyperbole perhaps, but it activated Ian Tuxworth [1942-2020], the N.T. Chief Minister of the day [1984-86], to give every encouragement to the appeal. A former northern Irishman, NT public servant Trevor Gargan, was put on the job to do what he could. Bishop O'Loughlin convened a

---

[23] "Looking for a new convent site," *NT News*, 18 February 1985.
[24] This editor was unable to locate the issue of NT News mentioned here.

public meeting at a large outdoor covered area on premises close to the convent. I think the owner was a former South African, prominent NT Catholic churchman Gene Scaturchio, who lived in the locality. He was present, as was Trevor Gargan. At that meeting there was much venting about the street antics of the temporally dispossessed husbands. The objectors were given food for thought. As I recall, no resolutions were passed.

Next in the chain of events was a visit to Darwin from Mother Teresa herself (1985?). Again, it was a Friday, but I knew nothing of this until at the end of difficult week after an expansive lunch with a few glasses of wine I returned to my office at about 4.40 to be informed by my excited staff that Mother Teresa was at the convent and would like to see me. I learned later that the bishop had elected to leave town to attend the funeral of a priest friend rather than face up to the saintly woman whose order he had invited to Darwin. Because of my earlier wine consumption, I felt no good could come from the meeting that Mother Teresa had asked for. Any confidence she might have had in the appeal outcome was likely to be eroded. Colin McDonald QC who had stepped in to present her case also had been invited. I explained the reason for my diffidence. He was strongly of the view I should attend.

The appeal was duly presented and argued before the 3-member Appeals Board. Nuns from the order gave evidence which was far from suggesting the impugned offensive street behavior was non- existent. The decision to uphold the Appeal was delivered swiftly.

It is not every day a lawyer has the opportunity to represent a living saint. But did I meet with Mother Teresa? I believe I adhered to my decision to avoid doing so. Colin McDonald, on the other hand, has a different recollection. According to him, we both sat across a desk opposite Mother Teresa who after preliminaries, reached across enfolding one of each of our hands in one of her hands and expressing confidence that we would do our best on behalf of the convent. I would like to believe the McDonald version, but I have absolutely no recollection of this scenario.

One dark cloud over Mother Teresa was in the form of uncomplimentary criticism from the sidelines from Christopher Hitchens. Hitchens [1949-2011] was a highly opinionated Anglo-American journalist and polemicist. From his teenage years he was a heavy smoker and drinker. He wrote or co-authored over 30 books at least some of which are little more than extended essays, pamphlets or transcripts of recorded discussions. In the later stages of his career, encountered his occasional featured articles in the week-end Australian edition of *The Guardian*. I found them so hectoring and uninformative that I gave up on them entirely. Nonetheless, his full-on style of debate made him an accepted, albeit controversial, public figure. Initially a socialist, Marxist, and anti-totalitarian he swung to a right-wing position over his personal disappointment and outrage at what he saw as the West's "tepid" reaction to the controversy over Salman Rushdie's *Satanic Verses*, followed by the left's embrace of Bill Clinton and the anti-war movement's opposition to NATO's involvement in Bosnia and Herzegovina in the 90s.

His books included criticisms of not only Mother Teresa but also Bill Clinton, Henry Kissinger, Billy Graham, and Diana, Princess of Wales. He publicized his homoerotic encounters at Balliol College in Oxford with an unnamed twosome who went on to serve in the Thatcher cabinet. It was apparently of no concern to him that his outing of the unnamed pair cast a slur over all of Thatcher's male cabinet who attended Oxford University while Hitchens was a student. His outrage over Mother Teresa caused him to devote the contents of an extended essay [25,000 or so words] published in 1995 as a book/pamphlet, devoted to her denigration under the "smart" in a juvenile sense, double-entendre title "The Missionary Position - Mother Teresa in Theory and Practice." He left the UK in 1981 to take up residence in the US.

Towards the latter part of his life, an essential part of Hitchens' psyche was a visceral hatred of religion. If indeed he was aware of it, Pascal's wager was not for him. His catch cry: "What cannot be proved by evidence can be rejected without evidence." The nature of that "evidence," whether primary, secondary, or circumstantial was never defined nor does it appear he was ever put to the test on this. For example, the British criminal law concept of circumstantial evidence being sufficient for a jury to find criminal guilt beyond a reasonable doubt appears never to have been embraced by Hitchens in his call for "evidence."

Hitchens classed himself as an antitheist - a word of his own creation. The rather precious and self- indulgent distinction he made was that "a person could be an atheist and wish that belief in God were correct" but that "an antitheist is someone who is relieved there is no evidence for such an assertion." A believer would question the assertion of absence of evidence of God and point to the Bible and specifically to the life of Jesus Christ and the resurrection as narrated in the gospels of Matthew, Mark,

Luke, and John as at the very least some evidence to the contrary. I interpret Hitchens' position as requiring a personal revelation of the nature granted to the apostle Paul [or Saul as he then was] on the road to Damascus for him to accept any belief in an all-powerful God.

Not only was Hitchens an atheist but he was intolerant of any who failed to acknowledge and accept his atheism. I classify Hitchens as a "metheist," one who rejected any idea of a supreme being and appointed himself supreme arbiter of everything. Consistent with this standpoint, when he was asked on a TV program what he considered constituted the "axis of evil" his answer "Christianity, Buddhism and Islam" was swift and clear, while being also glib and ignoring the fact Buddhism is non-theistic.

There is no evidence Hitchens ever met Mother Teresa or visited her Calcutta hospice. His attacks on her were a calculated denigration, a malicious construct of facts and innuendo. Individually, these facts were already in the public domain. His aggregated construct was developed over several years. His book/pamphlet reflects personal affront at the public and international adulation given to a person who failed to measure up to his undisclosed personal "antitheist" or more properly "metheist" standards. He offered the view of an opinionated man who seems to have chosen to ignore the Socratic observation/proof that the fact every human was born with an innate sense of right and wrong must mean we came from somewhere else and prove immortality of the soul. Socrates, in Phaedo, himself rechecked and approved his previous reasoning to this effect before drinking his fatal dose of hemlock.

So how was the professional controversialist Hitchens affronted by Mother Teresa? Firstly, her charity had been supported by some dubious but wealthy individual patrons, some with allegedly criminal connections. The interested reader may consult the comprehensive account of these controversies in Wikipedia. Teresa's response to these charges was, however, straightforward, that anyone, rich and poor alike, could make an offering.

Secondly, Teresa's medical facilities were adjudged by a *Lancet* editor to be not up to the mark. Hitchens' belief, based on supposition, speculation and innuendo, that she possessed vast financial resources, deliberately "pinched to preserve misery and second-rate physical facilities," led him to the bizarre overall conclusion that she

> "was less interested in helping the poor than in using them as an indefatigable source of wretchedness on which to fuel the expansion of her fundamentalist Roman Catholic beliefs."

Thirdly, she handled donations in a careless, possibly cavalier manner. Hitchens found fault with her for her handling of unimaginable sums. His slanderous innuendo hinted at numbered Swiss bank accounts.

Fourthly, Hitchens attempted to support his own controversial case by reproducing extremist Hindu claptrap to the effect that she and her nuns were baptizing their dying patients.

Finally, he disapproved of her position on abortion and contraception. Such a criticism should more properly have been directed at the Catholic church itself. Nonetheless,

Teresa addressed herself to these issues during her addresses to the US Congress in 1981 and to the American National Prayer Breakfast in 1994.

The Vatican in the lead-up to Mother Teresa's canonisation. *(ABC News)*

Hitchens referred to her ministry to the dying in the streets of Calcutta as a "death cult," but she justified her mission to the poor with the biblical pronouncement: "Whatsoever you do for the least of my brethren you do it for me."

Outliving Mother Teresa as he did, and after her canonization process had started, Hitchens conveyed to her Devil's Advocate, who was seeking information that might serve to discredit her case, his objections noted above. When she was nevertheless canonized as a saint in September 2016, Hitchens responded, complaining that the process to sainthood had been hasty. He disclaimed any quarrel with

Teresa, saying his argument was "not with the deceiver but with the deceived."

To the US Congress in June 1981, she spoke of newborn babies left in dustbins in Calcutta near the home of the Missionaries of Charity, with the mothers' unspoken hope that they would be found and saved. She spoke of her Sisters finding eight aborted fetuses, still alive, outside an abortion clinic, bringing them home, nurturing them. One survived, becoming a healthy child for whom they found an adoptive home. Mother Teresa and her sisters collected thousands of people from the streets: abandoned children, lepers, the sick, and the dying.

Every day in Calcutta, the Missionaries of Charity fed 8,000 people. Somehow, they never turned anyone away empty-handed. She told of a man who lay dying in a gutter, half-eaten by worms, rotting. Mother Teresa herself carried him to her home for the sick and dying. She laid him in a bed, washed his entire body using a basin and cloth, picked the maggots out of his open wounds and dressed them with ointment, laid him in fresh sheets and gave him a drink of cold water. He was given what he had not known until then: a clean place to lie, unconditional love, and dignity. "I have lived like an animal all my life," the man told her, "but I will die like an angel." He died soon after.

To the National Prayer Breakfast in Washington in 1994, Teresa addressed an audience of more than 3,000 people assembled from all over the world - Prime Ministers, Presidents, Ambassadors, Members of Congress, Supreme Court Justices, and dignitaries, the tiny nun spoke with a moral and spiritual authority eclipsing that of the holders of high office. Stepping up onto a footstool to be seen over the podium, she said boldly,

> "St. John says that you are a liar if you say you love God and you don't love your Neighbor. How can you love God whom you do not see, if you do not love your Neighbor whom you see, whom you touch, with whom you live? Jesus makes himself the hungry one, the naked one, the homeless one, the unwanted one."

Mother Teresa then threw down the gauntlet on behalf of the unwanted, declaring,

> "The greatest destroyer of peace today is abortion. And if we can accept that a mother can kill even her own child, how can we tell other people not to kill one another? We are fighting abortion by adoption, by care of the mother and adoption for her baby. We have saved thousands of lives. Please don't kill the child. I want the child. Please give me the child. I am willing to accept any child who would be aborted, and to give that child to a married couple who will love the child. Give me the child."

Her message that abortion was at the root of all evil may have seemed improbable, but her pleas plainly touched the hearts of her audience.

Editor Note: In the manuscript of this chapter, a lengthy discussion follows on the impact of Mother Teresa on Malcolm Muggeridge [1903-1990], journalist, writer, satirist, BBC TV interviewer and presenter. For space reasons it has here been deleted. Interested readers may consult Wikipedia or other online sources on the life and controversies surrounding Mother Teresa.

PART 5—Sailing

Chapter 11: Sailing, 1 [1958-2000]

Growing up in my parents' family homes in Melbourne suburban Surrey Hills and Mont Albert, I was about as far from the sea as a Melbourne suburbanite could be. Even so, boating, more particularly boats and the sea, attracted me. In the pressure university third terms, it was my habit to beaver away at the Melbourne Public Library, striving to compensate for a less than diligent application to study over the preceding months, There, I found two forms of pressure release.

The first was every so often a coffee break with a few other like tortured souls. The coffee shop was almost diagonally opposite the Public Library. Twenty minutes or so of animated conversation enabled us to return refreshed to the mental torment. Neale Hunter, Arthur McIntyre and Ananda Krishnan were like-minded coffee enthusiasts.

The second, usually of an evening when I was about ready to check out from the library, was to look out older bound volumes of the American yachting magazine *Rudder*. This was to study such parts of the plans as were made available for publication of the latest yachts from the 30s and 40s off the drawing boards of America's and England's leading naval architects. Names like Philp Rhodes, Winthrop Warner, Laurent Giles and Ralph Winslow come to mind as well as of course Sparkman and Stephens. My very limited knowledge extended very little further than that English yachts tended to have deep keels and narrow beam whereas those in America tended to be beamy and of moderate draft often deploying a centreboard- bronze of course with an equally costly bronze casing.

The library was just over the road from Technical Book Company where, passing by, I could pop in and browse publications like the English *Yachting World* Annuals and feast on the multiple yacht designs and nautical reportage. Browsing in the early fifties, one name stood out: Olin Stephens. If you wanted the world's best in yacht design of soundly engineered swift seaworthy craft, he was the man. Other standout names were the Australian Alan Payne and the Dutchman Ricus van de Stadt,

Stephens retired in 1978 aged 70 to apply himself to modern art, music, travel international yacht racing technical committees and writing. One of his special delights was to visit an Italian boatyard that specialised in restoration of yachts to his designs. Death overtook him 30 years later. His mantle seems to have been taken over by Argentinian German Frers, himself a graduate of the Sparkman and Stephens yacht drawing department. Other alumni from the same stable include notable US naval architects Robert Perry and David Pedrick. These days a plethora of sailing design information is available online.

Stephens gave some insights into both his design and personal philosophies when in his nineties he wrote his memoir "All This and Sailing Too." As to the former, he observed:

"In any design the most important factors of speed seem to be long sailing lines and large sail area with moderate displacement and small wetted surface. Then comes beauty by which is meant clean fair pleasing lines. Though, per se, beauty is not a factor of speed the easiest boats to look at seem the easiest to drive."

Added to this was stability via external ballast deep down in the keel. In a slightly earlier time it had been thought placement of lead pigs or other ballast about the bilges of a yacht was sufficient to add to any ballast in the keel to promote a smoother sea motion. The 28'Melbourne yacht Calore I was to purchase reflected this belief. Its bilges were packed with lead pigs. Its keel ballast was iron and this may have been a part explanation. At that time I decided to make no change. I suppose the best remedy for any inability to carry what an owner sees as "adequate" sail is to liaise with the yacht designer—a privilege of the deep pocketed few. The alternative for that great majority of boaters who buy second-hand or indeed off the shelf, is to acquire only yachts to established designs with proven seaworthiness and lead ballast all located at the keel base.

Or as physics textbook writer Arthur Beiser so eloquently put it in his hugely informative almost paganly worshipful book of the same name - "The Proper Yacht." The last report I read of Arthur was when in mid Atlantic, because of an underwater leak he was unable to locate, he had to abandon his magnificent Nicholson 70' yacht, epitome of properness, for the life-raft. His ultimate "proper yacht" disappeared beneath the waves.

Stephens questioned the seaworthiness of boats of his day whose hallmarks were excessive beam, high sides, extreme light weight and instability. Post the disaster filled Fastnet

Race of 1979, which saw capsized boats and 15 fatalities, he opined, in a very understated way in the circumstances, that some modern ocean racers and cruising boats derived from them were dangerous to their crews.

In the midst of the Fastnet debacle, it was noteworthy Lorelei a French skippered She [South Hants Engineering] 36' keeler to a Stephens design was under control and so manoeuvrable as to be able to take off the seven man crew from the life-raft of Griffin, a distressed 34' OOD [Offshore One Design] vessel. Griffin had been completely inverted for some time and when it finally rolled upright it was waterlogged. The crew had taken to the life-raft. With the wind speed gusting 60 knots, up until the first observation of a Griffin distress flare, Lorelei had been racing. Surfing under triple reefed mainsail and number 4 jib at 90 degrees to the apparent wind, she was standing up well and steering easily. Her helmsman had been enjoying a thrilling ride.

Stephens played an important role in transitioning yacht design from an art to science with artistic discipline. Scientific yacht design involved use of the test tank to observe towed hull models. While he achieved notoriety from the brilliant performances in the Bermuda Race of Carleton Mitchell's beamy centreboard 38' yawl to his design, he had no love for the diminished stability of the centre-boarder for serious oceangoing use.

As to his personal philosophy, he observed:

"In all phases of my work I was conscious of the need to find balance in both the long and short view. Broadly, I think

I can say I applied the principles of balance in design in business and in the pleasures I enjoyed."

To return to my story. Geographical location, let alone lack of money, had precluded yacht club membership and early sail training. Translating attraction to the water into sailing or even just boating, with any incidental yacht club membership, costs.

It wasn't as if I was utterly deprived of contact traversing water. When I was a child, at least one paddle seamer plied the waters of Port Philip Bay for tourist excursion hire on the Port Melbourne to Sorrento route. I recall violent seasickness on one such trip as the Weerona lurched its way on a return leg. And, for a brief time, in my twenties, I was an active but novice member of Melbourne's Banks Rowing Club. I was taken under the wing of an elder for some instruction in a scull. I enjoyed the physicality but had so much more energy to dissipate. Not surprisingly, there were routines to follow, especially for a novice member, to launch a scull and this was at a time in my young life when I thought I had no time to spend other than in physical activity or study. Looking back now, I have some regret I never applied myself to the oar and sliding seat. Sail eventually became more consuming and movement away from Melbourne put paid to any further serious consideration to rowing on the Yarra.

My first entry to actual boating as an owner in my own boat was via an American design 15′ plywood kayak featured in the magazine Practical Mechanics in the later forties. Two such had been built by a family in Brighton and were advertised for sale in the *Age* newspaper. The builder/seller was an alumnus of the Australian Naval

Academy. Largely attributable to his navigation qualifications, he had spent time in the US employed as skipper of a 55' centreboard yawl of timber construction. He showed me sobering before and after cyclone photographs of the US marina from where he had taken the yacht in his charge out of a cyclone path. The latter showed only the tips of masts breaking the water surface. Quite likely it was the suicide of the owner whose yacht he skippered that enabled a home break and the chance to sell his kayaks. While these were far from extreme lightweights, they were very well built and not bad looking. I was able to manage to carry one without assistance albeit awkwardly because of the shape. At the time of my purchase, I owned a Chevrolet tourer of about 1928 vintage. Improbably, its roof was able to support the weight of the two kayaks plus the associated stress from lashing both securely for the road.

A year or two later, I bought a used German built Klepper one man Aerius 15' folding kayak of roughly comparable weight. I think the word Aerius describes the inflatable rubber tube like belt just below and encircling the entire gunwale line of Klepper's kayaks so designated. This kayak conveniently broke down to 2 easily transportable packs. Kayaks are propelled by paddle. I prefer a rowing action, better still backed by a sliding seat. As to this, Keefers Boat hire at Beaumaris offered solid clinker-built rowing hulls for hire at very reasonable rates. No sliding seats were included. But, of all places it was on the water at Seymour that I discovered sliding seat rowboats of solid construction available for hire. Whilst I found that the more kayak paddling I did the more my endurance developed, few of my friends were interested in sharing the pleasures of kayaking in Port Philip Bay. But at least I was on the water. If my memory serves me correctly, I don't think I ever sold these 2 kayaks and they were about the family homes for years.

The kayak was not suitable for surfing, and I got the idea of trying my hand at a surf ski. This was about 14' long of plywood over timber frame construction, banana-ish profile at the bow and fairly weighty with no facility for easy retrieval via a Velcro ankle clip connected by a cord as with a modern lightweight surfboard. It was not something to lightly tuck under an arm as I see even the girls do these days [2018]. After its purchase, I became cautious about testing my skill in the surf with this ski. I came to worry about its weight and getting whacked in the head and/or losing the paddle if, or more likely when, I parted company with it in a tumbling surf. Furthermore, I never saw myself as a strong swimmer because I could never get any thrust from my leg kicking action.

The Klepper was not suitable for surfing for other reasons. While it was equipped with a foot pedal operated fold up rudder, placement of the paddler about amidships seated inside the shell was far from ideal, even for a wild day in what surf Port Philip Bay could muster. My proof was when, while revelling in such conditions and after several successful bouts of surfing, the bow dug in, pitchpoling me out of the hull. To compound matters, I was unable to climb back into the hull. Intrepid souls have successfully navigated huge ocean passages in Klepper folding kayaks but I was not so destined. That tumble caused fracture to at least one of the laminated ring frame members.

In earlier days I had envied the power of sail. As a child on holiday by the seaside beyond Mordialloc, I would enviously watch the owners of beach cabins launch their off-the-beach centreboard yachts to sail over the horizon to return hours later. Then, one day, when I did get out on my own bottom in Port Philip Bay paddling, as I thought strongly, I heard from behind a significant sound of hissing and splashing. The noise drew abeam. It was a lone sailor on a diminutive Moth sailing dinghy. He was travelling just that bit faster than me. Whatever extra effort I applied to my paddle, the Moth just sailed away.

Twelve months articles of legal clerkship further exposed me to the world of sail. My master in articles happened to be the solicitor for the Master Builders Association. He handled many serious building disputes and had a reputation for specialist expertise with them. It was not altogether surprising then that he was commissioned to act for engineer and yacht designer/owner Dick Wayman in a boat building action brought against him by a Philip Island boatbuilder named Manning. I had the privilege of sitting beside counsel in the role of instructing solicitor during the trial. My master in articles, John Adam, had done all of the hard yards and preliminary liaising with our barrister in preparing the court documents so the issues were defined. At the conclusion of each day's proceedings, I would report back to John with my impression of events in the courtroom. The litigation went for 8 days.

The boat involved was no ordinary craft. At a time when there were very few globally, let alone any at all of the 42′ length of Dick's, he had undertaken his own pioneering design exercise. Hull models had been tested and studied to reach what he found to be optimal shapes. Unbeknown to him at the time, sailboat designers in Hawaii had been working on a similar project Cross pollination of ideas would have been helpful to both parties. As it was Dicks vessel, VA-I- MANA had hulls rising considerably higher out of the water than its sleeker Hawaiian counterpart. Each hull offered comfortable stand up self- contained accommodation. The interconnecting deck structure was the platform for a spacious deck saloon and command post. Draft was quite shallow and there was no centreboard. Access to the hulls interiors was via this saloon.

Dick successfully defended his case. I never found out if Manning paid Dick's legal costs that were awarded against him. What I did manage though, was to secure an invitation to join Dick for a sail. There was comfort associated with absence of heel and spaciousness. Even conservatively rigged as it was, I found quite extraordinary the manner in which it slipped quietly through the water, faster than a monohull of similar length in the same conditions, with no sensation at all of speed.

The next phase of my sailing odyssey was the purchase of a used Gwen 12 sailing dinghy. To my eye, it seemed in fair condition. This was a seriously over-canvassed 12' sailing skiff with a bowsprit to help accommodate the sail area and an essentially flat deck apart from a modest self- draining cockpit. It was designed for two handed sailing. Later stages of the design incorporated a spinnaker as well as a trapeze. I joined the Sandringham Yacht Club [SYC] where there was an active Gwen fleet and boat storage racks for off the beach boats. The novice I was hoped to learn from my younger peers. This was about 1961. My Gwen was far from a boat that could be recommended for beginners. As it turned out, what I did learn was on a steep learning curve and sufficient base to carry on from.

I carried on my SYC membership as a country member after I left Melbourne. Though I had been nowhere near the Club for well over 40 years, I received in Darwin by post some kind of SYC trophy, I think for dedication, when I was in my seventies. Soon after, my country membership fee escalated dramatically. This was to incorporate an individual membership of the Australian Yachting Federation [AYF] of which I was already a paid up member through my then active membership of Darwin Sailing Club. I complained by letter. The only response was written advice from SYC that my membership had been cancelled due to non- payment of club dues.

By that time, I had no practical use for the membership anyway. Darwin located as I was, combined with age and a Parkinsonian problem with balance, so far as I could assess caused by exposure to International brand two pot polyurethane marine paint, had, since early 2008, by and large put paid to my active, let alone sailing, days. This was even though something like 30 years had elapsed since my first spray application of the debilitating paint to my Ranger 23 yacht in Darwin in 1975, before I developed dopamine deficiency symptoms. You could say it was an indirect consequence of cyclone Tracey wind- blown sand stripping away the port side gel coat of my yacht as it sat in its cradle at Darwin Sailing Club. Shortly post the Ranger repair, I had prepared and spray painted with the same paint my then recently acquired SandS 30 yacht, Stampede. Thereafter, I made extensive use of the same paint for each annual refit, plus a complete hull respray about every 10 years. When I was painting for Stampede at home, I would often put unused paint in my domestic frig to stop it going off by hardening. And when it came to cleaning my spray gun I found nothing bettered using a rag with my hands immersed in the paint thinners. One day when I spilled the paint thinners on my shirt, I experienced a severe burning sensation on the skin under the spill. The few local neurologists who have examined me are unable to make the link between the paint and my diminished neurological function. I hope my executor has the wit to collect on my SYC debenture which becomes redeemable only on death.[25]

John working on Stampede in Darwin (1990s?)

The Gwen had one especially memorable outing. As events turned out that was to be my last. I invited my non

---

[25] John's family did indeed investigate this but was assured that any such entitlement had expired "years ago."

sailor friend Brian Buckley to join me for a sail one Sunday afternoon. He left his very pregnant wife on the SYC breakwater to watch. In my limited experience, all under tutelage, exiting the SYC harbour area with the Gwen was always a dead beat to windward involving several tacks through reasonably densely moored yachts. It was not for beginners. I thought I knew enough even though this day the wind we had to tack through was gusting about 20 knots. On the occasions I had done so with my SYC tutor, it was always a fraught exercise with the Gwen. The problem was its spread of canvas meant it was a speedy thing in any breeze on all points of sail. In its day it was one of the fastest 12' sailboats in the world. In my experience, it was either almost stationery in the course of executing a tack or it was flying.

The yacht rigged and placed in the water, off we shot. The hull hummed and vibrated as it sped through the water. It beggars belief that the junior members by the dinghy racks were not looking forward to spectator entertainment. Au contraire Toni, Brian's wife, on the end of the breakwater, as I learned later, was expecting no more than to witness two gentlemen proceeding soberly in a sailboat. I think the first tack albeit eventful was managed successfully. The awful truth dawned on me that I had failed to properly secure the attachment point for the mainsail sheet [control rope]. Next this live vibrating thing conveying us was assailing with its bowsprit an elderly and dowdy looking moored yacht which I believe was a mooring saver. The tip of the bowsprit poked out one of its windows. Then it was off again, such that we somehow exited the mooring area and were abeam of the lifesaving clubhouse on the shore.

Next thing we were over. While we were struggling to right it, a lifesaver swam out to help. Suddenly, we were up and speeding out to sea. A bewildered lifesaver passenger was now on board. The further we sped out to sea the more concerned he appeared. I decided to put in a shoreward tack. This was done, after a fashion. When we reached roughly the position where the lifesaver had joined us, he elected to abandon ship. Our last sighting was of him swimming strongly shoreward. Unbeknown to me at the time, this drama was proximate to Toni's onshore position. As reported to me, she became almost helpless with laughter. It was time to retreat to the clubhouse. That course was almost directly downwind and easily laid. My confidence had been smashed. I needed more sailing lessons. The Christmas holidays were imminent. My plan for these was easy. I would master my Gwen 12.

The Gwen fleet in Australia died out in the eighties. As fibreglass hulls came in timber went out. Those that are sailed these days are restored older boats. But what a wonderful boat on which to learn to sail. Unfortunately, later events were to deny me this learning pleasure. What happened was this.

In late 1962, I bought a 1938 Oldsmobile. It came from somewhere in the Brighton area. As well as to my eye looking just right, American cars of this vintage were mechanically very simple and durable. A straight 6-cylinder side-valve motor transmitted power to the rear wheels via a 3-speed manual gearbox. It was in remarkably good condition save for unavoidable mechanical wear occasioned by light but consistent service. Even the original paintwork, lightish grey with a touch of green was in top condition. The all-steel body was tight. No rust. The doors closed snugly with reassuring clunks. The interior leather trim showed little sign of wear. All indicators that it had spent an undemanding life under cover. There was nothing about its mechanical condition to suggest its seller had done much other than to properly service the car with suitable lubricants since its original purchase. If things like brake linings, piston rings, the clutchplate and radiator were replaced it would be good for at least another 100,000 miles. The driver's door lock was non-operational.

Matt, Reg and Keith Bowen at Valonia Motors in Surrey Hills [now the site of a Chinese Restaurant] attended to all but the defective door lock. The car had been in my ownership for about 3 weeks. During the course of the repairs the cylinder bore wear was found to be inconsequential. No new car could have driven better after the work was done. Hills, of which there were many about Surrey Hills, Balwyn and Camberwell, were surmounted as if they were not there. Sure, it lacked the electronic gimcrackery of a modern car but that meant there was dramatically less to go wrong. In an ideal world I would have liked air conditioning, to substitute fuel injection for the carburettor, to convert the engine from side valve to overhead valve configuration and add seat belts and head supports.

But I was not to enjoy my marvellous car for more than a few weeks. In December 1962, shortly before Christmas, I parked it one evening outside the Rivoli Theatre at Camberwell. Scattered about the back seat and floor were my

Gwen 12 sails and a classy telescope I had bought at auction not long before. I had failed to remove the distributor cap. When I returned, to drive home, no car. I filed a police theft report that evening. To this day no Oldsmobile for me, its rightful owner. The car was not insured against theft.

Money always being tight for me, replacement of the yacht sails was out of the question. My learner sailing programme had been overtaken by events. However, I had heard it was not uncommon for yachts returning to the mainland after the Sydney to Hobart race to be short of crew. A new holiday plan was developed. I would travel to Hobart to attempt to secure a seagoing berth back to Melbourne. If I succeeded my planned sailboat learning would translate to a different level.

Among the magnificent craft tied up at Hobart's Constitution Dock - not least among them American Sumner [Huey] Long's alloy 57' state of the then art and Hobart race fastest time winner, the Tripp designed yawl Ondine - was the relatively nondescript and unassuming 30' timber-hulled Ailsa from Brighton Yacht Club in Melbourne. I was to learn she had been designed by noted US naval architect Philip Rhodes back in the thirties and built in Sydney. Her original build had included a bowsprit but this had been discarded. The powerful hull had shortish ends. She sported a 7/8 rig and a laid teak or white beech deck. This last was overdue for re-caulking. Hence the eventual trip to Melbourne up the Tasmanian east coast and across Bass Strait was rather wetter below deck than it needed to be. Because of its low rating for the Hobart race handicap purposes and how well it was sailed, Ailsa had been close to taking the coveted overall handicap victory for that year's race. In the event, Vic Meyer's Solo took out the handicap honours.

Although my credentials as a Gwen 12 yacht owner secured me a berth on John Marion's Ailsa, when the embryonic nature of that ownership later became apparent at sea, John was annoyed. He was concerned that the trip we were undertaking was not for beginners. However, once we were underway, beating to windward up the Tasmanian coast, the demands of the trip soon relegated John's concern as something to further discuss after we landed.

Before we got seriously under way, we stopped off for a regatta and party at the village of Orford. Red wine flowed freely. Early the next morning, it was up sails and off. A strong wind warning was no deterrent to John. I was not alone in paying the price for claret consumption. Even John, as he did a radio sked late that morning needed a bucket by his side. Yet no listener to John would have guessed he was other than gung-ho and enjoying the brisk conditions. The crew of the Jervis Bay Naval Academy 36' Tam O'Shanter having decided to wait out the strong wind warning, the tone of its master addressing John over the sked was distinctly respectful.

Thereafter, John was a serious passage maker. It was a dead to windward beat every inch of the way north up the coast. Each of the three of us took turns on the helm. It was wet on deck and not much less so below courtesy of the leaking laid deck. I succumbed to serious almost disabling dry retching. The blood red of the claret turned green with bile. My spasms were no fewer than hourly. I [barely] kept going as I stood my turns at the helm. Reefing about 3am one morning was a dour affair with our only other crew member Peter [Fewster?] electing to so accept the wet conditions both above and below deck that he undertook his reefing duty nude. The berths were damp but when the chance offered, we slept.

The weather turned for our Bass Strait crossing. It enabled an almost dead downwind run. Consistent with his full-on approach, John organised the setting of 2 headsails one poled out either side. We were flying. The leaking from the deck abated. My dry retching likewise. Our landfall was off the Gippsland coast in glorious sunshine and about 10-15 knots of wind.. By late afternoon we were closing the entrance to Port Philip Bay.

According to our pilot book, the difference between the tide going in or out depended on whether the lighthouse was displaying balls or cones. Certainly, there were some objects displayed. For the life of us we were unable to determine their shape. John's answer was to drop the headsail and stooge about the entrance until dawn the next day. Unable to determine the shapes any better that dawn, John put out a radio call for anyone on radio who had tide tables. The yacht Winston Churchill came through loud and clear. A healthy tide was ingoing, so in we went, with increasing wind behind us for a furious sail up the bay to the Brighton Yacht Club [BYC]. We arrived there in roughly mid-morning. Unless you were sailing downwind, as we had been, the weather was far from ideal for enjoyable sailing. We saw only the one well reefed down yacht exit the BYC. A strong wind warning was out. I had learned a major sailing lesson.

Back in Melbourne, all was not lost on my personal automotive front. Matt Bowen had a garage customer with a 1929 Nash sedan for sale. The car was sound. The price was 20 pounds. I was in. On the debit side that car body had issues. The left side timber framing where the centre-post connected with the roof had rotted. My solution was to rope together the doors and pillar on that side. The Nash had marvellous mechanicals and served me well for years. Even the brakes were up to the job. My more well- heeled friends assumed it was my preference over a more modern vehicle.

My next step involved a lovely, apparently rarely used, 28' yacht on the hard at SYC. It never crossed my mind to attempt to become more or less permanent crew on other rich men's yachts. This is the prescription offered by American Norris Hoyt in his entertaining book "Addicted to Sail." Norris didn't just crew—he crewed on elite yachts with the best in the business. His ex-Olympic swimmer background would have done him no harm when he looked for a berth. To enhance his desirability as crew, he often took photographs and presented copies to owners. A day job as an educator allowed him more free time than most. He was able to narrate how he was resting below on a newly launched 70' Olin Stephens design out for sea trials in heavy weather, with the designer on board. All was peace and tranquillity below deck. The hatch to the deck slid open. In a quiet understated tone, Olin Stephens, no less, politely asked Hoyt if he could go to help on deck. There he found another world, of gale force winds, turbulent seas, turmoil, and action aplenty. His help proved essential. On another occasion, he joined a couple on a Swan 40' yacht for a Trans-

Atlantic passage. Midway the weather blew up into a mighty storm. His heart quailed. He kept his thoughts to himself. Water was breaking over the bridge of a large ship in their vicinity. At the height of that storm, the owners innocently confided in him that, without his presence and experience, they would have been gravely worried.

The then sailing apple of my eye bore the name Calore. Built to a post-World War 11 Ralph Winslow design, including rarely published hull lines, that featured in the US *Rudder* magazine, the timber hull had been constructed to a very high standard by club member Maynard Mappin. Its white beech planking was such that it was difficult by external inspection to conclude whether the hull was not of fibreglass. I was to learn through ownership that the timber mast was far too tall and heavy for the hull and the interior was not much more than basic. All part of the learning curve. Calore's owner, builder Ken Wansborough, was asking what seemed to me to be a reasonable price on terms with 5% interest and quarterly rests. I was hooked. It became my pleasure to take John Marion out for a sail.

Calore was seriously over-canvassed. In stronger winds the result was acute weather helm. It was no exaggeration to say that, when the wind was up, the helmsman needed a block and tackle to manage the tiller. My naval architect mate, Ken Hope, drew plans for a new rig that saw about an 8' reduction in mast height. Jack Savage's Williamstown yard contracted to construct the new timber spar and the necessary new rigging. This was after a labour swap gentlemen's handshake agreement I had come to with German boatbuilder migrant Gert Leitzke had failed. I had pre-delivered his divorce, but he refused to meet any boatbuilding side of the deal. I removed the oversize spar at SYC. For all I know, it remains to this day in the yard there where I abandoned it. I then motored my mast-less yacht over to Williamstown for Jack to do the new mast.

I had thought for the short time involved in the water, I could avoid anti-fouling the hull. It was over a two-week period. Jack returned me a vessel that was infinitely more tractable. From its previous reputation as a tender boat, it was able to earn a new reputation as a stiff one. Acute weather helm was a thing of the past. So far as I was able to make out, the reduced weight aloft and consequent diminished sail area. in no way detracted from sailing performance. My assumption that a week or two in the water could not be harmful to my super smooth unprotected bottom was proven to be a serious error. It took the best part of another weekend to remove a remarkable shell encrustation and restore the bottom ready for anti-fouling. Another mainsail was needed for the shortened mast and for this sailing tragic mate John Michie put me in touch with a new sailmaker named Arnall. All in all it was a costly exercise, but it produced a dramatically better boat. Ken Wansborough knew something when he sold his boat. I was a wiser owner when assessing a boat with galvanised rigging, iron keel ballast and internal lead ballast and an excessive rig for the hull.

Sad to say, I never undertook any significant passages with Calore. One reason was my purchase agreement precluded me exiting Calore from Port Philip Bay until she had been paid for. About the same time as my purchase,

Karelia, a very similar yacht, possibly a sister ship, was bought by ex-Battle of Britain Spitfire pilot Jack Brookes. Early in his ownership, Jack decided to sail through Port Philip Heads one weekend. The unfortunate consequence, depicted on page 1 of the Melbourne Age the following Monday, was an image of the mast top protruding from the ocean as Karelia's completely submerged hull perched on the Corsair Reef.

Three of my Calore passages come to mind. The first, under the original rig, was in one of Melbourne's premier around Port Philip Bay overnight yacht races. My only crew was Gert Leitzke at a happier stage of our commercial relationship. Gert, as the more experienced, dictated no reduction in sail as we proceeded dead to weather in increasing wind. Calore was almost flat in the water before we reached the weather mark at the south of the bay. As we freed up for the next mark, we were treated to the magnificent moonlit spectacle of Tom Buza's snugly reefed-down Hereshoff 36 ketch Katrina storming by on a tight reach. We must have done something right to have been ahead of Katrina at that time. I was overtaken again by sea sickness. We returned to SYC the next morning with tails between our legs, albeit wiser. John Marion was to comment the weather and sea conditions for that race were more unpleasant than anything he had previously encountered in the ocean.

Calore was entered in another bay race under the new rig and with a favourable handicap. On this occasion as we were slipping the mooring at SYC to make the start line, courtesy of John Michie and his generous mate one Bryson, we were dropped off a loan Dragon class spinnaker. We were bowling along beautifully towards the south end of the bay when we ran out of water in the vicinity of the Pope's Eye mark. As Calore was lifted and dropped on the hard sand bottom by the modest swell we had to anchor and wait for the ingoing tide hoping withal the harsh bottom contacts would not cause hull damage. When we were freed some hours later it was back to SYC. Another lesson learned.

Then there was a rare, completely non-pressure, Easter cruise intended for around the Bay. I was accompanied by Peter Robinson. We set out around sunset on the Friday. Weather came up and we were hard on the wind. A few hours later and we were becalmed in dead still conditions. We were not that far from shore, but our navigation had gone to hell during the earlier blustery conditions. It was decided to lower the dinghy and send a lifejacketed Peter to row ashore and scale the cliff face fronting us to see if he could place our location. I was to wait on board the motionless Calore. The masthead light was illuminated. My wait was well over one hour. Peter was able to report we were close to Mornington. He had startled a car enclosed couple abutting his position as he scrabbled over the cliff edge to terra firma. The iron wind auxiliary motor was fired up and it wasn't long before we were comfortably anchored and sound asleep inside the modest-sized Mornington anchorage.

That turned out to be the far point of the Easter cruise. As luck would have it, the lovely timber classic yacht Nerida was tied up alongside the jetty. An elderly yachtie, who appeared to be its minder, invited us aboard that evening to help him consume what he described as his yacht's limitless supplies of Bells Scotch whisky. It came in beautiful bell-shaped bottles. We did our best and were the worse for wear for it. The next day the weather broke and strong winds prevailed. It was either press on or accept another invitation to help demolish the incomparable Bells. We chose the latter. Next we knew, it was time to return to SYC.

Had we but known it at the time, Nerida is a, if not the, grand dame of Australian yachting. She was from the design board of Scotsman Alfred Mylne, built for Tom Hardy in Adelaide by G.T. Searles and Sons and launched in 1933. Tom died in a plane crash in 1938. She then went through various hands until 1971 when she was brought back into the Hardy family by Tom's son Sir James Hardy. My visit aboard was in about 1962. She won the 1950 Sydney- Hobart race under the ownership of South Australian oenologist Colin Haselgrove. At one time converted to a yawl rig and from tiller to wheel steering, Sir James re-converted her to the original designed tiller steered gaff cutter. I think the Hobart race win was under the converted arrangement. Overall hull length ex bowsprit is 45'. Nerida has spent most of her life in Adelaide and later Sydney. We had stumbled upon her on what must have been a short sojourn in Melbourne.

Somewhere about this time, I took bushwalking mate and sailing neophyte Jack O'Halloran sailing on Calore. Jack, originally from Melbourne was to be burned out in the Hobart bushfires of 1967. He quit Tasmania to set up law practice in Canberra. It was there he bought his own yacht and undertook extensive Pacific cruising.

About late 1962, SYC member, retiree Stan Field, who owned the 27' sloop Kilki and who was cruising around the Whitsundays in Queensland, let it be known SYC members were welcome to join him. I arranged a visit for October when I joined Stan at Proserpine in the Queensland Whitsunday area. At about the same time Calore's builder, Maynard Mappin, joined us. Maynard was reaching the final stage of construction of a Trippe-designed 33' replacement for Calore.

Courtesy of SYC yard carpenter Jimmy Sly, Kilki had been given an interior fit-out modelled on that of renowned cruising yachtsman Eric Hiscock's 30' Wanderer 111. The North Queensland October was far from what I had been expecting. It was hot, mostly still and humid. I realise now it was about the worst time to go sailing in the tropics. It was build-up time for the wet season.

We tied Kilki up to careening poles and scrubbed and re-antifouled the bottom. Lunch one day was oysters straight off pilings. Late one afternoon, we visited a tourist resort island. There, Stan and Maynard's latent aggression was compounded by alcohol. I chose to sleep on the beach until they decided to return to the yacht. When I went looking for my comrades some hours later, they were nowhere to be seen. Apart from a sort of beachside staff knees-up to musical accompaniment, the resort was dead. I had to make do—this time under an upturned dinghy. I never slept well.

Come morning, there was no sign of Kilki. I made my way to the resort dining room to report. There, I felt a less than welcoming vibe. It turned out Stan and Maynard had become so aggressive they had been expelled from the island when I was in the first stage of my beach sleeping. While I was learning of the events of the preceding evening, a phone call came through from my shipmates. They had hoisted sail in the still conditions and woken up at daybreak off the mainland coast. For all they knew then, I had tumbled over the side. .They gave every indication of relief to hear my voice. Later that day I was picked up. The voyage continued.

My adventure to the Whitsundays concluded with an overnight trip to Bundaberg. En route, a swarm of houseflies boarded. Later, after dark, the sea and weather came up. As I was half sleeping, I heard one wave strike the bow with a resounding thump. That was shortly followed by the whoosh of a major fall of water in the cockpit with an almost simultaneous cry of anguish from Maynard who was on the tiller. Next morning, we wound our way up the Bundaberg River to the port and I disembarked.

About this time, I accepted an invitation of an afternoon sail on Sydney Harbour with Vic Meyer [1905-1993] on his redoubtable Alan Payne-designed 57' steel Solo. I learned a flogging sheet on a boat that size is akin to an iron bar, also that Vic was not sanguine about ever launching his craft when the hull welding was complete. But complete it he did, in 1955, to leave an indelible mark on the Australian ocean racing scene over the next 10 years. Better known victories included 4 Sydney to Hobarts [2 on handicap, 2 fastest time], 5 Brisbane to Gladstone and a Trans-Tasman Auckland to Sydney.

At the time of my sail, he had been forced into the realisation that Solo could no longer realistically compete for the winner's circle unless he incurred the considerable expense of converting his mast to alloy from timber. This was to be able to sustain the rigging pressures to minimise forestay fall off when beating to windward. His timber mast could no longer cut it. Virtually every competitive ocean racer had gone over to alloy to absorb pressures timber was unable to take. Subsequently, Vic took on a number of Australian circumnavigations, the first alone, followed by 3 all girl-crewed global circumnavigations. His last attempted Australian circumnavigation was with a lady by the name of Olga. Solo ran aground on Fraser Island. Vic married the 25-year old Olga in about 1965. He sold Solo about 1977 after notching up over 300,000 miles in her. Olga died in a motor accident while the couple were mango farming.

Sydney Harbour on a sunny afternoon even with a southerly buster was one thing. Traversing with Solo the wild waters south of Australia in the course of an anticlockwise circumnavigation of Australia was quite another. At the height of an especially nasty patch of weather, Vic's then sole crew was getting 40 Sundays churchgoing equivalence of proximity to and respect for God. Vic was on deck at the height of the storm, shrieking imprecatory challenges into the gale's crashing thunder and flickering lightning.

The last report available to me concerning Solo is that her steel hull was badly corroded, large unpaid storage fees had been incurred for her and she was threatened with the wrecker's torch. There were many prospective penniless user/purchasers for all manner of apparently worthy projects provided all the money came from the pockets of others. Sic Transit Gloria.

In 1963, about two years into my stewardship of Calore, I sold my law practice. I was free with a very modest sum in cash reserve. The operative word was freedom. I had worked hard over three years and learned much as a sole city practitioner, but I was not prepared then to embark on a life's work without exploring other options. The experience was to serve me well when I opened a law practice in Darwin years later.

Then it was I came into contact with Philip Wheat, the owner of the 44' (or thereabouts) Francis Herreshoff design ketch Windsong 1V. A son of the redoubtable wizard of Bristol, Nathaniel Herreshoff, Windsong's designer was from a notable Rhode Island US sailing family. Apart from yacht design, he was an idiosyncratic editor and author of books and magazine articles. My first contact with Philip was through meeting yachtie Neville Hoffman at the Melbourne Public Library, not long after Neville had recovered from a nasty fall. He was working at the masthead of his own slipped yacht when he found his perspective changing. The mast had not been properly secured. Neville was fortunate to survive.

I wound up as one of Philip's crew, with the title of bosun, for his imminent planned voyage to the US west coast. The decision was made to sell Calore. I met Melbourne Tech librarian and ex-Antarctic expeditioner Jack and architect Dick Holden. Together with Neville, we pitched in helping prepare the boat. I bought and packed an old Bolex 16mm reflex clockwork movie camera to record something of the voyage.

Windsong was of timber hull construction, 44' to 46' ex bowsprit in overall length and of moderate displacement. Beam was about 13', draft about 6' and the rig was Bermudan ketch with heavily sternward raked masts, A clipper bow with bowsprit, bold sheer-line and counter stern showed above the water. A distinctive feature was a substantial timber framed glass screen ahead of the helmsman's position, designed to shield from spray across the deck when going to windward. The underwater shape was of a long keel and slackish bilges with external lead ballast. As was characteristic of the design type, the rudder was angled back from the vertical and attached to the rear of the underbody. She was what is described as a character yacht. At the time, many of her smaller ilk in the form of Herreshoff 28s were sailing regularly in club yacht racing in Port Philip Bay. You might say she was a blown up H28. Fit out down below was basic but all essentials were there. At the time in my limited experience it was not uncommon to find yachts equipped with Brooke and Gatehouse style wind speed and direction instruments, an electronic log or speedo, but Windsong had none of these. There must have been an SSB radio. A more contemporary and more pleasing, albeit considerably more expensive, fibreglass representation of the Herreshoff 44 character yacht concept of about the same overall dimensions, is the Cherubini 44 yacht built in the US.

Calore was sold to SYC mate, advertising man Cy Cater. In short order Cy commissioned SYC yard boat builder Jimmy Sly to modify the interior to mirror as much as practicable that of the Hiscock's Laurent Giles-designed 30' Wanderer 111. A new, even shorter, mast, his time alloy, at the time rather avant-garde, was installed. She finished up as lovely and seaworthy a 28-footer as you could imagine. Last I knew of Calore, she appeared for sale in Queensland in the pages of Australian boat sale publication Trade A Boat.

It was some time towards the end of January of 1964 we set sail. The plan was to make New Zealand our first stopover. All was well as we were proximate to Refuge Cove a small inlet around Wilsons Promontory. I got out the Bolex and from a position on the end of the bowsprit filming back towards the cockpit secured what turned out to be some crystal sharp Kodachrome movie footage. The westerly wind driving us was picking up. Philip floated the possibility of sheltering in Refuge Cove. I was far from enthusiastic. After all, we were en route to the remote reaches of the Pacific. Looking back, we could have hove to until the weather passed. I am not sure if we had any up-to-date weather forecast for Bass Strait or, if we had, that it did justice to the weather system that came up behind us.

As Refuge Cove receded, the weather intensified. Overnight, it reached such a state and the following seas become so steep that all sail had been doused. During the day, warps were trailed over the stern to slow down the boat speed. Helming was far from easy. As the following sea became progressively steeper, the hazard was that the bow would dig in and we would pitchpole.

In 1956, off Cape Horn, the much-travelled adventurers/litterateurs Miles and Beryl Smeaton accompanied by John Guzzwell aboard the 1939 Hong Kong built 46′ Bermudan ketch Tzu Hang were fortunate to survive such a pitchpole event. Beryl, who had been on the helm, was tossed from the boat and injured. Tzu Hang was dismasted, partially submerged, and the topsides were severely damaged. Miraculously, the three managed to navigate the damaged vessel to Chile for extensive repairs. A year later, the Smeetons set out again to round Cape Horn. In approximately the same position, beset by storms, another pitchpole related dismasting took place. Again, they managed to make the coast of Chile. The name Tzu Hang meant under the protection of "Guanyin," the Daoist goddess of the sea and protector of sailors.

Much worse was the fate of the 52' Winston Churchill in the 1998 Hobart race. Crossing Bass Strait, she was caught beam on to the massively built up near vertical seas and dropped into the trough. The drop impact dislodged the caulking from her carvel planked hull causing her to founder and sink. Three lives were lost.

Our survival depended on keeping the stern at as near as could be managed to a right angle to the following sea and reliance on the warps to slow us to a less dangerous speed. A steering breakdown, as likely occurred on Winston Churchill, would have been disastrous. Before the system eased, everything on board that was able to be added to the warps was being trailed. Still the weather built up. Well into our ordeal, architect Dick Holden estimated the distance from trough to crest was about 80'. I saw no reason to disagree. Gazing back at the massive wall of water as waves came up astern, I quailed at the power of the sea. I looked back no more than I had to. My measure of wind strength was my ears being blown forward—and this when we were moving at hull speed before it. In the troughs it was dead still. Then, the oncoming almost vertical wave would lift the stern and up we would be taken as Windsong plunged down the face of the foaming wave. I was relieved from one of my turns in the galley preparing food after something like 3 dry retching episodes over 15 minutes,

There may have been another way of coping with our weather system. Bernard Moitessier [1925-1998] a French colon from Vietnam, was an intrepid sailor of considerable celebrity achieved through his voyage writings. One claim to fame was, when victory in the 1978 first Golden Globe single handed round the world yacht race was within his grasp, he decided to turn his back on adulation. In the home stretch, heading north in the vicinity of the Falklands, he turned south, doubled the Horn and set course for Tahiti. Arrival at his destination completed another half circumnavigation. He claimed that decision was in the interest of his spiritual development. Another explanation he gave to a confidant was to avoid an obligatory victor's kiss from Charles de Gaulle.

On an earlier late 1965 voyage from France to Tahiti via the Horn [the subject of his second book, *Cape Horn the Logical Route*, still in his 40" steel-hulled very long-keeled ketch Joshua, he found himself in survival mode in the Southern Ocean running under bare poles before a weather system similar to ours. Crew comprised his wife, Francoise. The self- steering system had broken down. He helmed from below deck positioned under a perspex observation dome. Five warps the ends of which were weighted with iron pigs and old rolled up fishing nets were trailed astern. Joshua's decks were regularly wave-swept end to end. Twenty-four hours into the system, steering difficulty in a by then gigantic sea caused Joshua to broach and be knocked down. Later, as the stern was kicked up by an oncoming wave the bow buried up to the mainmast.

The danger of pitchpoling was acute. Withal, as the hull was steel, it was dry below decks although the boat's violent movement had thrown much stored there into a chaotic jumble. It was then Moitessier, with his wife's help to look it out, consulted his on board copy of a book authored by Argentinean Vito Dumas. In it was detailed a method of dealing with similar conditions in a much smaller boat. This was to maintain some sail and keep up with the following sea by surfing before it at speeds of up to 15 knots. This measure was supported by another chronicler Pilot Bohlin, a schooner skipper from Massachusetts. Intellectually unable to accept this proposition and after more than 24 hours continuous helming, Moitessier then reports hearing the voice of Dumas telling: "Here, I'll show you." The voice was followed immediately by a wave causing Joshua to surf, then yaw and heel heavily, topsides forward in such a way as to have them act like a ski, bearing her up. Needing no more demonstration, impetuously and perhaps in the circumstances unwisely, Moitessier went on deck and cut the warps. Fortunately for him and his wife, Joshua's handling was transformed. Steered so she took the waves at about 15-20 degrees off dead astern, she heeled, resting her bow in the trough and all but planed. Steering was easy. The seas came under her quarter. As he wrote:

"Everything had changed because a dead seaman had replied to my insistent question. Five blows with my knife had freed Joshua from the chains she had been dragging. A small gesture but what a difference."

In the third day of our massive weather system, I was on the helm. As Windsong rose to the crest of an especially nasty wave, the breaking crest surfed over the stern flinging me through the toughened glass of the screen in front of the cockpit. Were I not wearing a safety harness, it is likely I would have been washed overboard. My violent wave-induced forward shove ripped me from the tiller. It must also have brought me into contact with the motor start button. The immediate aftermath saw Windsong surfing at a 45-degree angle across the face of the errant wave, dangerously assisted by the full power of the activated motor. While I was regrouping from the cabin top, where the surf left me, back to the helm, the hatchway accessing the yacht accommodation slid open to reveal a startled face. I shouted above the weather to explain what had happened. Fortunately, the sea had removed all broken glass from the deck and I had suffered no cuts. Bruising was another matter.

Jack came on deck to assist so that one of us either side of the tiller could reduce the workload and make it safer. I still recall Jack's words: "You are steering for your life" I needed no telling. Philip was operating the hand bilge pump below decks. I could hear the pump action for long after there was any indication of water being picked up. By the time I came off watch, I thought I could detect some very slight abatement of the weather. With hindsight, I believe the breaking wave crest was the high point of our ordeal. If the hatchway had not been closed Windsong would have been pooped and sunk by that breaker. I was relieved to be able to return to my reasonably dry bunk. Curled up there was reassuring, even if, as was the fact, such a feeling was utterly unfounded. The feeling accorded with the observation of Windsong's designer made many years previously:

> "The cabin of a small yacht is truly a wonderful thing. Not only will it shelter you from the tempest, but in the other troubles of life which may be more disturbing it is a safe retreat."

Equally appropriate, was another observation from the same source:

> "If you spent the night alone in an open boat in a thunderstorm it will bring you closer to God than going to church 40 Sundays."

Amid my fitful slumbering, I mentally made ready to struggle for access to the yacht life-raft if Windsong went down. This was despite my reservations about how any life-raft could weather the conditions. I may have been drawn closer to God but I had no desire to meet him in the hereafter just then. One cameo I remember is of Dick climbing out of his sodden forward bunk to stand and proclaim his wetness. None of us said a word. A chastened Dick returned to his bunk.

Windsong endured the dangerous conditions for about 72 hours in all. As the wind abated, a still hazardous lumpen swell was left over. Another yacht about 40' in length materialised not far distant from our position. The hopelessly tangled warps were drawn in, Philip attempted a sextant sight that put us around Alice Springs. A radio call was put through to the Deputy Director of Navigation. The advice: "Steer northwest and you will hit Australia." That course was laid. Food was prepared. Sail was raised. No more than about 24 hours later, we entered the fishing boat harbour at Ulladulla and tied up alongside. We could dry out the boat. Dick was off to Melbourne to re-establish contact with his girl- friend. Philip played a number of stirring single track records of Greek fishermen vocal tunes. We had been very fortunate.

At the height of the weather, I had failed to get the Bolex out of its protective wrapping. My reason for passing up recording imagery of what we had faced was a combination of near totally disabling sea sickness and a mental prioritisation of survival over all else. Moreover, there was so much water about the deck it was very likely the Bolex would have been seriously if not irretrievably salt water damaged if it had been brought out. The conditions we had experienced must have been similar to what caused death and havoc to the Sydney-to-Hobart ocean race fleet a few years later in 1998.

Lessons learned? The older rudder design, attached as it is to the trailing end of the long keeled underwater shape is too far forward for controlled running at any speed downwind. The angle at which it is set back from the vertical doesn't help. Cruising yacht doyen and writer Eric Hiscock had his last yacht built of timber in New Zealand. Thirty eight foot in overall length, it was a beautiful object to behold. But, Eric's joy of ownership was dramatically diminished by acute and almost uncontrollable weather helm. The ultimate diagnosis was the attachment of the rudder to the rear of the underwater body and its abnormally acute rearward angling. Rectification extended to the complete repositioning of the rudder to a vertical position with a new rudder post well aft.

Windsong's builder Captain Walker asked Philip later, after the storm was described to him: "Why didn't you heave- to until the weather passed?" If I had to resail that storm in a full underbody long keeled monohull ketch with conventional rudder placement that is what I would consider, at least initially. I would also be mindful that the likes of Moitessier would never consider heaving to in the Southern Ocean.

The Moitessier solution? Relevant considerations are that Joshua was all boat and once the decision is made to tow warps it is not easy to decide to change. Not every sailor can rely on direct supernatural assistance. As to the first, Joshua sported a transom hung rudder at the end of a canoe stern and the underwater profile being almost rectangular.it was utterly devoid of any pretensions of reduction in wetted area. If anything, it would have been difficult to increase this wetted area for its overall boat length of 40'. The ballast ratio was modest to say the least. The rudder could not have been further aft. This fact, together with the extraordinary length of underwater body meant Joshua had a high degree of inherent self-steer. But, given its steel hull and considerable weight in the hull rather than as ballast, Joshua would have been an absolute dog in tropical trade wind passages, if one was to design a vessel for use limited to the Southern Ocean it had few obvious disadvantages other than that there were far better modern approaches to hull design and sail handling. It was a sort of sailing submarine.

I suppose the answer here is, if one has no wish to heave to, the "suck it and see" approach should work. Or in ultimate adverse conditions heave to until that is impracticable bearing in mind Moitessier never would consider such a course in the Southern Ocean. Then, traverse the following sea at an angle of about 15 to 20 degrees from dead astern being prepared to trail warps or a Jordan series drogue– always bearing in mind the essential design elements of Joshua could not be more different to those incorporated in a cruising yacht of modern design such as the centre cockpit single-masted Najad 380 of Madame Socrates. And, at all times be aware that other iconic deep-water sailors like William Robinson, the Smeetons and the Hiscocks consider application of the Moitessier/Dumas principle would be foolhardy.

A word on Jeanne Socrates is called for. Born in 1942, she and her late husband had never sailed before they took up sailing in their fifties. she came to hold the record for the oldest woman to have achieved a single-handed non-stop circumnavigation.[26] As I write [Dec 2018] she has rounded the Horn and is en route to South Africa in the course of a planned non-stop solo circumnavigation via the 5 great capes aboard her centre cockpit Najad 380 Neriad [loa 37.89', lwl 32.48', sail area 691 sq ft, beam 11.97', draft 6.4', displacement 20,052lbs, ballast lead 6334lbs, ballast ratio 34%]—an exponentially superior vessel to Joshua although of about the

---

[26] Katy Stickland, "77, and sails non-stop around the world," *Yachting Monthly*, 7 May 2020. Jeanne Socrates: 77 & solo non-stop around the world - Yachting Monthly/

same length. In ultimate storm conditions and given sufficient sea-room, she is fulsome in her praise of deployment from the stern [where it is always stored at sea] of the Jordan series drogue. This drogue comprises a line up to several hundred feet long to which is attached a number of cones. Jordan, a retired aeronautical engineer, devised a freely available formula, involving length and number of cones, for construction of the drogue dependent on the dimensions and weight of the craft using it. If it is to be used, the sailor would be well advised to prepare in advance the point or points of attachment and the manner of retrieval. Celebrity professional yachtsman Skip Novak, who conducts sailing operations around Cape Horn, decries the use of a drogue as much for any other reason that laying it out in ultimate conditions is not for the faint-hearted, let alone retrieval.

It would be remiss of me not to supply some background to the Moitessier/Joshua story.[27] Bernard Moitessier [1925-1994] grew up as a gilded child of a well to do Vietnamese colonial family. He was a top tennis player and winner of an Asian Games 100 metre freestyle swimming event. As well as being up to modern playboy standards with wine and women, he had received a good education, especially in the classics and could write well. As a solitary sailor in the fifties he lost two sailboats named Marie Therese on reefs, the first, a Chinese junk off Diego Garcia and the second off the West

---

[27] See "Bernard Moitessier" in Wikipedia: https://en.wikipedia.org/wiki/Bernard_Moitessier/

Indies. Marie Therese 11 was to his own design, of timber construction with a canoe stern, 28' in length.

Soon after, in France, while he worked first as a medical detailer and later a boat salesman, he wrote and had published his first book "Vagabond of the South Seas." That book enjoyed runaway sales. Post publication, he was approached by naval architect Jean Knocker with whom, over 12 months or more, he resolved the dimensions [39'6" loa, 32'9" lwl, 12' beam, and 5'3" draft, ballast 6,610 ponds, displacement 15 tons, ballast ratio 21%, sail area, ketch, 1,100 square ft] and style of Joshua. The nature and placement of ballast is not given leading me to suspect it is iron mixed with cement placed in the bilges. I am not able to say whether the design was intended for steel construction.

About the same time, Moitessier was approached by a Monsieur Fracaul, a French metalworking industrialist and yachtsman who had devised a novel method of minimum framed steel yacht construction. The key was heavier than usual steel plate. Fracaul would build Joshua as a prototype, using the new method and charge only the cost of materials. So Joshua came to be launched at Marseilles in 1962. The name is a tribute to the original global single-handed sailor and writer Joshua Slocum. It would be 3 years before Moitessier would embark on Joshua's first voyage in 1965.

Australia's McIntyre Marine is sponsor of a 2022 rerun of the original Golden Globe Single Handed Around the World yacht race. Its name appears on an undated online offering from a Turkish boatyard to construct to a set specification a lookalike Joshua described as a GGOD [Golden Globe One Design] class for E300,000. US yacht designer Stephen

Waring is of the strong opinion that, for a modern, build Joshua's performance numbers are irrational. Her displacement to length ratio for example is 394 among some of the heaviest boats ever drawn. The offered price comes in at an amazingly cheap US$10 per pound. In Waring's view a purchaser would be very fortunate to build the boat for anywhere near E300,000. But as he says why would one anyway, to be stuck with a lump of a double-ender man-killer that'll guarantee you spend a year of your life soaking wet and going slow around the world. And, for mine, when a top spec Najad 380 can be purchased for US$225,000.

With Solo's success in Australian yachting Alan Payne was consulted by concerned yacht owners who had constructed steel, ocean racing yachts from plans for timber hulls. These boats floated well below the designed waterline. The explanation was the extra weight of the steel hulls. I have studied images of Joshua alongside those for a GGOD under construction. The waterline of the real Joshua is well above that of the GGOD. The topsides of Joshua show appreciably less freeboard than painted on the incomplete GGOD. There is nothing corklike about the flotation of a steel hull until its length gets up around 50' or so. Aluminium at any cost would have to be preferred to steel. After all, the hull represents no more than 30% of the cost of a properly fitted out sea going yacht.

It was Olin Stephens who brought rearward yacht rudder positioning into the mainstream. He moved Intrepid's from the rear of the hull underbody to a vertical position attached to a skeg further aft. In so doing he reduced wetted area and enabled more control with more precision. His example was so widely followed that very few, if any, yachts built for competition today incorporate an angled back rudder as an adjunct to the hull underbody.

I have sailed downwind in brisk conditions but a non-comparable sea state in a Mull designed Ranger 23 canoe-type, flattish-bottomed yacht hull body with a fin keel and separate well aft spade-rudder and been under effortless control. On a near run with a full spinnaker set, the bow has dipped slightly as wind strength and sea conditions combined to cause exciting bouts of utterly controlled surfing. The counter-side is my later acquired Olin Stephens designed S&S 30 yacht was always far from easy to manage in similar conditions to those I have described for the Ranger 23. The S&S 30 had a wineglass section underwater shape with a separate skeg mounted rudder positioned well aft. For running and reaching conditions in my view the Ranger 23 underwater configuration is streets ahead. Perhaps the height of the mast on the tall rig S&S 30 meant it was not suitable to carry a full spinnaker in heavier winds. When we did carry it, helming required more concentration than my skill was up to for more than about 10-minute intervals when it was evening, the wind was up, the weather overcast and the only point of reference to steer to was the masthead Windex wind direction indicator.

On one Ambon trip with Woetar, an Indonesian guest crewman, we had a wild period on deck with spinnaker control at night. Stampede was all over the ocean and spent some time dramatically heeled to port. When things were settled, Woetar was found curled up in the bow studying a survival manual entitled "Stay Alive." Woetar was a very experienced and competent seaman unaccustomed to and suddenly immersed in a new kind of sailing. A heavy weather spinnaker may have been a valid option, but I had none such in my sail inventory Eventually, I came to make my choice in heavier conditions by poling out the genoa and deploying a shooter on the other side. I experienced plenty of surfing with this rig but control was manageable. I doubt if my hull speed was reduced.

My S&S 30 with over 45-per cent ballast ratio was a marvellous yacht climbing to windward, as well as being feather light on the helm withal. I have covered long distances to windward under small jib and double reefed main with over 30-knots continuous being recorded on a slow wind gauge and the helm has been feather light. The problem then was twofold- driving through and falling off the backs of waves and coping with the cutting stream of eye level spray. I read about the modern monohull 50 to 60 foot round the world racers achieving over 800 nautical mile days running before gale strength winds in the Southern Ocean in yachts configured underwater in a similar fashion to the Ranger. I gather the trick here is to lock on to a weather system like Windsong encountered and endlessly surf before it. The last word on this subject is the framed quotation, attributed to Sir James Hardy and fixed below decks on Nerida: "Gentleman do not sail to windward."

As Windsong lay alongside at Ulladulla, Philip became preoccupied with preservation of Windsong's substantial tinned food stores. Water ingress during the storm had caused the labels to start disintegrating. All the many tins had to be coded for identification so the labels could be disposed of. Then the individual cans were coated with varnish to prevent rust. To fail to do this now would make the contents of every subsequent can opening a mystery. All indisputable sound practice, which probably should have been undertaken before departure from Melbourne. Meantime, I was mulling over Philip asserting, after he first saw my Bolex, that he would require an assignment to him of the copyright to any film taken of the voyage. In an earlier life, Philip had been a finance journalist on the staff of the long defunct Melbourne *Argus* newspaper when it folded. I assumed it would be only a matter of time before this issue was raised more directly. For all I knew, he had instructed solicitors to prepare the assignment document. As I saw it, Philip had become so preoccupied with monetarising the voyage in his sole interest that if I was to continue on his terms I would be likely to wind up as his unpaid employee. My vague opal mining plan came into clearer focus. For me, it was a better choice than attempting to please Philip. The result of this thinking was to lead me to challenge Philip's authority over me to join the canned food preservation team. As I had expected and hoped, that led to my dismissal from his crew. A free man again, I withdrew to Melbourne to regroup.

With Captain Walker added to the crew, I was to learn later that Windsong proceeded eastward from Ulladulla. How far she went is not known to me. However, some years later she was in Australia whether back or having never left I know not. I read in yachting magazine scuttlebutt of a festive event staged for the "Friends of Windsong." I was not invited.

Thereafter, my sailing life was put severely on hold until I arrived in Darwin ex Andamooka Opal Field in the latter part of 1968. If you think the geographic proximity of Andamooka's patch of hills, close as it is to the edge of the salt lake, Torrens, meant that it was close to a substantial body of water think again. Lake Torrens as one of Australia's inland salt lakes, has no depth of water. As I write this the thought occurs to me that the Lake may be a suitable venue for land yacht sailing when the surface is dry. Fat buoyant tyres would be de rigour for any experiment. I suspect Lake Hart near Woomera with a firmer dry surface is a better bet.

It wasn't long before I joined the Darwin Sailing Club. I was made most welcome. Neil Fowler designed [in some instances in collaboration with Roy Martin/] off the beach catamarans from 11' to 20' were big there. There was somewhat of a misguided view that the harbour with its big tides was sailable only with a catamaran. As Darwin developed during my residency from 1968 to 2013, that Club grew to a membership of over 3,000, making it numerically one of the largest sailing clubs in the world. Before long, I had bought an 18' catamaran and trailer from Kim Nicholls. It was named Mini B. This plywood centre-boarder was an exciting boat to sail, equipped as it was with a jib and trapeze. My prospects for racing victories with it were somewhat diminished by my ignorance of locations of racing marks in the Darwin Harbour. I had to follow a boat that seemed to know the way. Next, it was on to a Olympic one design 18' cat rigged fibreglass hulled A class Australis catamaran sold to me by Mark Hookham, the designer of the Australis class. This was a lovely looking boat with deep blue hulls edged with white and varnished timber decks. Instead of a centreboard there was a dagger board in each hull. The hull connection was via two alloy bars, the foremost supporting the mast and the deck between hulls was of stretched terylene. When it came along, there was a small fleet of identical yachts to compete with.

With both of these boats, steering while out on the trapeze was by a long rod connected via a universal joint to the mid- point of the bar connecting the rudders on each of the hulls. If the sailor was not on the trapeze this rod was left to trail over the stern and the bar alone sufficed to steer. My prime recall of the earlier boat is only not knowing the marks of the race course. And, as I dragged it down the beach at a Darwin wet season low tide to launch, being asked nicely by World Airlines flight attendants if they "could have a ride on your boat." Of my second catamaran, christened ID, two incidents come to mind.

In the first I was out on trapeze, trying to overtake another older, obviously not slower, design A class with its sailor likewise on trapeze. My cat was designed with very sharp bows. My rival's bows were quite the opposite. It was mid-afternoon and the breeze was fresh. We were on the fastest point of sailing a reach across the wind. I had looked under my boom to see how my rival was faring I was chuckling to myself as I saw the bow of his lee hull submerge slightly, thereby slowing him. In that same instant, my narrower and sharper lee bow did much more of the same. The hull became so buried my cat came to an abrupt halt from about 15 knots. Like a large pendulum, I was flung forward on the trapeze and pulled the boat right over in a complete pitchpole. I was abraded and bruised by the rigging. The boat became completely inverted. The trick to righting in this situation was to extend out the trapeze harness hook, attach it to the lee hull and then supporting my feet on the weather hull lean back. Eventually the lee inverted hull comes down correct side up and hopefully not on top of the sailor. Whilst I was so engaged, my competitor disappeared into the distance.

The second was more dramatic. I was out just sailing for the joy of it. Much of that joy was in the sheer sensation of speed over water. I was on my trapeze and on a screaming reach. There was no other vessel in the vicinity until, slightly ahead of my course, a Minx class catamaran appeared. It was sailed conservatively. Its sailor, Jack Haslam, was not using a trapeze. I made to pull around his stern. Simultaneously, he slowed to become almost motionless in the water. As I pushed on my tiller extension rod to pass across his stern it parted company with the rudder interconnecting bar. Out of control as I then became and almost in the same second, my lee bow struck at some speed and wedged itself some inches into the plywood weather bow of the other stationery vessel. When the cats were prised apart it became apparent my quite sharp bow was split. Neither of us was injured and we were able to carefully sail our soggy boats back to of the clubhouse. Repair work for Neil Fowler.

Not that many years later, I was to be on the receiving end of a hole punched in the port quarter topsides of my later purchased S&S 30. This was shortly after completion of a complete respray and paint of all the hull from keel to cabin top. Stampede was on its moorings and unattended. A heavier long-keeled timber-hulled racer about 40' long of an earlier generation was sailing among the yachts moored off Darwin Sailing Club [DSC]. As it was given to me, the helmsman found himself bearing down on Stampede. His sails were trimmed for windward sailing. He attempted to make a critical change of course without any sail retrim. Of course, his helm was unresponsive. I suppose I was in some measure fortunate the hole was punched above the waterline.

My next boat was the De Havilland Rambler 18'6" trailer-sailor, Bete Noir. It finished my catamaran days. (On this, see also below, chapter 12, "Bathurst Island Weekend"). Likewise, how I came into ownership of an American built fibreglass Ranger 23. In Many respects, Ned Kelly, as I named her, was an ideal small keelboat for north Australian waters. It was one of over 700 produced by Ranger Yachts of the US.

But of the boats I have owned my top ranking must go to the Rambler (Bete Noir). Like all trailer-sailers I know of, the Rambler could be inverted and remain stable. I had inadvertently established that fact. The penalty for an inversion in an isolated beachside location was the risk of being unable to return to human habitation and death. Death was a more probable consequence if the inversion occurred in open sea. Perhaps an instant inflatable masthead float as was used in earlier seagoing multihulls was the answer. Then, if the Rambler was flat in the water the crew, even one person who knew what he was doing and had a trapeze harness, must have a chance of righting it. The 880 pounds hull with built-in buoyancy was otherwise unsinkable. In the instance of my inversion, this was proven up to the job. I don't think attempting to convert the Rambler to a ballasted keeler answers any sensible question. An ultimate plan for the more daring voyager could be to emulate the aged single hander round the world racing yachtsman Tony Bullimore and find a dry perch in the inverted hull whilst sending out a signal from an emergency position locating beacon [Epirb].

Sailor/visitor to the Darwin Sailing Club, six times married, writer and self- described artist of words and wind, Webb Chiles, was in the course of a circumnavigation, later all but successfully accomplished, in a completely open 18' Drascombe lugger, Chidiock Tichborne. Completion of that voyage was prevented by his imprisonment as a spy by Saudi Arabia in 1982. The same Webb Chiles lost Resurgam, his Stephens designed proper ocean going She36, off Galveston in the Bay of Mexico in moderate conditions. He was relaxing, all the boats hatches were unwisely left wide open, loud music was playing. A lazy green wave washed over the boat. Next thing he was treading water as Resurgam made its way to the bottom. Over the next 26 hours he reported he was Gulfstream borne something like 125 nautical miles before he was able to rescue himself by clambering aboard a moored fishing boat. On both occasions, he was denuded of all his possessions. As he wrote of his dispossession:

"I mention this only partly in pride that I lived on the edge and risked everything for so long - as I once wrote, almost dying is a hard way to make a living - but also it explains omissions. Possessions can usually be replaced, but some of my writing and many photographs were lost and can't be."

In this vein, I recall the story of quirky former Victorian policeman Colin Watson. Colin owned a larger trimaran—I think to a Hedley Nicholls design about 38′ in length. I knew him only from the encampment he established with and under his boat in the outer reaches of the Darwin Sailing Club inner boat park. The Club committee wanted him gone. The right to expel him was hindered by the fact the portion of boat park he occupied was outside the area of the Club's lease. So, not unlike the jolly swagman of Waltzing Matilda fame, Colin philosophised and drank under the decking of his trimaran, impervious to the world. To be fair though, I never heard him sing and most of what he drank never came out of a billy.

Absolutely unaccountably, one day he craned his boat into the water and set sail for the East Coast. Now trimarans are not load carriers. Contrary to best advice, Colin was something of a bower bird and he had stuffed his trimaran, including the floats, with possessions. Several hundred miles out of Darwin, in the vicinity of Croker Island, Colin sailed into moderately severe weather. An essential stabilising outrigger hull, to leeward at the time, broke up. The contents spilled into the surrounding ocean. It wasn't long before all the rest of the trimaran broke up. As Colin readied his life-raft he was surrounded by a veritable sea of possessions that the ocean was claiming. He was fortunate to survive courtesy of an aboriginal settlement vessel. When I met up with him after, he was to claim the loss of all his possessions was cleansing.

It was at the Darwin Sailing Club in late 1972 or early 1972 that I met Frenchman Alain Colas [1945-1978]. Having sailed singlehanded and non- stop from Tahiti, he was bone tired. A quiet-spoken, modest but obviously a determined and driven soul, he was on route to London to start in the 1972 single-handed English Transatlantic race. His 20.5 metre alloy, ketch rigged rotating masts trimaran Manureva [ex Pen Duick 1V] won that event. The Transatlantic crossing was something of an anti-climax to his voyage to the start line.

His boat had been built originally for French yachting hero Eric Tabarly [1931-1998] who had won the same event in 1964 in an earlier Pen Duick 11, a timber monohull ketch. Colas had not been a sailor until he met Tabarly in Sydney about the time of Tabarly's victory in the 1967 Hobart race with the 17.45m clipper bowed alloy schooner Pen Duick 111. After some crewing with Tabarly, it wasn't long before he resigned from his teaching position at Australia's St. John College to devote himself to sailing full time. Colas, or more accurately his father, had borrowed heavily to purchase Manureva for 23 million old francs and he had learned the only way to generate money sailing was through headlines.

Perhaps it was to this end and while he still owned Manureva, he commissioned the construction of the 236' monster 4 masted monohull Club Med for ultra- competitive single-handed racing in the 1976 edition of the English single handed Transatlantic. While construction was underway, he all but had a foot severed in a boating accident linked to Manureva. The foot was saved after a fashion, following many surgical procedures. A series of storms devastated the fleet. Vessels were sunk. Colas put into Newfoundland to repair broken halyards. He finished second 7 1/2 hours behind Tabarly but was penalised 58 hours for assistance associated with the shore visit. This relegated him to fifth place.

In the inaugural storm ridden Route de Rhum Transatlantic race in 1978 Colas generated his largest headline. He and Manureva disappeared off the Azores. No trace has ever been found of either. The boat's alloy structure was later revealed to have been subject to much painted over micro fracturing. A fellow competitor reported a sighting at the height of a storm. Manureva had been making astonishing speed. In a previous such incident, Colas had written his philosophy had been to set up his trimaran for absolute maximum speed and then pray it held together. The most likely cause of death was said to have been stress related disintegration of Manureva's hull structure. Tabarly himself was lost at sea in 1998, when he was knocked overboard by its boom from the deck of the original Pen Duick, his family's 1898 40' Fyfe cutter.

Very few Ramblers were built. Mine was in due course sold to a local building contractor. He sold her to a buyer who air freighted her from Darwin to a remote island where he was employed. Before it was sold, I bought for racing a used Soling class spinnaker which was [just] manageable. I spotted another on Perth's Swan River on a blustery Fremantle afternoon from the cockpit of a Herreshoff 28. It was sailed two up with the crew on trapeze. My Australis 18 also left Australia.

Darwin-Dili Race, 1974

The 1974 Dili race saw me just make the start line in time. I was in the midst of work- related complex client negotiations that didn't seem to be going anywhere. Race morning I was contacted by the client. He had heard that a resolution to the deadlock was in the wind and all that was needed was my contact with the solicitor for the other party. When that contact was made, it became apparent to me eventually, after much toing and froing, the move was pure mischief on the part of the other solicitor designed for no other purpose than to cause me maximum stress and inconvenience on race morning.

The race set an intriguing course. There were no rounding marks after exiting Darwin Harbour. Tiny Jaco Island, just off the easterly point of East Timor was not mentioned in the race instructions. This meant rounding Jaco was optional. On Ned, our conclusion, after reading most unpromising reports of pilotage of the Strait in our pilot book, had been to round it anyway, rather than sailing through the quite narrow [no more than I mile] strait. If the navigation was accurately plotted from afar there would be very little in it, In the event, we sighted Jaco about mid-morning. Chris Rae, our navigator, thought we were proximate but no land had been visible from deck level. It was only after Peter Chilman had been hoisted to the masthead that we had confirmation.

Our landfall was about noon. We had enjoyed a good reaching/running breeze to that point. In fact, at its peak, crewman Lawson Beatty sought advice on the location about the boat of the components of the rubber dinghy I had chosen over my life-raft to save weight. My life-raft had sailed in the same event, on loan to another competitor. As soon as we had made the north coast of Jaco, our wind fell away to almost nothing. Perhaps current came into it, but without Satnav that was impossible to say. Offshore from the north coast, we were doing little more than drift. It took most of the rest of that day to find ourselves about abeam of the northern end of Jaco Strait. Then, to our chagrin, another competitor, Geoff Chard on Balladier, his 24-footer, materialised, still carrying the wind that we had lost after rounding Jaco. As we watched from our essentially becalmed position, Balladier traversed the no more than two nautical miles length of the Strait to take up a position comfortably ahead of us. From there it was a drifting match for the 80 or so nautical miles to Dili.

Drifting, as we were, stock had to be taken of the yacht's uneaten curried beef. I had organised this culinary delight with Charlie Cagnetti of Darwin's Charlie's Restaurant. There was no refrigeration on board and the dry ice we had used to keep it had long since run out. The uneaten portion was beginning to develop a life of its own. It had to go. As the plastic bag was thrown over the side something quite extraordinary happened. Like a cricketer catching a ball, a very large fish surfaced to take the parcel into its wide-open mouth.

Well- deserved victory in that race went to John Altman on his Hood 23 (Gypsy ll). We saw nothing of John until after we finished. To compound my chagrin, shortly after we crossed the finish line and were anchoring, Chris Rae became so preoccupied with getting hold of an ice-cold beer from a Portuguese official welcoming motor launch that he released our primary anchor and all its chain without securing the bitter end.

Ed Note:

<The outcome of this 1974 Darwin to Dili race, for the monohull division was, first, John Altman on Gypsy ll, in 121.82 hours; fifth, John McCormack on Ned Kelly (with crew comprising L. Beattie, C. Rae, and P. Chilman), in 135.62 hours. Geoff Chard's Balladier came 8th in 142 hours. (Full details in <https://sailtimorleste.org/rally/>)

Like my Rambler Bete Noir, Ned Kelly had no inboard motor. A 6hp Johnson Outboard motor sufficed. When returning from Dili, on my only seaborne trip there for the last Dili race in 1974, dead calm conditions prevailed for most of the return to Darwin. Apart from the occasional stop to top up the fuel tank and maybe clean the sparkplugs, the Johnson just purred away. There may have been a sailable breeze for the last 70 miles from Cape Fourcroy, but that was it.

For that return trip we were able to see the Strait, at that time of year [July] as essentially benign, flanked as it was at the northerly end by a then deserted village on Jaco and an enticing sandy beach on East Timor. I have learned since that the US consul based in Dili made this beach one of her favourite destinations—access in her case by road.

The Portuguese and Timorese in Dili treated us handsomely. A race fleet banquet saw us sitting at table in a vast hall with an individual waiter for each diner. Portuguese wine was cheap and plentiful. We set sail for the return voyage with a substantial opened cask of vino verde on the cockpit floor. Dili then was basically a sleepy hollow.

After 8pm a dog could fall asleep safely in the middle of the main road. Post the cessation of Portuguese colonial rule and the subsequent brief Indonesian colonisation, stability seems to have returned.

The following year, civil war in East Timor precluded a return of our race. Before the official cancellation, the Darwin Sailing Club had the offer of a visit from East Timor political supremo Jose Ramon Horta who was in Darwin. He was spurned. Within weeks the same man was addressing the General Assembly of the United Nations in New York. An alternative race was substituted.

A number of Darwinites have more or less settled in East Timor. Ex Rotarian Saqib Awan has established a trading and restaurant presence and included US Secretary of State Condaleezza Rice as a diner at the latter. Saqib's military officer brother is in residence as Pakistan's military attache. Former Customs chief Wayne Thomas has been busy with a building programme. A former Territory policeman cum lawyer has set up legal practice. Another Darwin lawyer, Jon Tippet, found a bride there. Tragically, the brother of former NT Chief Minister Stone was knifed to death when he misread the measure of tolerance for the social activity of an errant local wife. The killer was never charged.

The Dili alternative race was over a wonderful course of about 350 nautical miles anti-clockwise around Bathurst and Melville Islands. Local surgeon Jon Wardell, who, with his 57' timber pocket maxi yacht Australian Maid has sailed and competed in yacht races world- wide, maintains this course has no peer. Unfortunately, many Darwin sailors find it either too challenging or the cost of safety requirements for their boats too costly. The dilemma for race organisers is how to reduce the cost of these safety standards without compromising safety. What had become an annual event after 1975 looks like slipping off the yacht racing calendar. Expressions of interest were sought for the proposed 2018 race. Later the race was cancelled. Caution with respect to the sailing and navigation challenges may have played a part, but the cost of complying with mandatory offshore yacht safety requirements, without actually going foreign, must contribute.

I agree with Jon Wardle that this circuit is brilliant for the sailing challenges it offers. On the occasions I have competed in the Round the Islands, the start time has been such that there has been the opportunity to get help from the tide to make the passage through the Vernon Islands about dusk. Then, if the sailor is lucky, he can catch the ingoing tide as far as the Rooper Rock midway through Van Dieman Gulf and then ride the next outgoing tide to round the northeast point of Melville Island. With more luck, the unlit Rocky Point at the Northwest tip of Bathurst Island can be rounded before dark after a run across the top of the course. The next leg is usually a tight reach to Cape Fourcroy at the southwestern tip of Bathurst followed by what is usually a 70 nautical dead beat to the finish line off the Darwin Sailing Club [DSC]. Truly a brilliant circuit set up by nature. More use should be made of it.

I have tried enough but never been able to win this race on handicap. A wonderful start for my S&S 30 Stampede one year saw us at sunset, the tricky passage through the Vernon Islands behind us and well on the way through Van Dieman

Gulf. The next yacht could not be seen. We had risked grounding by sailing to the Vernon Islands via the narrow shoal channel close inshore out of the tide. For me, all this had come at the end of a hard work week. The evening prior until 3am I was installing a new motor. I was exhausted and came off watch about 10pm. Instructions were left that Stampede should at all costs avoid the wind hole of the east side of the Van Dieman Gulf we were traversing. Short of a wind hole, I expected dawn should find us at least close to rounding the east coast of Melville Island.

I slept heavily. Awoken at daybreak I was baffled about our location. Eventually, this turned out to be close to where I had turned in. My helmsman had gone over to the eastern side of the Gulf into the wind hole. We were becalmed. The rest of the race fleet was advancing on us under spinnaker. I will never know how we would have managed if my helmsman had followed my instruction. We re-joined the fleet. As we rounded the northeast point of Melville Island and freed up for the run across the top of the course it was discovered I had failed to pack the chart with the salients for the rest of the course. Crewman Martin Rijkuris, now Captain Rijkuris, relying on the on-board pilot book, prepared a rough facsimile chart incorporating these salients. The less written about the remainder of this race the better.

Probably the greatest challenge navigationally is the narrow passage through the Vernons. I have been navigating a course through the main-lit channel and found myself, courtesy of big tide-related currents, irretrievably albeit felicitously in the shorter north channel. On another occasion, against a strong tide which rendered us all but immobile over the ground and following yachts that were pointing up to high northerly courses, I was encouraged by crewman Neil Plumb to free off. As a result of visiting the location at low tide he had formed the view we were being over careful. For a short time, I heeded his advice. Then sinister looking mini-whirlpools showed about us. I returned to high pointing. Neil fell ominously silent. We got through.

The next challenge is any night rounding of unlit Rocky Point off the northwest tip of Bathurst Island. Ordinarily I am glued to the depth sounder for this rounding. My most diffuse rounding was as crew on the same Neil Plumb's quarter tonner Invincible. No depth sounder was operational. Neil was helming on deck with Bob Jackson. Chris Rae and I were half asleep below. Chris and I were peremptorily called on deck to take over. As soon as we stumbled up Neil and Bob vanished down below. Invincible was amid breaking seas close to Rocky Point. Neil and Bob disappeared below deck. My solution was to retrace our path until we had left broken water. Invincible had no victory to record for that race.

I have found sailboat racing in Darwin Harbour on a big tide day to be a marvellous experience—especially if the breeze is light. It is not unusual for a sailor to find himself with his bow pointing 90-degrees away from a rounding mark while the tide on his flank brings him up to it. There can be a downside. On one less than happily memorable day, on my S&S 30, as the wind fell away, the tide brought us into a robust beam on collision with a floating harbour light. That race later included the bizarre spectacle of Stampede's spinnaker being flown upside down.

My tall-rig S&S 30, Stampede, was an Olin Stephens design built by Swarbricks in Perth. It was designed as a cruiser as distinct from the more well-known S&S 34 racer. Not only did Swarbricks build the complete boats, under licence, they hired the moulds at very reasonable rates to those who thought they could manage a complete build. Swarbricks supplied the materials and the construction shed. They offered even a third option, to build to lock up stage. By today's standards, their prices were crazy cheap. Both hulls sported separate skeg mounted rudders set well to the rear, wineglass underwater sections and tumblehome. Tom Swarbrick has showed me how the hull drawings to the same scale shared identical above-water profiles as far as the rear of the cabin top from which point the extra 4' of hull length was drawn. Both had high [lead] ballast ratios. The 34 has a displacement of 13,000 pounds as against 9,700 pounds for the 30. The stationary waterline lengths were almost identical, and the hulls were equally solid. Below decks one would be hard put to identify by the beam differential which vessel one was on.

The difference was in the extra sailing hull length that the 34 could pick up when heeled, and the extra stability and sail carrying power the 34 gained from 12 inches more beam, extra ballast, up to a foot of extra draft and the additional reserve buoyancy of the 34 from the substantial bustle at the stern of the hull under the cockpit. Because of the moderate underwater shape of the stern of the 30 and in the interest of having her sail on her designed lines the preference has always been to locate the auxiliary engine amidships essentially under part of the dinette. The original owner of

Stampede, my next-door neighbour Bill Burroughs chose the 30 over the 34 because he considered with its shallower draft he had a better prospect of pushing off if it grounded.

I am uncertain if the moulds were made locally. In the case of the 30, save for absence of convex curvature to the counter, the local tall rigged 30 is identical to the US built Yankee 30 Mark 111. In the instance of the 34, the only difference from the English built identical vessel is the absence of a doghouse at the rear of the deckhouse. Yankee Yachts ceased production in 1990 when it refused to compromise quality to attempt to meet the market after a sudden big increase in the cost of fibreglass materials. The English 34 builder ceased production about the same time. My bet is that the US and UK moulds have been used for local production.

John Swarbrick, from the same family as the boatbuilders, has achieved international recognition as yacht designer. He came up with a radical new concept, narrow waterline beam, very fast, easily sailed, high-ballast, mono-hull, drop-keeled 30' yacht. The hull was developed in Perth from a plug. For protection of his design, he relied on artistic copyright. Somewhere along the way, he gifted a large proportion, but not quite the entirety of the moulds for the new concept yacht to two employees. These were sold to a potential competitive fibreglass yacht producer. That producer employed the Swarbrick ex- employees to manufacture the yachts from the originally gifted moulds. The missing moulds for production of the complete yacht were stolen from John's factory. When John injuncted the competitive production of his design from the gifted moulds the matter eventually reached the apex of the Australian judicial system, the High Court of Australia. There, it was determined copyright legislation gave him no protection and that if, as was the case, he had failed to register his concept under registered design legislation, he had no claim against his rival producers. Because of the work of Olin Stephens and his ilk, the series production from fibreglass moulds taken from a plug has been determined to be more akin to a science than an original artistic work. As John commented, the architect draftsman of a set of plans for a prosaic suburban dwelling can claim the protection of copyright but a yacht designer cannot.

Stampede can claim some affinity with the same High Court. I had located her on a custom-built steel trailer in the carpark of Frank Lam's Capricornia Restaurant on East Point Road, Fannie Bay. This was after the sale of my Darwin law practice. Jim Brawn, a former client was driving cabs at the time. I was unaware Jim knew my whereabouts or connection to Stampede. About mid-morning one day, I was surprised to have Jim and taxi descend on me in the car park. It turned out he was taking a passenger sightseeing. That passenger was the recently retired High Court Chief Justice Harry Gibb—fortuitously not a member of the Murray Gleeson High Court that presided over the Swarbrick case.

The S&S 34 moulds used by Swarbricks to produce the S&S 34 are now back in Perth courtesy of Mike Finn of Cottesloe Yachts. They were deployed to the east coast in 1986 where at least one 34 was built. By all accounts the moulds are in excellent condition. In consultation with Sparkman and Stephens they have been refurbished to accommodate the latest vacuum infusion technology. The current generation S&S 34 is built by Swarbrick and Swarbrick Composites located in Henderson WA under licence from Cottesloe Yachts and Sparkman & Stephens.

Construction has been re-engineered from the original hand layup fibreglass to foam core vacuum infusion using 100% vinylester resin. This is said to produce an extremely strong, stiff, lighter hull and deck with top impact resistance. In 2010, the price for a complete hull to lock-up stage ready to fit out was A$158,000. A hull represents no more than about 1/3 of the cost of a completed boat. More tellingly, the advertiser for the sale, at A$220,000, of Blondie, a comprehensively fitted out new generation used S&S 34, disclosed over A$450,000 had been expended on his part for the build. That ad on the S&S 34 Association web site is stamped "Sold."

In the days when the Round the Islands race was held, a skipper who had the time could brush up crew work and boat familiarity for the crew by competing in the 140 nautical mile or so race to Cape Fourcroy and the 350 nautical mile Round-the-Islands preparatory to participation in the 600 nautical mile race to Ambon. Political instability caused by orchestrated religious rioting resulted in cancellation of the Ambon race in 1998, well after my last voyage there. But I believe politics have stabilised in Ambon and moves are afoot to resurrect this race.

The Ambon race-course instructions used in my races left it open to a skipper to leave Bathurst and Melville Islands to either port or starboard. Selection of the former involves travelling an extra 35 or so nautical miles and navigation through the Vernon Islands passage. I believe I was the first to choose to sail this longer course in about 1978. At the morning radio the next day, I was relieved to find Stampede was level-pegging on latitude with the leaders of those sailing the obvious shorter course by rounding Cape Fourcroy.

The advantages of the longer course are the potential to ride the tides to clear Australia by daybreak on day 2; being well up to weather of those choosing the shorter way; and avoiding the wind hole that can develop in the lee of Bathurst and Melville Islands. The windward

John sailing Ned Kelly, under the Indonesian Flag, Darwin to Ambon Race, 1978?

position offsets the ocean dry season set from the east to the west. Using a satellite navigator, I have measured this set returning dead into the prevailing wind from Darwin to Ambon as pushing me 20 degrees below the actual course sailed. Terry Coulehan, my navigator for the longer course, sailed his own yacht over this same course a year or two later. Spectacular good fortune rewarded his choice. All the race fleet remainder were becalmed in the lee of the islands for something like 24 hours while he was bowling along in reasonable trade winds from 24 hours after the start. He had an emphatic racing monohull win.

Work took me to Katherine some months after my sail and, despite nothing being actually said, found myself being treated with great enthusiasm by local bookmaker Paddy Fitzgerald.

I recall several incidents associated with sailing the Ambon course. Due to freakish conditions, I was able to chalk up one win in the racing monohull division in I think my third and last attempt—all made on my S&S 30.[28] That victory happened like this.

On Stampede we had sailed the longer route. At the end of the fourth day out, we laid the east side of the Ambon harbour entrance in the morning. Then the wind fell out altogether. As we lay becalmed, we could see the main fleet blocking up about the western side of the several nautical miles-wide harbour entrance. The finish line is about 8 miles up harbour. As our competitors arrived, they, like us, were becalmed. The scattered fleet spent the day waiting for wind. Thoughts of victory were forgotten. The probability was the same wind, when it came, would favour the smaller boats. Late in that afternoon, while we waited, chatted and practised our very limited Indonesian language skills, all 10,000 pounds of Stampede started to move into the harbour. It was an ingoing tide. As the movement generated wind

---

[28] This could appear to indicate 1978, after racing earlier in the decade on several occasions on the Darwin-Dili course.

over the sails, they filled and as we moved with the tide, we were creating our own apparent wind. As we progressed noiselessly up the harbour the sights, sounds and smells of a busy harbour-side community assailed us. We breathed slowly and softly and spoke little lest the spell be broken. We crossed the finish line at about 8pm.

Flush with my instant Indonesian language take-up while we were becalmed, I introduced myself as Kepeting. The hosts appeared mystified. Kepeting, as I should have known, translates to crab. I was Capitano. No other yacht crossed the line until mid-morning the next day.

Ambon boasts one of the world's great harbours. It is where the Japanese forces mustered for attacks on Darwin during World War 11's Pacific war. There was a Russian interlude around the fifties. Submarine pens were at least partially constructed at the northernmost point of the harbour. To the best of my knowledge, Darwin visitors have never been made less than welcome. On my first visit it rained almost continuously although not monsoonally. It was on the cusp of (Indonesian) Independence Day celebrations. Undeterred by the rain, groups of marching locals preparing for the big day were everywhere.

I don't know how often the locals stage what they call the Crazy Bamboo Pole Dance. It was performed during my second Ambon trip, with the props bein a lengthy bamboo pole, probably the longer the better, dependent on the number of people concerned and the land area available. Add a few mobile drummers and shovels, red hot coals and some substance that reacts with the coals to give off thick fumes. The dancers are spaced evenly over the pole length and with arms bent at the elbow grasp the pole. The mobile drummers commence their rhythm and the handlers of the gas producing shovel heads move along the dancers so that they inhale the fumes produced. The more the tempo increases, the greater twitching movements of the pole. For the dance I witnessed, volunteer yacht crew also danced. It made an entertaining spectacle. NT cabinet minister and spectator Tom Harris was mildly ambivalent about having witnessed, and implicitly approved, the use of hallucinogens. No photos were taken.

Which reminds me of my lost photo opportunity, as we were approaching Saumlaki in the Taninbar Island group for a visit on route home to Darwin. It was the day after Independence Day. At the time, my still camera had been stolen from my car parked in my own driveway. All I was able to pack for that trip had been a Canon Super 8 movie camera which I hadn't used for years. As we tacked through the Eggeron Strait it was early morning. A flotilla of heavily passenger laden large sailing vessels was exiting the port on the reciprocal of on our inward course. They were departing Saumlaki after the celebrations. The colourfully dressed passengers, about 40 in number per vessel, were noisily and happily animated. They made a wonderful spectacle. I grabbed the Canon out of its case. I could not activate the lens auto focus or for that matter manual focus. The camera had been tampered with since my last usage. Autofocus, the only focus, had been de-activated. I had forgotten how to reset. The best I could manage was a blurry image of a wonderful spectacle.

At the time of our arrival for that visit, the inter-island ship arrived. A crowd awaited it on the wharf. In front of a group of excited children, the Javanese island policeman spoke with us. So as not to undermine his status, we made as if he was one of us linguistically. Undoubtedly, he spoke better English than we did Bahasa. The sole fluent English speaker was a resident Dutch priest. When he graduated from his seminary, he was fluent in 5 languages not including Bahasa Indonesian. He was assigned to Saumlaki. Within a matter of a few months, he was preaching in Bahasa. The Bishop of Ambon, another Dutchman, had arrived on the ship for a visit. The policeman wanted no photographs taken.

One morning, at the invitation of the resident priest, we set out with him for what he termed a quiet walk. It may have been so for him. It was from the coast at Saumlaki to the coast on the southeastern corner of the island. There were no motor vehicles, not even a motorised bicycle. The track was well defined and consisted of a number of what we found to be testing hills. Coconut palms lined the wayside at the edges of which were a number of grottos dedicated to Christian saints. About three-quarters of our way, there was an enormous, wooden, cathedral-dimensioned Catholic church. We never met another soul on the track. The priest set a brisk pace. This was his parish and walking was only mode of transport. He was a very fit robust 6-footer, such that the lady in our crew commented, not to him, on the loss to the fair sex occasioned by his priestly celibacy. Wearing indifferent thongs as I was, I was not equipped for a serious walk. We carried no drink. The weather was typical tropical.

I doubt if any of my crew were better set up than I was. I suppose we reached our destination in about 2 1/2 hours. Then we had to look forward to an equally sweaty return.

Along the way, I learned that every free-hanging coconut belonged to someone in the community. As to the massive church, our host had no explanation for it. It was obvious this was a deeply Christian community. At the end point, we were invited into a modest home and offered tea, which we gratefully accepted. Then, our steps retraced, we found ourselves at what was probably the only store. Cold beer was available. Our host enjoyed his share. About 1 hour into our libations, we were joined by an apparently censorious Javanese understudy priest. Our host openly confessed to having been found out.

One evening, we invited the priest and his visiting bishop for tea on board Stampede. The priest from an outlying island of Ternate may also have been in attendance. The policeman was invited but chose not to attend. Jenny Simondson and Tom Pauling turned on a wonderful meal. Despite Stampede's modest dimensions the 5 of us and the three guests were comfortable in the cabin. The oil rubbed teak glowed. The dinette was called into play, the cooks were busy and mostly on their feet and we passed a very pleasant few hours. The bishop made comment how the universal Bahasa language had transformed travel and communications in the archipelago. When he arrived in Indonesia quite some years earlier, any traveller around the islands had to cope with a profusion of dialects. As to this, despite having been born in Java, Darwinian Nick van Eyck found the Javanese language quite beyond him when he left as a young man. Bahasa was a different matter.

Before that trip, I had tucked aboard a copy of the novel *The Thornbirds*. My understanding then was the novel had been well received and would be a good read if there were idle moments. As our next port was Darwin and the priest was isolated. I decided to leave the book with him. At the time I dropped it off, the bishop only was at the residence. Only after I returned to Darwin and bought and read another copy of the same book, did I come to understand that my well-meaning gift had been monumentally unsuitable.

Another year was memorable for the return trip to Darwin from Ambon. At the northern apex of the harbour, where Stampede was located, all was still. Reports filtering through suggested the wind strength outside the harbour was well up. We had decided to depart that evening anyway. The Customs and Immigration formalities had been completed. My crew, Clive Colenso and Terry Coulehan, were as aware as I that we faced a fair chance of a more than usually formidable 600 nautical mile beat to windward. Clive had been something of a noteworthy English windsurfer afficionado, but I suspect his trip to Ambon had been his first oceangoing passage in a small boat. Our last meal was served at a Chinese restaurant adjacent to where Stampede was anchored close inshore. At about 8.30pm there was no further excuse for delay. We boarded and deflated the rubber dinghy. Anchor lifted and stowed, the engine was fired up. As we proceeded down harbour, the rig was made ready for the rumoured outside conditions. The heavy weather small jib was hanked on the forestay and two reefs put in to the mainsail. Little was spoken.

Sure enough, there was wind aplenty outside the harbour. My wind gauge, always to my mind pessimistic, was reading 30 knots. The motor was switched off. In the ensuing silence Stampede was snug albeit well- heeled as it bashed its way to weather. The weather runner was secured to support the mast upper section from flexing. Always a prey to seasickness I swallowed my first dosage of stugeron. The tiller was light. Watches were allocated. Terry was setting up at the chart table to navigate our passage. This was in the days before I had installed a Satnav receiver. As the bow smashed its way through the seaway, it was increasingly wet for the helmsman on deck. The water was tropical warm, windchill the real enemy. We forged ahead into the blackness. It looked like a dour struggle with the conditions to achieve our objective of Darwin. Tacking, as we had to and taking the north-west set into account, we could look forward to travelling well in excess of 600 nautical miles over the ground. All the auguries were for a passage in excess of 6 days. At best, meal preparations, for any of us inclined to eat, would be basic. Snacks and hot drinks would be the order of the days and nights ahead.

In the night watches, I checked the wind speed indicator from time to time. It may have indicated a smidgen over the 30 knots but never really close to the 40 knots I could have sworn we were experiencing.

On either the first or second night out, I was off watch asleep below in my bunk when Terry, I suspect mischievously, woke me in the small hours for a course consultation. How close did I want to go to the Nil Desperandum reef? This reef, that we had never seen but joked about, was in the offing. My answer was to steer the course that gave the reef the widest berth.

I think it was mid-one afternoon when Clive had to relinquish the helm. He had brought no oilskins and until I pressed upon him a spare waterproof top, had been helming by day bare chested, with no regard to wind chill. Stampede had been driving through and falling heavily off the backs of waves. Were it not for the recently fitted mast runners that kept the mast in column it surely would have failed. I took over the helm if for no other reason than to bear away when I could feel Stampede lurching in readiness for a fall off a wave back. Clive reported he needed a meal. I offered him freedom of the galley and the provisions. Stampede was at about a 30-degree angle of heel. It was like being strapped to the back of a bolting horse. Clive had no galley ambitions. Some hours later he had recovered and offered himself for helming duty. About the halfway point, the Indonesian island of Babar offered us a respite for a few hours as we traversed its lee. Then it was back to the banshee. That wind never abated until we were almost home. Seventy or so miles out, from our rounding of Cape Fourcroy, it had eased.

Another year, when I was not competing, proved disastrous for Brian Bottger's 30'yacht Sfida. Brian always was an aggressive competitor. His Sfida seemed to have about the same boat speed as Stampede, so I loaned him a spinnaker for that event. Pre the race, one of Sfida's sheets [ropes] was let dangle in the water when the yacht was motoring. It caught in the propeller. The shaft transmitting engine power to the propeller was bent. Water ingress from the point in the hull where the shaft exited was prevented by a seal. However, on the return voyage to Darwin, Sfida was dis-masted. Relying then on engine power alone for the rest of the return, it wasn't long before the bend in the shaft damaged the seal. This damage must have been severe because eventually Brian's yacht succumbed to the deep — about 2 miles of it. Michael Maurice on his 30-footer had been dis-masted in about the same location. Both Michael and Brian had commissioned new rigging from the same rigger for their respective yachts especially for the rigours of the Ambon race. Michael was standing by when Sfida went down. Brian's crew transferred to Michael's crippled but auxiliary engine powered mast-less yacht.

That night, a rendezvous was arranged by radio link with Hans Voss' 45' concrete yacht Antipodes. The plan was to transfer the Sfida crew of 4 or 5 to the more spacious accommodations of Antipodes, Michael was positioned in an anchorage somewhere in the location of, if not actually on, the halfway Babar Island. A signal flare was to be shot by Michael at midnight to enable Antipodes to take a compass heading. Close to the appointed hour, the deck watch of Antipodes observed a light in the approximate heading of where the planned flare was expected. A course was set for the light. Soon a after the 18 tons or so of Antipodes became seriously entangled with the Indonesian sailing vessel that had displayed the light to alert Antipodes to its presence. Michael and Hans and the Sfide crew all made it back to Darwin without more maritime drama. I hope the same went for crew of the Indonesian prahu.

About one year later, as I was casually observing yacht racing off Darwin, I spotted my loaned spinnaker. It was being flown. Another mystery of the [very] deep.

There has been for me a mystique about long distance single-handed sailing. At the time of my last Ambon jaunt, I resolved to sample it for myself by returning to Darwin alone. The crew were told well in advance. I bought an electric-powered Auto helm. Although I had a backup sextant and tables, my primary position fixing was to be through Satellite navigation. Unlike the around A$200-300 current [2018] cost of a GPS receiver, the cost of a Satnav receiver then represented a significant capital cost of just over A$3,000. It was after I had discovered stugeron to utterly allay any symptom of seasickness. To my knowledge, it is not available in Australia and, when I last tested local medications quite some years back, they were ineffective. I ordered mine online through ebay.

The Auto helm was a single unit designed to operate directly on the tiller. It was fixed at one end to the cockpit side with the other end connected to the tiller. Pre-race there was no time to do the simple installation. It would have to be done in Ambon. When I came to do the job, no Auto helm could be found. With the many in and out charter flights to Darwin, I managed to retrieve it. I can only conclude it had been removed intentionally. The installation took a few hours. By the time I was ready to leave, there was only the one other yacht left. This was a Brandelmeyer-designed 44-footer owned by an ageing retired farming Canadian couple. They were waiting in remote Ambon on a funds transfer from Merrill Lynch.

Weather for my solitary voyage was moderate with a wind speed range of 15-20 knots. The new auto helm installation was successful, and I never had any steering problem. All of the passage was to windward and the autohelm gave just that extra bit of balance to the yacht that otherwise I was to later find unachievable. In this respect my earlier yacht Calore with its longer keel could be set up relatively easily to steer itself to weather. I found my biggest problem initially was being able to relax to sleep of an evening. To a certain extent, this was at least partially resolved by the need to get up and position plot after the Satnav had noisily calculated a position. Interval lapses of 2 or more hours between positions were not uncommon.

By the second night I was more relaxed. The evening might be pitch-black, but I could have confidence I knew my position and was well clear of any land or reef, So it was I was drifting into dreamland, rocked on the bosom of the deep, when there was a momentary reduction in momentum. This could only be attributable to a glancing hull contact with something with give. I never had long to ponder this mystery before a massive quantity of water forcefully landed on the cockpit area of the hull. The whoosh and thump were consistent with that water coming from some height.

I had to investigate urgently. The night was black. Torchlight revealed the cockpit was unprecedently filled to the brim with water. Up to then and in the wildest weather I had encountered with Stampede, the self- draining cockpit may have been wet but only with a smattering of water in the bottom. Even my experience on Windsong when a wave surfed me through the cockpit glass screen never left more than a modicum of water in that boat's self- draining cockpit. Stampede's cockpit was a touch over 6-feet long with a depth of about 2 feet and a width of about 3 feet. I shone my torch into the blackness. Nothing. I concluded that my boat had struck, fortunately glancingly, a basking whale, of which there were many in these waters. In an earlier year, on route on a dead beat from Ambon to Banda Island, a whale about a mile to weather had been proceeding on a parallel course. The thumping body of water dumped on the deck could only have been thrown up by the flukes or tail of an irritated whale. Luckily that was the end of the matter. The cockpit was draining as it was designed to do. Back to sleep.

I clearly remember half waking on another morning when the cabin was brightly lit by the sun. In my drowsy state I processed the whir of the Autohelm as the buzz of cockpit chatter. It would be my turn on watch soon enough. I snuggled up to return to dreamland until I was called. It was then I heard a child's voice: "Get up." As my location filtered through my consciousness, my ears pricked up for any imminent disaster like the resonant thump of the engine of an approaching ship. I scrambled to the hatch to check. Nothing. The objective of the voice had been achieved. Time for breakfast.

Not that my course was devoid of merchant shipping. Traversing a gap through the chain of islands around Babar Island in order to pass to the Arafura Sea. I seemed to be bucking an adverse tide. A tack was decided upon. With the runners having to be freed on the new lee side of the mast and set up to weather this took a little time. The new tack set up, I tarried in the cockpit to admire the Autohelm doing its job. Lo and behold, there was a merchant ship not more than 1 mile away on my port quarter. It was steering a course parallel to the northern fringe of the islands. That was my first intimation of its presence.

Throughout this voyage, I had maintained once a day radio contact with a daily schedule maintained by the scattered Darwin fleet returning home. An apparently well-connected American driving a nicely set up Olin Stephens designed Tartan 37' took a particular interest in my movements. He had done intermittent passages solo, but much preferred company, in his case that of his girl-friend, Francesca. They tended to argue but he had concluded a passage with her was much to be preferred to one without. In Ambon Francesca had set up on board his yacht more-or-less a shrine dedicated to his achievements and decorations as a professional officer soldier. He had also tried his hand at stock-broking. Darwin Sailing Club member, builder Roger Collins had crewed on the American's yacht for the Ambon race. Since then, Roger has built a family with a French-born wife and cruised extensively *en famille* in a Farr 37 yacht. Another Darwin couple cruised their yacht to the Philippines for their annual vacation.

At the time of the whale episode, it crossed my mind that there might have been water damage to the electrical circuitry of the Autohelm. But no, all appeared in order. That happy state was not to last. It ceased to operate about the time I made my landfall off Rocky Point on the north-west tip of Bathurst Island. My provisional diagnosis was belated water infiltration from the whale episode. I had no alternative but to manually helm until I reached Darwin. The wind had dropped out and the balance of my return was done under the auxiliary motor.

About the time the steerer dropped out a large blowfly entered the cabin. It proceeded on its noisy path until I managed to extinguish it. Then, when I looked out, Arthur Hall's returning 35-footer glided past still under sail. I was in no mind to remove the headsail that was set to instead fly my lightweight genoa sail as I suppose I should have done. If I had been racing, there would not have been two ways about the issue. On reflection now, perhaps that would have been a faster way home. It was not until around 11pm when I tied up at Q buoy. There was no sign of Arthur's boat then, so I assumed he had been cleared.

As I understand it, the serious long-distance, single-handed yacht racers don't have sail changes. They have large cutter rigs which they can reduce by part or complete rolling up of any of the 2 headsails or the main at the touch of a rope or even a button. In Sydney I once watched the start of a leg of a single-handed, round the world race. Competing yachts were 50 or 60' long. One competitor had well- wishers on board taken off at the last minute. When the gun went off the sheets were winched in and in an astonishingly short time the fleet was hulls down on the horizon. I venture to opine that fully crewed Hobart-bound racers would have struggled to outpace these specialised single-hand yachts.

Anchored off the Q buoy and cleared by Customs and Immigration, Stampede was so in the grip of a swift flowing tide I was unable to break out the anchor to return to my mooring off the Sailing Club. Just when I thought I would have to start my engine another Darwin lawyer, John Withnall, was passing by in his much-used Sharkcat, Nulla Bona. He could see my problem. He drew alongside to enable boarding by several strong males who soon upped the anchor.

I sent the Autohelm to the Sydney agents to be checked. They found no problem. I could only conclude whatever water had ingressed had dried out. I never had cause to re-use that unit before I sold Stampede.

My most idyllic yacht passage was one evening on Ned Kelly over the 70 nautical miles or so to Cape Fourcroy. It was in the course of a race. The moon was full and its glow suffused all like a giant electric globe. The tiller was light. The spinnaker was up. A gentle breeze from abeam kept the boat moving nicely. That breeze was increasing to brisk and moving further behind. The water was flat. A phosphorescent wake was astern. The only sound was the burble of the boat slipping through water. When I came off watch I was entranced. I remained in the cockpit, drinking it in. By dawn we were surfing. The return to Darwin was another matter—a most ungentlemanly going to windward in 20 knots plus.

My Darwin sailing life was maintained as one balance to a busy and often stressful lawyer's life. My race associated overseas trips were always to a tight schedule of the order of about two weeks. Some more fortunate sailors had months of free time to spend cruising the Indonesian archipelago after the Ambon race. When I left Darwin, the Ambon race was a vehicle to traverse the Indonesian archipelago. Overseas yachts had got the message. Yacht entry permits for the race automatically extended to all of Indonesia.

The advent of two marinas in Darwin's Cullen Bay and Frances Bay has added a new but costly dimension to northern sailing. Certainly, it is very pleasant to stroll down to board a yacht for a sail, or to attend to its maintenance without having to employ a dinghy. But it costs. And exit to and entry from the harbour must be progressed through a lock. I was never able to justify that cost over and above the other costs of yacht ownership like insurance on top of upgrades, maintenance, and repairs.

For a brief period and only at the apparent offer from Alan Dale of free use of his unused berth, I occupied a berth in the fishing boat marina in Stuart Park. This berth was visible from the roadway. To my surprise, as I was passing by late one evening, I noticed the hatchway on Stampede was open. I stopped off to investigate. The hatchway had been broken and forced open with tools from my cockpit locker. The hatchway of John Wilkin's yacht tied up next to Stampede was likewise open. This was about 11.30pm. I phoned John. He knew of no reason for his boat to be open. On coming down, he found an intruder slumbering below. Meantime, I found on Stampede the contents of a bottle of overproof rum had been drained. With assistance John went below to awaken the sleeper. He was dragged on deck soon to be in the water. While the intruder never said one word throughout, he was pursued in the water while the police were called. In the course of that pursuit, he spent some time with his head underwater. He was arrested and taken away in police custody. The forced and broken hatchway was a complicated and expensive repair. To cap cost off, I was phoned by the financial controller of the fishing boat harbour and asked for the money for my berth usage.

I was to learn later the thief was one of two mourners in Darwin for the funeral of a mutilated murder victim of one the press had christened the Butcher of Parap. Courtesy of the NT Museum Director Colin Jack-Hinton, they had both been accommodated in an Indonesian-built Prahu Hati Marega that had been sailed to Darwin as part of the 1998 Australian bi-centenary celebrations. Hati Marega was positioned at the end of one arm of the fishing boat harbour. Possessions and money had been disappearing from many boats after the arrival of the pair. Next day the thief was bailed and was last heard of hitching a ride out of Darwin.

Apart from the apparent mysterious resurrection from the deep of my spinnaker, my inventory of stolen effects includes two near new 12 alloy dinghies, a wonderful near new Hood NZ 125-per cent genoa sail, and a bottle of OP rum. On a free swing mooring off the sailing club, in the latter days of my ownership it seemed to me there was little to dissuade a thief from boarding in the small hours to inspect for anything that might take his fancy. I have on occasion come aboard to find my boat has been systematically gone over.

Chapter 12: Sailing, 2, Bathurst Island Weekend

I am not quite sure how long I owned my DeHavilland built Rambler 18'6" trailer sailer, but I know I sold it before Cyclone Tracey on the night of 24 December 1974 and early morning of the following Christmas Day. I sold it with regret to buy one of two Ranger 23s brought to Australia and six distributed world-wide for shooting the film "Dove" about a global circumnavigation.by Robin Lee Graham. Robin was just 16 when in 1965 he set out from Hawaii in a Cal 24-ft stock yacht and 21 when he returned with a different Allied built Bill Luders designed 33' yacht he bought in the West Indies. [Then] about 19 years young Ron Wilson of latter-day Sydney TV host fame bought the one used to shoot Darwin footage. It was in immaculate condition having been used as a backdrop only. I sailed with Ron on several occasions and was mightily impressed by this yacht. But I digress. This is about my Rambler.

Designed by Alan Payne the doyen of Australia's sailboat naval architects, the unballasted hull weighed in at about 880 lbs. "Unballasted" meant that if the vessel was capsized as occurred to me once there was no ballast keel leveraged weight to right it. It had a large mainsail with reefing points, a large area tilting rudder to facilitate retrieval to a trailer and a characterful and immensely strong fibreglass hull that was quite unlike that of any other trailer sailer. Beam was about 8', the cockpit was very large accommodation below was limited but enough for camping style living. It was built for sailing.

As to the hull shape I rate it as perhaps Alan's best yacht design and that includes his Americas Cuppers and winning ocean racers. There was no rule governing its dimensions. Perhaps it might have been argued the sail area to weight ratio was excessive as it may well have been for the disabled or elderly but that meant it was quite lively. With the beam flaring out to the gunwales a hard turn to the bilges the bluff flaring almost plumb bow wide side decks and a very moderate coach roof reducing in height as it went forward the visual impression was of jauntiness. On deck and sailing it was difficult to believe it was only 18'6". Not only did it sail like a witch it was in my experience far faster than any other of the admittedly bulky and under canvassed trailer sailers in Darwin. I recall one morning whilst on a reach effortlessly zooming past a chagrined Fred Ridge in his Hood 20 centreboarder on the same point of sail. With built in buoyancy, it was unsinkable. Even the rig ran to a 21 ft tapered alloy mast and the boom protruded well beyond the stern. Two large metal external flaps at the stern cockpit rear facilitated easy and quick drainage.

Mainsail area was 135 square feet. Compare that to the admittedly higher aspect ratio 110 square feet for the 3,499 lbs Ranger 23 keeler a far from dull sailboat & 195 square feet for my later owned Swarbrick S&S 30 weighing in at 10,000 lbs. Draft with the duralium centre plate down was just under I metre.

Bete Noir [BN] as I named her after she came into my possession just arrived and sat unloved and unused in the Darwin Sailing Club boat park for months. It was a complete set up: hull with bunk cushions, mast & rigging 6hp Johnson outboard mainsail, genoa. No 2 jib. It was rounded out by a nice, galvanised tilting trailer. For all practical purposes the kit was new. It was different to all the trailer sailers many with home built hard chine plywood floating caravan style hulls with ludicrous "full headroom" appearing in Darwin at the time. I am unable to recollect whether any "for sale" notice was attached.

Eventually I learned it had been brought to Darwin by Clem Chilman's Darwin Group Developments, it was for sale and from memory the asking price was $3650. It just looked right. Not without difficulty finding the readies including selling my 18'Australis one design racing catamaran it became mine.

Sadly, I don't believe I have any photographs of Bete Noir [Black Beast] or Black Betty as she came to be known. When I was on board the last thing on my mind was photography. Even trawling online it is difficult to find one acceptable image of the DeHavilland Rambler that anyway does her justice. How it never became more popular in its day escapes me. My suspicion is that few were built. I recollect one "expert" yacht magazine writer characterising the design as solid but slow. Built as it was by DeHavilland to an obvious high specification perhaps it was a question of cost. One thing I have picked up online is that it is a much sought after vessel by those who are in the know.

For me I have seen only one under sail, two if including one on trapeze one windy afternoon on the Swan River. A few years after I sold Bete Noir I heard she had been transported to a remote Pacific outpost by her new owner. When I left Darwin in 2013 there was certainly no sign of her about that town. A similar fate befell my 18' catamaran after I sold it.

So, it came about that one beautiful Darwin dry season Saturday I loosely arranged for one or two mates to sail to Bathurst Island. I had used the boat to compete in Darwin Sailing Club in Harbour events for trailer sailers, was reasonably familiar with its handling characteristics and the weather was perfect, with a breeze of about 12 knots. As I learned later, there were strong wind warnings, and the warning may have been picked up by my sailing invitees. Nobody having turned up, I had to make the choice to sail or not and if so to where. I had no enthusiasm to just jilling about Darwin Harbour however aimlessly pleasant that might have been. Whatever choice was made no preparation could go into it. I had tea making facilities on board & a small amount of snack foods about me. On board, there was a compass and some life jackets but no chart or radio. Ill advisedly, I chose to sail in the direction of Bathurst Island.

Up to then I doubt I had ever sailed Bete Noir with other than 2 or more crew, full main and genoa. So that was my rig for the day. As to direction, I seemed to recall that the Bathurst Island mission was on a course not far short of due north. In the event 290 degrees seemed to fit my bill. On reflection and allowing for set my true heading must have been nearer 280 degrees. Certainly, on such a heading I calculated the worst that could happen to me was to hit the south coast of Bathurst Island to the west of the mission. Armed with these navigational profundities, time of departure was late morning. From memory, the distance to Bathurst mission was about 40 nautical miles and to Cape

Fourcroy at the Southwestern tip of the island 75 nautical miles. Wind was from the Southeast.

As the day wore on and the breeze kept freshening to at least an estimated 25 knots in gusts I began to have reservations. BN was handling brilliantly. I found myself surfing in regular bursts down the faces of significant waves. Doubt assailed me regarding the home trip. And still the wind kept freshening. It was about 2 or 3 pm when I decided to press on and take stock when I made landfall. No land was visible then. I was in the middle of Beagle Gulf.

It was late afternoon when I dropped anchor in shoal waters on a deserted beach. With the centreboard retracted and rudder up this was in water no more than knee deep — one advantage of a trailer sailer. I could see nothing of the mission or Cape Fourcroy. All I could be sure of was that the mission being situated at the southeastern tip of the island I was somewhere between that point and the Cape. Estimating now with my speed and time taken and allowing for set I reckon the distance travelled at 50 nautical miles. By now the wind was still gusting well over 20 knots. I walked ashore and contemplated my return to Darwin. BN bucked in the incoming waves. The sun was low in the sky. I don't recall even carrying a torch.

Obviously, I was in for an overnight stay. In many ways the beach was attractive but wild buffalo or pigs might be lurking in the hinterland. With no firearm, I had no wish to risk what could well be a life-threatening encounter with either. So it was the boat. Such food as I had was limited and of non-cookable snack type — nuts and cheese. I had no cooking pot anyway. Also no fishing gear to perhaps haul in a choice fish. An uneasy night ensued on the boat. I tossed and turned fitfully,

When daylight broke there was no sign of the wind abating, so I thought I would try the full mainsail and the no.2 jib. A perilous and short-lived passage ensued. The boat was making good way but I was on the point of capsizing. Unwisely, I had allowed a beautiful Zeiss binocular to lay in the cockpit to leeward. As I came close to capsizing, the binocular was washed away, and my control so limited that retrieval was out of the question. Deciding discretion was the better part I decided on a return to shore to regroup. Then followed two more attempts firstly under main only and then under jib. Both hopeless. All the while I was being set well to the west of my overnight anchorage. So, the final endeavour was to be a reefed main and jib. I am unable to recall whether the mainsail which was standard kit incorporated one or two reef points. If the latter, I very likely used the second.

Bliss. Bete Noir was perfectly balanced, requiring almost no helm and standing up effortlessly on its bilges to the weather. It was barrelling to weather. And it was dry. I am reminded as I write of the owner of a nice looking 35′ steel hulled yacht reporting to me that going to windward in up to about 20 knots of wind his vessel was quite stiff, sailing on its bilges. That changed as the wind came up and ballast had to be relied upon. It then heeled quite suddenly and dramatically. Early mainsail reefing was the order of the day. The weight of its steel hull precluded maintenance of a desirable ballast ratio.

Albeit hard to windward it was delightful sailing. The wind kept up at much the same strength as for the previous day. The blanket of concern with how I would manage a return was lifted. Thus passed the day until I laid the no.5 farewell buoy off Charles Point at the mouth of Darwin Harbour well after sunset. BN had no lighting, but the night was clear, all was quiet and no other marine craft was visible. By now, the wind was easing to about 15 knots in the gusts, but Bete Noir was far from feeling under-canvassed. From then, it was just a matter of following the lit passage.

On route, I saw in the moonlight somewhere off Nightcliff, a Darwin northern suburb, what appeared to be a topless heavy breasted woman swimming breaststroke and high out of the water. It must have been a dugong.

I arrived off Darwin Sailing Club about 10 pm. Bete Noir was put on her trailer. It being Sunday, even the bar was closed, the restaurant likewise. But home was just up the hill. I slept well.

Epilogue

While such a trip is not to be recommended, I learned so much about Bete Noir over that weekend that the associated spasms of angst became to me insignificant compared to the delights. That being said, I realised then and even more so today that it had been the most personally dangerous trip I ever made under sail.

Nonetheless, there are clear lessons to be learned from such a sailing jaunt. I was aware of them, and all was well in the end. I had learned much about BN and what I had learned pleased me immensely. The crisis point was when I lost my beautiful binoculars. A capsize was narrowly averted. If it had occurred, I was nor so far from the beach as to be unable to make it back. That assumes there was enough depth of water for a complete inversion. If the mast had prevented a full inversion, the windage on the hull its weight and the sea state in combination would surely eventually have broken the mast. All this assumes I would not have been pinned underwater. But then, with only the clothes I stood in, no water and the mission probably at least 20 miles away, I would have been in trouble. Nobody had been notified of my jaunt. Part of the reason for the trip solo was irritation that no crew had turned up. It was a lovely day for sailing. With no firm plan in place, I just started in the general direction of Bathurst and let events overtake me.

It was not so long after that I actually did invert Bete Noir. It was just off the Sailing Club on a breezy Sunday morning. Unwisely, I had up full sail. It was a race day and yachts in all directions of all shapes and sizes were milling about. I regarded myself as being in complete but not effortless control. Then, a shackle pin was dislodged from a deck fitting. A moment of inattention to the boat's inclination to the wind whilst attempting to replace the pin and I was over. Bete Noir was completely inverted. As I scrambled to climb on to the hull as distinct from hanging on, I cursed the times I had lovingly applied polish to the underwater aspects of that hull. But get on I eventually did.

There was an outgoing tide. I was being moved quite quickly by the current. I rounded East Point and was being propelled in the direction of the harbour channel. Fortunately, young Paul White was assisting various starts in a club launch powered by two large outboard motors. After about half an hour he was able to deal with my plight. A line was attached to the lee gunwale plenty of power was applied and over Bete Noir rolled to the upright position. She was awash with water below, up close to the level of the bridge deck. The two large drains at the rear of the hull saw the cockpit drain quickly. The inbuilt buoyancy was doing its job. Luckily the bunk cushions had not floated out. All I had to do was climb aboard and bail out the interior. The rig appeared undamaged. The only water damageable item on board was a portable gas burner. It was never the same.

I gave much thought to enabling Bete Noir for more adventurous ocean-going activity. Concepts like adding a lead bulb to the centreboard base were considered. The pitfalls were possible fracture of the duralium centreboard material let alone inability to retract. This in turn led to thinking about a much heavier centreboard. Whichever way I thought about adapting there was considerable cost let alone time and any experiment could go disastrously wrong. Very likely Anan Payne in the design had calculated that once the initial not inconsiderable stability from the great beam and hull form was overcome extra weight of the centreboard in mid boat would be unlikely to tip the scales in favour of more stability. Almost certainly any later resale of an adapted boat would have been problematic. And the whole concept and purpose of the design would be likely lost.

Accordingly, when I heard another of the 6 Ranger 23s which had been sent to Perth by the production company to film storm & a dismasting sequences was for sale at from memory about $6,000 the somewhat risky sight unseen decision was made to sell and replace. At least the Roly Tasker organisation in Perth assured me the Ranger there was in acceptable condition. As best I can remember now, my Ranger 23, renamed by me from "Dove" to "Ned Kelly," arrived via the WA State Shipping Service sometime around mid-1973. Unlike Ron's which was a product of a US west coast factory my hull was moulded in New Jersey. It was considerably rougher around the edges than Ron Wilson's "Dove" but then Ron or more accurately his mother, had paid much more money.

Ron's boat was on display outside the Darwin Cinema for the screening of the "Dove" film. She was still there when cyclone Tracey hit Darwin on Christmas eve and early Christmas Day of 1974. Wind gusts of 240 kms per hour were recorded. "Dove" still supported by its cradle, was blown over by about 45 degrees, when the mast lodged on a building behind her and she could go no further without failure of the mast or rigging. After several days left so askew, the stub fibreglass keel to hull join failed. Eventually the damage was fixed and "Dove" sailed again, at least as well as before and quite likely with a hull to stub keel join stronger than previously.

I venture here to opine that although young Graham set out in 1965 in a Cal 24 the Ranger, being only built from 1971 to 1978, was a later and superior design at least as capable of dealing with the perils of the sea. The Ranger was designed by the late Gary Mull [1937-1993] to what was then thought to be the future of ocean racing the Ton Rule or in her case a subset quarter-ton rule. Principal dimensions are: length overall 23.67'; waterline length 20' ; beam 7.92'; draft 3.75'; displacement 3400 lbs ; ballast 1500 lbs; ballast ratio 44%; mainsail area 110 sq ft. Between 1971 and 1978, 740 Ranger 23s were produced.

Mull himself came from an interesting background. Starting out at university as an English Literature major, he graduated from a different university as a mechanical engineer with a minor in naval architecture. In between he took time off to participate in an ocean yacht race from the US west coast to Tahiti. He died aged 56 from cancer in 1993. Not long before his death he was attempting to purchase the moulds for his designs from Ranger yachts. Between 1969 and 1987 Ranger built 10 yachts to Mull designs. Mull's endeavour was thwarted when Ranger which by then had withdrawn from yacht building destroyed all its fibreglass moulds.

PART SIX—Looking Back

Chapter 13: Upon Retirement[29]

You might say I drifted into my second incarnation of legal practice (Darwin in 1970). Yet when I look back and despite its vicissitudes and stresses my choice, if that is the correct word, was inspired. Sure, it took me a while to find my niche, by which time I was well down life's road. But, for one who was never fearful of venturing down untraveled perhaps lonely pathways, it provided me with a discipline of difficulty, surmountable only by intelligent hard work. The methods I chose to run the forms of professional practice I adapted to and adopted over the years provided a sufficient, albeit erratic, income to enable an idiosyncratic and more importantly independent, life that was never easy. Easy is the deadliest drug of dependence.

As I look back, to define life guiding principles to explain why my life end point is as it is, the best answer I can come up with is a disregard for wealth as such and money as an end in itself. Much the same applied to people—I was never able to see naked emperors as resplendently clothed. While I am not averse to money, I never had any ambition to devote my life to any all-encompassing endeavour of whatever stripe in the name of large regular personal income. My temperament was ill suited to the typical lawyer life.

---

[29] This was originally part of the long draft chapter (ca 38,000 words) entitled "The Vineyards of the Law," most of which for reasons of space has here been deleted.

Most lawyers in the game for wealth make their big money doing repetitive work perhaps involving large sums of money working in a narrow, highly specialised segment of the law. Nor did I ever aspire to social position or standing just for its own sake. I was criticised by my mother for always choosing to achieve any goal only in what she saw as the hardest way possible.

You might say I was preoccupied with personal freedom, but if that was the case it is unlikely that I would have so effectively enslaved myself in the name of challenging litigation on behalf of clients unable to afford to engage a lawyer by paying their way. So, I leave it to any readers who would bother to agitate such matters.

To me the key to life was personal satisfaction. I never saw that as achievable in a conventional setting, although most who would consider themselves as satisfied live and work within conventional structures. Maybe I was just born under a wandering star in a free country, and at a time where that option to follow it offered more fulfilment for the likes of me than any alternative.

Two people played a big part. Keith Gale brought me to Darwin (see Chapter 7, "Transition to Darwin"). At a time when I was thinking of returning to Melbourne to try my luck at the Bar, Geoff Samuelsen convinced me Darwin had an active legal scene with potential. They never made me rich in money terms, but the real name of the game I chose to play was being able to function in adversity. They opened the door to this game. Peace to their spirits.

I was able to manage what I had no choice but to manage after choosing to take up what I did. Perhaps my ever-varied modus operandi could not have worked in other than Darwin at its then stage of development. As I saw it, the key was my willingness to explore unconventional legal avenues that more established lawyers or law firms had no stomach or capacity for and to undertake intensive research before entering any fray. Another factor was being a one-man band where I was both solicitor and counsel and sole controller of the business side of the office. My initial professional staff problems were inimical to my eventual end point.

Oddly, over the years, I had links to individual members of what I believe was Australia's mega legal firm in Sydney. In the earlier days it was Cec Coleman who had tired of the never-ending pressure that he was finding made any semblance of family life impossible. His work-related trips, as to the US, were so paced he was unable to savour the country other than from his hotel room and out of his taxi windows.

He was to turn his back on a partnership in the firm even the best and brightest young graduates could only dream of gaining entry to and set up his own shop in the Sydney suburbs. He had hosted me on a tour of the firm's offices. No light switches. I was introduced to the unique billiard cue style operation of the electric lights.

In later days it was a retired senior partner who came to visit as a representative of the International Commission of Jurists. I inferred from his observations that what he was enjoying most about his retirement was freedom and the ability to be his own man.

I have little doubt that many lawyers have found satisfying niches operating conventionally often as non-specialist barristers. Here I call to mind Victorians Brian Bourke, Woods Lloyd and Joe Kaufman. My niche, often in my later years representing clients teetering on the edge of financial extinction, was always personally fraught. Yet, to the best of my knowledge, no client was aware of my personal angst so far as cash flow went. Not for me the almost sinful love for the job that barrister Woods Lloyd was to proclaim. As I write this in 2019, I appreciate more now than ever that it is very difficult for a lawyer who is dependent on the income from a law practice to be truly independent unless he has a touch of madness.

Bringing a personal professional negligence action against the lawyer/Chief Minister is no part of a prescription for professional advancement in the Northern Territory. The same may be said of running against the Chief Minister for his parliamentary seat. For good measure, I publicly opposed then Chief Minister Marshall Perron's euthanasia drive.[30] I did all three. The first was because if I had not responded there was every chance no one else would. The second arose out of a sense of having been personally wronged, for reasons blurred now by the passage of time. Perhaps familiarity with Paul over lunches at Charlies prior to his Chief Ministership had made my action easier than they might otherwise have been. As to the third, I am strongly of the opinion doctors should attempt to preserve rather than extinguish life. All that said, I would go so far as to say that

---

[30] On euthanasia, see above, chapter 8.

unless a lawyer has practised on his own account with direct responsibility to clients over a period of years he cannot be said to have ever practised real law. Real law is a dangerous but heady and addictive wine.

Given that I needed income to be able to pay my way, you might ask why I chose a different path to my legal peers. My answer is that the path was ever evolving as external circumstances changed. My guiding star was to attempt to prevent effective denial of access to justice because of poverty in the sense of being unable to fund civil litigation. These days, that means all but the rich. Clients who became rich tended to be wooed into the clutches of larger more gnomish and more expensive legal firms. Always, if it was going to be worth my while and I was to be able to continue, there had to be a jackpot. Invariably, that was the opponent's resources.

As my knowledge and skill developed over the years, I began to appreciate that many lawyers who line up behind the clients who have money inevitably find themselves using the weight of that client money in the litigation as well as the overall legal process. One way is to attempt to crush smaller entities by deploying costly procedural niceties. To such clients the lawyer is a well-paid pawn in their life game of accumulating money at any price.

That pathway had no allure for me. I suspect for those who follow that path there must be a deliberate mental block of conscience and or judgment regarding the consequences of much of their work. As Socrates noted and used as his cardinal proof of the immortality of the soul, humans are born with such an innate sense of right and wrong as to prove they came from somewhere else.

The astrologers would explain my personal proclivities in terms of my Sagittarian star sign. Never having any concerns for astrological prognostications, it was only in the course of preparing this memoir I turned up what was for me this surprising Sagittarian overview:

> Independent and strong-willed, Sagittarius personalities are all about going off the beaten path. Sagittarius isn't afraid to step away from the pack and is a natural born leader who goes after what he or she wants, regardless of what other people think. Sagittarius is a born adventurer, and loves solo travel and exploration. Sagittarius also loves exploring the inner workings of their minds, and love stretching their horizons through a good book or movie."

I had several advantages, none of them financial, when I hung up my "shingle" in Darwin. It was 1970. I was aged 37. I had practised law for 3 years on my own account in Melbourne between 1960 and 1963. I was in the rudest of rude health courtesy of several years of survivalist but generally unprofitable toil as an opal prospector and associated abstemious living. Undoubtedly though, my association with Gollin Kyokuyo Fishing Company and the linked evening entertainments for the benefit of incessant corporate visitors from Sydney and Tokyo had blunted my edge somewhat.

My 12 months articles of clerkship with middle-tier Melbourne law firm Weigall and Crowther had provided a solid foundation in the practicalities of Supreme Court civil law built on by 2 stints, each of about 12 months, as an employed solicitor. My employed work experiences in Melbourne after articles fail to resonate much in my memory. In the second, working in the Melbourne suburb of Elsternwick, I was able to gain some insight into, and understanding of, the Jewish community, as well as developing a good working knowledge of probate practice.

My work and political experiences at Andamooka Opal Field broadened my life view. I had some knowledge of Darwin town (population then about 25,000) and its economic life through working for Gollin Kyokuyo Fishing Company (an Australian/Japanese joint venture). On the debit side and, as my first Darwin bank manager and former London policeman Dennis Humphrey once bluntly told me, "You haven't accumulated much in the way of wealth." How right he was.

www.ingramcontent.com/pod-product-compliance
Lightning Source LLC
Chambersburg PA
CBHW051417290426
44109CB00016B/1337